SAQIYUQ

Stories from the Lives of Three Inuit Women

Praise for *Saqiyuq*:

"This book is a living text." *Geist*

"An absorbing collection of stories from the lives of three Inuit women." *MacLeans*

"Invaluable [to] anyone interested in Inuit culture. The implications for the future from generation to generation are enlightening, and at times, overtly frightening." *Edmonton Journal*

"*Saqiyuq* is a delightful and inspiring work – delightful in its readability and inspiring in the example it offers of how good multi-generational histories can be produced." *Choice*

"*Saqiyuq* is a thoughtful and important tribute." *The Montreal Gazette*

"A moving account of three generations in the Arctic that sends a fascinating mixture of messages about its hardships and it riches." Hugh Brody, Canada Research Chair in Aboriginal Studies, University College of the Fraser Valley

"*Saqiyuq* gives an intimate view of these women's lives and of their essential ability to adapt and survive." *The Left Atrium*

NANCY WACHOWICH is a lecturer in the Department of Anthropology at the University of Aberdeen, Scotland.

APPHIA AGALAKTI AWA spent most of her life on the land in the Eastern High Arctic. She died in September 1996.

RHODA KAUKJAK KATSAK currently works in Pond Inlet as the director of Community Operations in the Qikiqtaaluk Department of Economic Development and Transportation of the Nunavut Government.

SANDRA PIKUJAK KATSAK (now Omik) was among the inaugural class of graduates from Nunavut's Akitsiraq Law School. She is now employed as Nunavut Legal Counsel with Nunavut Tunngavik Inc. in Iqaluit.

SAQIYUQ

❊ ❊ ❊

STORIES FROM THE LIVES OF THREE INUIT WOMEN

❊ ❊ ❊

Nancy Wachowich
in collaboration with
Apphia Agalakti Awa, Rhoda Kaukjak Katsak,
and Sandra Pikujak Katsak

❊ ❊ ❊

McGill-Queen's University Press
Montreal & Kingston · London · Ithaca

© McGill-Queen's University Press 1999
ISBN 978-0-7735-1887-2 (cloth)
ISBN 978-0-7735-2244-2 (paper)
ISBN 978-0-7735-6801-3 (ePDF)

Legal deposit fourth quarter 1999
Bibliothèque nationale du Québec

Printed in Canada on acid-free paper that is
100% ancient forest free (100% post-
consumer recycled), processed chlorine free
First paperback edition 2001
Reprinted 2003, 2005, 2010, 2013

McGill-Queen's University Press acknowledges
the financial support of the Government of
Canada through the Book Publishing Industry
Development Program (BPIDP) for its activities.
We also acknowledge the support of the
Canada Council for the Arts for our publishing
program.

Canadian Cataloguing in Publication Data

Wachowich, Nancy, 1966–
Saqiyuq: stories from the lives of three Inuit
women

(McGill-Queen's native and northern series ; 19)
Includes bibliographical references and index.
ISBN 978-0-7735-1887-2 (bnd)
ISBN 978-0-7735-2244-2 (pbk)
ISBN 978-0-7735-6801-3 (ePDF)

1. Awa, Apphia Agalakti, 1931–1996.
2. Katsak, Rhoda Kaukjak.
3. Katsak, Sandra Pikujak
4. Inuit women—Nunavut—Biography.
5. Inuit women—Nunavut—History.
6. Nunavut—Biography. I. Awa, Apphia
Agalakti, 1931–1996. II. Katsak, Rhoda
Kaukjak. III. Katsak, Sandra Pikujak.
IV. Title. V. Series.

E99.E7W33 1999   971.9'5   C99-900996-6

Typeset in 10/12 Sabon by True to Type

CONTENTS

In September 1996 as this book was being prepared for publication, Apphia Agalakti Siqpaapik Awa, who suffered from congestive heart failure, took off her oxygen-therapy machine and made a patchwork quilt – her granddaughter Sandra's wedding gift. She died on 16 September 1996, two days after Sandra's wedding. This book is dedicated to Apphia Agalakti, to her ancestors, and to her descendants. May her strength and good humour carry on through the generations.

CONTENTS

⬧⬧⬧

ACKNOWLEDGMENTS

❖ ❖ ❖

This book has been over five years in the making. We want to extend especially warm thanks to Lucy Quasa, Bernadette Dean, and Apphia Killiktee for spending many of their valuable evenings in Pond Inlet during the spring and fall of 1993, helping translate Apphia's eloquent Inuktitut stories into spoken English for the book. We are grateful to the editors at McGill-Queen's University Press, Aurèle Parisien, Joan McGilvray, and Maureen Garvie, for their guidance in getting this manuscript into its final form. Patricia Badir, Gretchen Brundin, Bette Wachowich, Leslie Robertson, Kerri Wylie, and Andrew Stewart all read versions over the years and offered sound editorial advice. Thank you to Mathias Awa in Pond Inlet and Kenneth Bragg at Ground Control Geotechnologies for the place-names maps and Leah Otak in Igloolik for her help with Inuktitut spellings. Rhoda's aunt, Koopa Maktar, her brothers and sisters, her husband, Josh Katsak, and their children were reassuring audiences throughout several rounds of editorial changes. I also want to thank my parents, Allan and Bette Wachowich, for their ongoing support and inspiration. The original impetus for this project came from the Royal Commission on Aboriginal Peoples and some of the material initially collected for this book appeared previously in a report prepared for the Royal Commission. Many of my ideas for shaping this book came from conversations and seminars with Julie Cruikshank at the University of British Columbia.

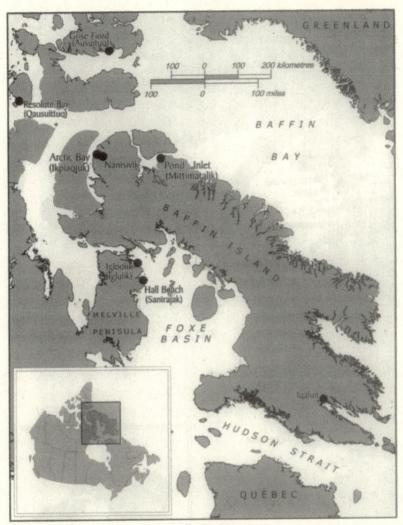

Baffin Region

Some of the camps and settlements mentioned in Apphia Agalakti Awa's stories

SAQIYUQ

"Saqiyuq is our word for a wind that blows across the land or ice,
a strong wind that suddenly shifts its direction but still maintains its force."

Rhoda Kaukjak Katsak, 1997

INTRODUCTION: The Life History Project

*I keep things in mind, stories from my life, so that I can live a very
long time, not forever but a very long time.*
                    Apphia Aglakti Awa, 2 September 1993

*I moved in off the land and went to school when I was eight years old.
That is when they started trying to teach me to become a Qallunaaq.*
                    Rhoda Kaukjak Katsak, 15 April 1993

*There are lots of things going on here. There are lots and lots of
changes always happening. The modern world is hard for us today,
for us young people. It is hard.*
                    Sandra Pikujak Katsak, 20 August 1993

"Saqiyuq," Rhoda Katsak explains, is a North Baffin Inuktitut word
for a wind that whips across the land or ice, changing directions but
maintaining its speed. This book is a collection of stories from three
Inuit women's lives; together, the stories offer one family's experience
of almost a century of shifting winds in the Eastern High Arctic. The
Inuit have developed and pursued cultural practices that ensured their
survival in a difficult, often erratic Arctic environment. Most recently
Inuit culture has met with globalization and the forces of modernity;
snowmobiles, televisions, video games, and teen dances now assume
their place alongside traditional hunting, skin clothing, bone tools, and
dog teams.

Storytelling

For generations, storytelling has been an integral part of Inuit social
life. Oral traditions range from anecdotes of events and historical
accounts, to elaborate legends, myths, epics, origin and creation
stories, proverbs, poems, and versed songs. Stories that transmit
knowledge about family and local histories, about connections to the
landscape, about complex and complementary animal-human relations, and about Inuit conceptions of the universe have been recounted
for centuries in imaginative and rich detail in a number of settings.

Curled up on the corner of her flowered couch one evening, her face glowing in fond recollection, Apphia recounted to me her childhood memories of being tucked into a bed of warm caribou skins with her brothers, sisters, and cousins listening to her grandmother Kaukjak's stories. Tracing shapes with her hands, she described how she watched the shadows from the qulliq flame dance on the sod-house walls as her grandmother filled the dark winter night with tales. Stories like these were told to the beat of women's hands, cleaning and scraping skins in igloos, sod-houses, and skin tents. They were retold to the rhythm of sled runners scraping on the snow during long spring trips on qamu-tiks. They were harmonized with the incessant buzz of mosquitoes during summer treks inland in search of caribou. In fall and winter camps when groups congregated, night-time gatherings would take place in large ceremonial snow-houses called qaggiit where elders would recount celebrated hunting stories and Inuit legends, and people would sing songs and drum dance.

Apphia Agalakti Awa was born in 1931 in a summer caribou hunting camp in the Northern Foxe Basin region of the Eastern High Arctic. She spent most of her life until 1972 travelling with her family across tundra and sea ice between hunting camps, fishing spots, and trading posts. Her sixth child, Rhoda Kaukjak Katsak, was born in 1957 and raised on the land until the age of eight, when she was sent to federal day school and boarded in hostels in the settlement of Igloo-lik. Rhoda's eldest daughter, Sandra Pikujak Katsak, was born in 1973. She has grown up in Pond Inlet, a community continually in flux, where Inuit and Western cultures have established an uneasy co-exis-tence.

I first came to know Apphia, Rhoda, and Sandra in the summer of 1991, two years before this project began. I was in my mid twenties and in the High Arctic for the first time, spending three months in Pond Inlet doing fieldwork for my Master's thesis in cultural anthropology. My research that summer was moving at a disconcertingly slow pace. I felt the awkwardness of having to balance my status as temporary resident – a generously tolerated guest – in this close-knit indigenous community against my need to negotiate a path through the academic world. The first month had passed, and I still hadn't worked up the nerve to conduct "formal" interviews. I had met all three women in my first week in the settlement, and during that initial fumbling period they were among the first to graciously volunteer to take part in my small project. We held a few interviews together, but as the summer passed, we became companions. I took comfort in the family's hospi-tality and spent more and more evenings and weekends in the Katsaks' living room having coffee with Rhoda or her daughters, chatting, reading, watching TV, or simply being silent. When the summer ended, I left Pond Inlet to go back to the University of Western Ontario. We corresponded through letters, phone calls, and an exchange of Christmas cards. A year later, in July 1992, I returned to the settlement to follow up on my study and to visit.

In the fall of 1992 I obtained my Master's degree and it was at this time the Royal Commission on Aboriginal Peoples circulated a notice to Canadian universities calling for proposals to record three-generational life histories. The idea of documenting the perspectives of Apphia, Rhoda, and Sandra on the dynamic relations of the Eastern High Arctic's colonial history interested me immediately. Not only did I see this as an opportunity to record on tape and in writing a collection of rich Inuit oral traditions like those I had heard during my visits to Pond Inlet but I also recognized the historical value of bringing Inuit histories into dialogue with the large body of western accounts of Arctic peoples written by cultural outsiders. With the notice in hand, I telephoned Rhoda; we drew up a proposal and six months later I returned to Pond Inlet.

While storytelling remains important to contemporary Nunavut communities, changing lifestyles have altered the shapes and themes of Inuit oral traditions. The different ways in which Apphia, Rhoda, and Sandra draw upon their life histories testify to the change in Inuit women's experiences and storytelling practices throughout the generations. Their stories were recorded in Pond Inlet during the spring and fall of 1993.

Apphia's life experiences travelling and living in camps on the land with her family helped form and polish her particular narrative techniques – her lyrical style, her use of repetition, and her rich stock of images. Rhoda and Sandra's involvement with western institutions has fostered different (albeit also colourful and revealing) narrative styles. Their accounts are more linear than Apphia's, influenced perhaps by their exposure to western conventions of historical biography. This book builds on the Inuit storytelling tradition, but in a different way. All three women told their stories in the context of modern Arctic settlement life. They recounted them in bustling kitchens while carving meat and boiling noodles for dinner. They taped them while kneeling on floors and stretching, scraping, and sewing caribou and seal skins, while sitting cross-legged on beds in small, dim bedrooms and nestled on couches late at night. Memories were recalled amidst the sound of family and friends talking, playing games, and watching television. They were jotted down on looseleaf paper and clarified over the phone. While these accounts illustrate rich intricacies of Inuit life, their themes, their articulation, and their effects on audiences (both listeners and readers) are clearly not the same in the 1990s as they were in the igluvigait, tents, and sod-houses of their ancestors.

Words on Tape: Recording the Stories

Apphia, Rhoda, Sandra, and I held a meeting as soon as I arrived in Pond Inlet in April 1993 and decided to work together in determining the mechanics of the storytelling and the themes that might be addressed. The settings for Apphia's interview sessions were varied. Often we would meet at her house in the afternoons, after she had made lunch for her children and grandchildren. Sometimes there were just three of us: Apphia, our interpreter, and me. At other times her husband, children, nieces, nephews, grandchildren, or visiting neighbours would be there, listening to her taping her stories, asking questions, commenting on what she was saying, watching television, or talking among themselves. When the sound of the television or the noise level in her busy household became overwhelming, all three of us would pile onto Apphia's battered snowmobile and move the recording session to the interpreter's house or to the living room of the house where I was staying, down the hill from the Awa residence.

Close to a dozen taped sessions were conducted with Apphia that spring. These would often begin with Apphia taking the tape-recorder from me; she would turn to our interpreter or others listening in the room and begin to tell stories from her life. She spoke reflectively, and often passionately. Sometimes remembering happy events in her life made her laugh so hard that she had to turn off the tape-recorder. At other times her memories made her cry. Some days she would speak for three or four hours at a time, and occasionally she brought a folded piece of paper on which she had written herself notes in Inuktitut syllabic script. Her stories were told in Inuktitut; the translator provided me with a sketchy recapitulation of her words after the session or during breaks when Apphia stopped recording to pour herself some tea, eat, or most commonly, cough. The tone, cadence, and emotion in her voice, and her body language, combined with my limited understanding of Inuktitut, gave me a vague idea of the meaning of her words. And yet, apart from those brief overviews, I had to wait until much later, once the tapes were translated into English, to learn the vivid and intricate details of her stories.

Because of the language barrier between Apphia and myself, interpreters were central figures at each meeting. The person filling this role, however, changed all the time. Pond Inlet was a busy settlement during the spring and fall months I was there, active with the hustle and bustle of the hunting and fishing seasons and with people juggling family, work, and school responsibilities. Finding a person with a strong command of both the traditional Inuktitut spoken by elders and of English, a person who was close to Apphia and with whom she felt comfortable sharing her memories, was a difficult task. The first woman Apphia called in to listen to her stories and translate our conversations was her forty-year-old adopted younger sister, Lucy Quasa. Lucy was Apphia's younger brother Maktaaq's daughter. She had been adopted as a baby by Apphia's mother, Suula Atagutsiak, and was eager to work with her oldest sister and hear her life stories. When approximately one-third of the recording sessions were complete, Lucy was offered a full-time job at the Northern Store (formerly the Hudson's Bay Company) and Sandra took her place. Rhoda also sat in on her mother's stories with me and acted as translator on several occasions, as did a twenty-nine-year-old second cousin, Bernadette Dean. In the last few weeks, a fifth interpreter, a family friend and neighbour, Apphia Killiktee, was solicited to listen to Apphia's tapes and convert them into English.

While Apphia's stories were often told to me as long Inuktitut narratives with few interjections, my recording sessions with her daughter were of a different nature. Rhoda recounted her life stories to me directly, in English, her second language. Rhoda had been translating both English and Inuktitut since her childhood; she was heedful of the resistance of certain concepts to cross-cultural translation. Thus, the stories that she chose, as well as the way she told them, were consciously shaped to fit verbal expressions and expectations of English speakers like me. Constantly juggling the demands of her hectic life – her job at the hamlet office, her six children, her correspondence courses in accounting, and frequent unforeseen commitments – she recorded her life stories not as a series of long narratives but in bits and pieces, recollections slipped here and there into her cramped schedule. While the imagery and rhythm of her stories reflect the storytelling skills of Inuit raised on the land, her voice also shows the influence of western narrative patterns to which she was exposed in federal day schools. Some of our earlier recording sessions, for example, took on professional qualities with Rhoda sitting face to face with me relaying crisp, directed testimonies of her experiences. Later narratives became more candid and were peppered with jokes, inquiries, and vibrant asides. A few times, in an attempt to balance time constraints, she took equipment home with her to record stories by herself. While she considered this more convenient – she could do it late at night, when she found a minute, or once all of her children were asleep – she later told me how difficult it was to keep her train of thought when speaking to a grinding tape and a flickering red recording light. She said she wanted to have someone who would listen to her when she spoke, someone she could look at, someone who was interested and who would keep her focused, someone who would nod and ask questions. We held the rest of the sessions together.

Sandra Katsak grew up in a settlement inundated by southern media, schools, and government institutions. Even more alienated from the oral traditions learned on the land by her mother and her grandmother, she initially found it difficult to narrate episodes and memories from her life in one-on-one or group storytelling sessions. After the first few taped sessions she told me that she wished to write out her life history privately on paper, as she would an assignment at school, and present it to me in sections. An avid reader of English literature, she has strong writing skills and had been recording her thoughts in diaries for years. She spoke of using portions of her diaries to structure her contribution. At her request, I wrote out some generic questions I was asking both her grandmother and mother, such as: "Where were you born?" and "What are the things you remember most about your childhood?" I also listed possible broad topics such as birth and childhood stories, schooling, health care, life in the settlement, Inuit traditions, and cultural change. Sandra came to the house where I was staying on a number of afternoons and evenings and, over coffee and between conversations, used my lap-top computer to type out portions of her narratives. She also gave me handwritten stories and sent me letters when I returned south after this first visit. Portions of these are included in this collection.

I returned to Edmonton in May 1993 and began transcribing the tapes into several hundred manuscript pages. I assembled lists of questions pertaining to stories whose fragments, details, and people/place names had been lost in the translation from Inuktitut to English and from spoken to written word. Returning to Pond Inlet the following September, I spent another dozen or so afternoons and evenings with Apphia reviewing with an interpreter my English transcriptions of her stories. Apart from the last two evenings when I recorded her closing contributions to the book, these autumn meetings were more interactive than our spring storytelling sessions. I usually sat on the floor or at a table, with my inch-thick pile of transcripts and questions spread out around me, and asked Apphia to expound on certain stories which she had recounted earlier. Sessions with Rhoda and Sandra were similar. Sandra, feeling more comfortable with her life history as it evolved, grew tired of writing and came over to my house for several taped interview sessions. She also filled an hour and a half of tape independently. The night before my departure from Pond Inlet she stayed up late recording stories in her bedroom and singing Inuktitut songs on tape with her sister Mona. She presented these cassettes to me the next morning at the airport and asked me to add them to her contribution.

I mailed a new set of transcripts to Pond Inlet in November 1993, and Sandra flew to Edmonton that same month to review with me the first draft of her family's life history collection. I returned to Pond Inlet in the spring of 1997 with one of the later versions of this book in hand. Apart from these trips, our communication and collaboration has been through the post, and over the phone, fax, and e-mail.

From Spoken to Written Words: Editing Oral Histories

Apphia, Rhoda, and Sandra recounted their life histories as events and images, linked but not always chronologically ordered. This reflects fundamental differences between stories told (the oral tradition) and stories written down. Each of the three collections of stories in its own way illustrates distinguishing features of oral tradition: a poetic quality, an oscillation between the present and an ever-changing past, and (sometimes bewildering) ellipses of memory. Stories were told and later retold to me within the context of other stories, or in combination with new tales, with different details and emphasis. Properties of time and place changed quickly as memories provoked new thoughts and recollections. Each narrator connected past, present, and future in her own way as she tapped into her own distinct ordering systems for events in her life. In one afternoon, for example, Apphia switched from a story about when she was four to a related story that occurred when she was in her twenties and then back again. Rhoda and Sandra made similar shifts.

In my attempts to translate oral histories into written narratives, I have worked to preserve as best I can the associative threads spun by Apphia, Rhoda, and Sandra. However, transcribing and editing the stories posed for me a number of methodological problems. At issue is the balance between the need for these testimonies to remain as much as possible in the women's own words, and the need for life histories to be comprehensive and "reader friendly." Perpetually conscious of the fact that editing (along with translating and transcribing) is a concentrated act of interpretation, one that plays a critical role in the reproduction of narratives such as these, I have tried to keep the accounts as close as possible to the spoken words recorded on tape. I have also attempted to preserve the sentence structure originally used by Apphia, Rhoda, and Sandra, including the repetitions, colloquialisms, pauses, and framing devices (such as: "here I go," "eh," "that's all," and others) that distinguish oral from written discourse. At times, however, ideas raised in conversation with Rhoda or Sandra, or translated by interpreters from Apphia's Inuktitut narratives, were expressed in bits and pieces or in fragmented English. Complicating this further is that Apphia's Inuktitut stories were translated into English through the voices of the five different inter- preters, all using English as their second language and each with her own individualized command of both the traditional Inuktitut spoken by elders and English vernacular. Sometimes eloquently expressed Inuktitut phrases suffered in translation.

In an effort to avoid confusion and to present the stories as intelli- gibly as possible, I have moderated the vernacular of the translators and made minor corrections to grammar and syntax. Apphia, for example, told the story of the birth of her first child, Oopah, on four separate occasions during our recording sessions. I combined these tales into one story, and changed as few of her original (translated) words as possible. I have removed parts of the interviews, including questions and statements made by myself, the interpreter, or by other people present in the room. I have also edited conversational quips made "off topic" by the storyteller. In consultation with Apphia, Rhoda, and Sandra, I have cut elements of their original recorded life histories that they did not want included in a public account.

The stories appear here in loose chronological order. Although at times, breaks in the chronology, repetitions, or puzzling statements occur, these do not signal false recollections on the part of the story- tellers, but instead the subjective nature of Inuit orality and the creativ- ity of memory. In my attempts to bridge Inuit and non-Inuit knowledge, I have added contextual information in endnotes and appendices. These sections provide information about the spellings and meanings of Inuk- titut terms; they list the stories, historical events, and principal people, and provide an outline of the socio-cultural context of the stories.

Presenting the stories

The 117 stories that follow were told to me in 1993 by Apphia Agalakti Siqpaapik Awa, Rhoda Kaukjak Katsak, and Sandra Pikujak Katsak. Each section begins with a brief biography of the storyteller and an outline of the prominent themes that emerge in each life history. The collections are divided into life stages, starting with childhood memories and ending with reflections on contemporary life and changes brought about by Euro-Canadian involvement in the Arctic. The stories offer a multitude of points of comparison and con- trast; the index has been organized to assist those who wish to read this book thematically.

I have not yet mentioned how privileged I feel to have participated in the recording of these three women's life histories. My afternoon and evening teas and coffees with Apphia, Rhoda, Sandra, and members of their family have taught me much about graciousness and generosity. They have shown me how people can face adversity and still find things to laugh about.

Nancy Wachowich
Vancouver, 1998

PART ONE

Apphia Agalakti Siqpaapik Awa, 1993.
(Photograph, Nancy Wachowich)

Apphia Agalakti Siqpaapik Awa

❈ ❈ ❈

Looking back on my life, the stories that I have told,
a lot of them are from tough and difficult situations that I went through
when I was younger, from back when I started remembering things.
I had a very difficult life back then.

INTRODUCTION

When I first met Apphia in the summer of 1991 she was sixty years old. I arrived at her house, with Rhoda's sister-in-law Rosie Katsak working as my interpreter, to ask her a series of questions related to my Master's research. While Apphia's health improved considerably between the day of my first meeting with her and the start of our life-history project in 1993, I entered her house on that day to the sound of her wheezing and coughing. She was sitting on the edge of a flow-ered couch with a box of Kleenex beside her, mending a sealskin kamik. Two of her toddler grandchildren were playing at her feet. On the walls to either side of her were a number of family pictures and large, handmade "No Smoking" signs coloured in crayon. Churning on the table in front of her was an enormous oxygen machine.

Rosie introduced us, and we smiled and formally shook hands. I explained the premise of my research to Rosie, who summarized for Apphia. Although Apphia understood some of the English words I was using, she, like all women of her generation in Pond Inlet, was a unilin-gual Inuktitut speaker. As I was about to launch into my series of written questions, she intercepted my prolonged gape at the oxygen machine and began talking to me about the various problems she had with her lungs. Her lungs, she told me, had been bothering her for many years, but these problems had not always been with her. When she was young, before she started smoking, she had been able to run and play and to walk on the tundra for days and days carrying children and gear. She recounted how, during the previous spring when she had been out camping on the land for several weeks with her family, "far away from the noise and the dirt and the Qallunaat," she had "breathed just fine."

Apphia Agalakti Siqpaapik Awa was born 13 August 1931 in a camp in the Amittuq region of the Eastern High Arctic around the current-day settlements of Igloolik and Hall Beach. Her mother, Suula Atagutsiak, was then a young teenager. Soon after Apphia's birth, Suula and Kublu, Apphia's biological father, following the custom of Inuit adoption, offered her to her uncle, Arvaarluk, and his wife, Ilupaalik, who at the time had no children of their own. Apphia (then known by her Inuktitut names, Agalakti Siqpaapik) lived with her adoptive parents until Ilupaalik died in 1939. Apphia was then eight years old and spent the next five or six years travelling on the land around the Northern Foxe Basin region with her father, Arvaarluk. When she was about thirteen, a marriage was arranged for her with a man named Awa. Leaving her father and her extended family, she moved to her husband's family's camp. She never again saw Arvaarluk, who died two years later at a camp outside Hall Beach.

Apphia and her husband spent the next thirty years travelling to camps, trading posts, and hunting spots around the Amittuq region. They were baptized as Anglicans by a visiting minister when Apphia was in her early twenties and were given the Christian names Apphia and Mathias. Between 1946 and 1968 they had eleven children: a daughter, Oopah, a son, Arvaluk (also known as James Arvaluk), then Martha, Simon, Jacob (also known as Jakopie, Jake, or Jako), Rhoda, Solomon, Joanna, Salomie, Phillip, and Ida. Each of their children was named following the Inuit custom of passing on names from a recently deceased relative or community member (without regard for gender), but the younger six children after Rhoda were addressed by their Christian names. Apphia and Mathias adopted a twelfth child, a son, Nary, in the fall of 1972. All of the Awa children (except for Oopah and Solomon, who stayed on the land, and the youngest two, who were raised in town) left their parents as youngsters to attend either residential school in Churchill, Manitoba, or federal day schools in Igloolik and Pond Inlet. In the 1960s Canadian government pressures on the Inuit to move into year-round settlements intensified. Apphia and Mathias Awa moved into Pond Inlet from their camp in September 1972. They were one of the last families in the area to move off the land.

When her daughter Rhoda and I approached her about this project, Apphia was enthusiastic about the chance to document her life and share her knowledge. Her early stories are graphic and personal and touch on her childhood, her adoption into another family, and her relationships with her siblings and both sets of parents. She describes her life spent travelling between hunting camps. She tells of her arranged marriage, her initial feelings for her husband, living with her in-laws, her experiences with childbirth, and the way she raised her children. She discusses her first contact with Qallunaat missionaries, traders, and the RCMP and explains how relationships with Qallunaat have changed over the years. She describes epidemics of measles and tuberculosis that spread through the Arctic during the 1940s, '50s, and '60s and the hardships she and her family endured. She recalls her first plane ride in 1955 when a crew of government officials landed at her outpost camp to round up her family for tuberculosis testing. She relates the pain and powerlessness she felt in later years when Qallunaat administrators took away her small children to residential and federal day schools.

Apphia also retells stories told to her by her parents and grandparents about life at the turn of the century, anecdotes about traders and whaling ships that visited Inuit camps. She documents traditional Inuit burial practices, healing practices, shamanism, hunting strategies, tattooing, and Inuit methods of conflict resolution. She talks about traditional naming practices and the numbered disks or "dog tags" given to the Inuit by the federal government in the 1950s, along with the impact of money, alcohol, and settlement life on her family and friends. She discusses changes to the way elders are treated. She also relays stories of local historical figures from the region – individuals such as her father, Arvaarluk, who could run "as fast as a caribou," and her famous aunt Ataguttaaluk, dubbed "the Queen of Igloolik," who died when Apphia was a young adult. Her stories demonstrate in vivid detail the countless changes in Inuit life over the last hundred years.

At the time of our work together recording these stories, Apphia was living in a house on the edge of Pond Inlet with her husband, her son Solomon, his wife, and five grandchildren. A friendly, jovial, kindhearted woman, she was known in both Igloolik and Pond Inlet as the woman who sang "Happy Birthday" to people on the community radio. She was also a renowned artisan, a skilled designer and seamstress of caribou clothing who spent much of her time teaching this craft to her daughters, and granddaughters and school-children. She arrived at my house the afternoon the first story was recorded driving her beat-up snowmobile with our interpreter Lucy (her adopted younger sister) hanging on to the back. She was wearing a new purple parka Sandra had purchased for her from a catalogue, a flowered skirt and kamiks; in her hand was a plastic bag full of mending and a crumpled paper on which she had listed in syllabics the names of her relatives and some dates. She told me that she was eager to record her life history because she wanted the younger generations to learn and remember how Inuit used to live. She looked at me intently that first afternoon and, pointing to Lucy and then to a group of small children playing outside the window, she said:

"I want to let them see what our lives were like back then. I want them to see what it was like for us. I want them to know."

GROWING UP ON THE LAND: I START TO RECOLLECT BITS AND PIECES

MY ANCESTORS, MY FAMILY

Okay, yes, I will start talking now. I am Apphia Awa. Now I will start. I will start with a description of my ancestors, my family. How is it? Just a minute. I have to think of where to start ... who to start with ... Just a minute now ...

Now my ancestor family, it goes like this. The Arvaarluk family was my adoptive family. Arvaarluk and his wife, Ilupaalik, they were my adoptive parents. My adoptive parents were Arvaarluk and Ilupaalik. The husband was my adoptive father and his wife, Ilupaalik, was my adoptive mother. Arvaarluk had a mother named Aqaaq and a father named Attaarjuat. Arvaarluk's brothers and sisters were Nasaq, Alasuarq, Maniq, and Naqitarvik. There may be more, but that is all I know. Now, Arvaarluk's own children were from both his first and second wives. His children were Qajaaq, Qattalik, and Kuutiq. I never heard who Ilupaalik's parents were. If I tried hard enough to find out who Ilupaalik's parents were, I could.

I was adopted, but I consider these people my family. We are like that when we are adopted. Since we grow up with these people, we feel like they are our family. We feel distant from our own family, the family we were born into. Anybody can have that feeling if they are adopted.

Now for my actual relatives: Kublu was my real father, and my real mother was Suula. I don't know all of Kublu's ancestors, but I do know who his parents were. His mother was Quliik, and his father was Ippiaq. These were his parents who I know, but I don't know his distant relatives or his ancestors. As for Suula, my real mother, her father was Nutarariaq and her mother was Kaukjak. Those were her parents, and again I don't know who her ancestors were. I am the eldest in my real family, then a second, a younger brother, Maktaaq, then a third one who died young, Pikuk, no, Quliik, then a fourth one, Thomas Nutarariaq, and then a fifth after Thomas, Quliik – Paul

Quliik – also deceased, after that Bernadette Koobloo, then my youngest brother, Leeno Koobloo. These are my actual relatives, four brothers and two sisters. The other one died at a young age. That is how we are as a family. There are lots of us now, including cousins and grandchildren. I have twelve children, six boys and six girls. Maktaaq had twelve children also, but one died not too long ago. Also Thomas, the fourth born, has children, but I am not sure whether he has eleven or twelve. My brothers and I have many children, so our relatives go on and on.

That is how we are today, alive and well even though we had such hard lives back in the old days. Sometimes we struggled to survive. We survived when we had only country food to feed ourselves.

🎴 🎴 🎴

We barely saw Qallunaat when we lived around the Igloolik area. My adoptive parents are from that area, Amittuq. My real father, Kublu, he used to travel a lot. He would travel all around the High Arctic, also to areas around the Keewatin. He even went to Churchill. He used to travel everywhere.

A long time ago, before the Qallunaat arrived among the Inuit, or even when there were just a few Qallunaat around, shamans were the spiritual people. Inuit had never heard about Jesus or God at that time. There were no Bibles. People tried very hard to please the spirits, to be good to them, because if someone angered them or committed a sin there might be a shortage of food and the whole group might go hungry. The shaman would help the people by telling them who it was who had caused the bad things to happen. Like, for example, if a young woman had a miscarriage without letting anyone know that she was pregnant, if she didn't tell her parents that she had a miscarriage or if she didn't tell them when she had her first menstruation, then animals might not come. The only way to clear this up was if her parents or the shaman confronted her and they dealt with the problem. That was the way it was at that time.

Back at that time the Inuit used to name their children after animals. I remember one of my adoptive mother's names was Tiriganiaq.[1] They never used to use the Bible when naming their children. They never used saints' names.[2] They never heard about God or Jesus at that time so they didn't have Bibles.[3]

I was born when they started to believe in Jesus and God. When I talk about these beliefs, I am talking about way, way back. I am talking about before they heard of God. Even my mother, Suula, was born when they had started believing in Jesus and God. It was long ago that

Inuit believed in shamans and followed their strange rules, back around the 1600s, 1700s, and 1800s, maybe even at the start of the 1900s. They used their shamans to cure a sick person or to fight an enemy. And they were asked to love one another, especially orphans. They gave blubber and meat to those without fuel or food, those who had less than they had. So they lived through times of happiness and sorrow just as we do now. When the first Qallunaat arrived by ship to live among the Inuit, that is when they finally realized that they had to be Christian. That is when Inuit were asked to forget their old beliefs, to forget their beliefs about the powers of the shamans and other things like that.

People used to travel a lot. They travelled by dog team or they walked. Some even went as far as Greenland. If they knew how to hunt, Inuit could go almost anywhere without starving. Just as long as they caught animals, they could survive and keep on travelling, miles and miles and miles. They never stopped for very much time because they were always looking for animals to hunt. They never really settled down in a camp. People would starve and die when the animals weren't around to hunt. They had really hard lives. In some camps people starved, and people would hear about this in other camps. Starving did not happen every day, not every year either, but every once in a while.

This story could go on and on, but from what I know, it is real. In the old days there was happiness and there was sorrow. We used to play games, like tag and other games – that is how we were. We weren't always just trying to survive, we used to have fun sometimes too. We would have challenging drum dances, and sing Ajaa jaa songs.[4]

❀ ❀ ❀

I was born on August 13th, 1931, not too long ago. When I was born there was only one Qallunaaq man around – the Catholic priest.[5] When my real parents, Kublu and Suula, went to the outpost after they had me, the priest marked my name and my birth date down. That is how I know my birth date.

In my real family, Nutarariaq was my grandfather. His wife, Kaukjak, gave birth to my mother, Suula. Nutarariaq had a sister named Ataguttaaluk, and she was the eldest in the camp. I recall that their mother was Arnarjuaq, but I don't know who their father was.

My mother got married very young, and when she was pregnant with me, they migrated to the mainland towards the Keewatin District. They started in the early spring and moved through the summer.

My parents had another family with them, Tullik, Tasiuq, and Qamukaaq.

At that time my mother, Suula, was just a girl, not even fit to have a husband. Her family gave her to a man who was old enough to be her father. His name was Kublu. That is what she used to tell me when I asked her the story about herself. She didn't have a baby sister, and she was desperate to keep me because I was a girl. Her real parents were separated, and her real father kept her and left her mother, Kaukjak, to go live with another woman. He went to live with his atiq's wife, Arnaarnuk. Her adoptive mother, Arnaannuk, couldn't have any children so she raised another woman's daughter. My mother was desperate to keep me when I was born because I was a girl and I was her first child. Her new husband, Kublu, my father, didn't want to keep me. He was hoping for a son and I turned out to be a girl so he wanted to give me away. My mother was not a very bossy woman and she was having a hard time at that point, so she had to listen to her husband. He was so much older than her. She couldn't say no to him even though she was crying so much inside at the thought of having to leave me.

My father, Kublu, didn't want to keep me because I was a girl and he had another three daughters from his first wife. He had never had a son, and when he married my mother and I turned out to be a girl, he was disappointed. That is why he wanted to give me up. My mother felt shame in front of her new husband when I was born and thought to herself, "If I keep having girls, what will I do?" That is how my mother felt when I was born. She felt better, though, when her husband said he wanted to give me to Arvaarluk, because Arvaarluk was my mother's uncle. So they gave me up when we came off the ice, when we got to the seashore to start caribou-hunting. The camp that they gave me up at was called Akkuniq. My mother had me for a month or so before she gave me up – she was breast-feeding me at the time. When Ilupaalik, my adoptive mother, found out how much it hurt my mother to have to give me up, she let my real mother keep breast-feeding me, even when I was living with my adoptive mother. She fed me for another month or so, up until when I could smile.[6]

All of the sudden my real father, Kublu, wanted to leave to go to the Keewatin area and the Repulse Bay area. That is when she finally gave me up, even though she really wanted to keep me. She told me later that on her way to Repulse Bay she had a really hard time. She had been breast-feeding, so her breasts were swollen and filled with milk.

The reason that my real father, Kublu, wanted to leave all of a sudden was that he had committed a crime and he needed to escape to the Keewatin area. I am not sure what particular crime my father committed ... I asked Suula much later on, much later I asked her, "Why did you leave me all of a sudden? Why did you go away? Why did you have to leave so fast?" Suula did not know. She was very young at the time. She did not question her husband.

They were gone for a long time. I began living with my adopted family, and they had another child after me. My real mother, Suula, also had another child, a son, Maktaaq. Before Maktaaq was born, my real mother had lost a baby. Maktaaq was born after. During that time they reached Churchill and Chesterfield Inlet. So between Maktaaq and I, my mother gave birth to a boy, but he died at infancy. My mother got pregnant very soon after this second child. Then she had my brother Maktaaq.

So I was born when there were barely any Qallunaat around the Igloolik area. I recall that there was only one Qallunaaq man. He was the priest. He had a sod-house and a qulliq, and he used to run out of tobacco because he smoked. He used to make us look for cigarette butts when the sealskin tents were taken down, and when his qulliq ran out of oil he made us light it. He was the only Qallunaaq around, and his nostrils were always filled with smoke.[7]

At that time we had caribou skin for our clothing, nothing else, just caribou skin. Even during the summer we wore caribou-skin clothing since there was no other choice. Even when there were hardly any caribou around, we had to make do. There were no fabrics back then for us to make clothing, nothing at all, only caribou skins.

FIVE YEARS OLD

I start to recollect bits and pieces after my real parents came back from the Keewatin area. By this time I was about five years old, and Maktaaq, he was about two years old. By this time I really thought that Suula was my older sister. Her husband, Kublu, was just a stranger to me. He was not like a father to me at all. Every time he left to go hunting, I stayed overnight at my mother's house. My adoptive parents really loved my mother. She was their niece and they loved her very much, they treated her like their own child. They made a fuss over her even when she was older and had a child of her own. In my adopted family I had a younger brother, Alurut, but when we camped together, my real brother Maktaaq and I usually played together. My brother in Arvaaluk's family was maybe three years younger than me.

One time when we were playing together, the three of us, we heard that some hunters had come back from hunting caribou with meat, so we went to where the hunters were to eat it. We were in Siuraarjuk, by the shore. It was kind of windy that day, and I remember all of us holding hands with our two mothers because we were so small. We were different ages but we were all about the same size. Since I was a girl, I didn't grow very fast. I was quite small and my brothers had grown faster than me, so we were the same height. I was a lot weaker than my younger brother. Every time he used to push me, I fell down. It was like we were twins.

The people who caught the caribou were Kunuruluk, Arulaaq, and Niaqukittuq. After we ate some of the caribou meat, we went back home and started to play. My brother Maktaaq used to play with his father's rifle. On that day his father hadn't emptied the rifle. He had forgotten to empty it. The rifle had been sitting in the entrance-way to the igluvigaq so he started to play with it. His father let him play with his rifle because he was his first son, and he spoiled him rotten. Maktaaq used to play with it when his father was feeding the dogs. I remember Maktaaq would imitate shooting the dogs while they were being fed.

On that day his father didn't empty the rifle. As soon as we came home from eating caribou at the neighbour's house, we started playing with the rifle. We were playing with my little brother, my adoptive brother. We were playing with him. He went inside the igluvigaq. We had a door on the igluvigaq and an entrance-way dug about two feet deep into the ground to protect the inside of the igluvigaq from the cold. That is how they used to make an iglugivaq if they planned to stay in it for a long time. My little brother was leaving the igluvigaq to come back outside again. He had a cup of hot water, and he wanted to put some ice in it to cool it off. My other brother Maktaaq and I started playing a game. We were pretending we were walruses trying to defend the shore from each other. My brother was on his way out of the igluvigaq. Maktaaq pointed at him and said, "He is the walrus going down to the sea!" I said, "I'll do it, let me catch the walrus!" As I was trying to pull the rifle out of Maktaaq's hands, it went off with a big bang. We were so young we didn't know about shooting, and we were not scared. We didn't know what it was all about.

Then my younger brother, Alurut, went falling down with the cup in his hand. My real mother, Suula, came running out of the igluvigaq with her kamiks off. She came out and screamed, "He's been shot!" I became very afraid all of the sudden, and my mind went blank, maybe because they started to yell at me or something like that. When I regained consciousness, I remember seeing lots of legs around the door of the igluvigaq and it was kind of dark. I started to crawl through the legs and realized that there was slippery ice on the floor. My own mother always kept the floor clean, but at that time it was slippery from the water that my brother had been carrying before I shot him.

I must have fallen down again because when I woke up the snow had melted where my face had been and I had a nosebleed. There was some blood in the snow. No one had been watching over me since they were tending to my adopted brother who I had shot. Then I tried to crawl through the legs, and someone pushed me aside and told me not to go inside because I had just shot a person. They pushed me away. I was really cold and I was crying because nobody seemed to care for me now. Then all of the sudden someone grabbed me and threw me inside roughly and put me face to face with my little brother. He was alive at that time. They yelled, "Look at him! You shot him!" They started to scold me really loudly. They were yelling and it was then that I realized what I had done. I saw the blood. He died the next day.

It was spring, and the day after it happened and the sun was shining outside, I was out playing with the other children. I didn't realize I was wearing my dead brother's mittens. Some adult came up to me and grabbed the mittens I was wearing and yelled, "Your brother died, and now you are wearing his mittens." He took the mittens and didn't even give me another pair to wear. I don't remember if there was any funeral.

After the accident, maybe a week or so, my real parents left the camp, Siuraarjuk, without warning. They went to the Pond Inlet area to escape from the RCMP.[8] My real father, Kublu, was afraid of the RCMP and he was ashamed because I had shot and killed my little brother with his loaded rifle. He didn't want to be blamed for what I had done. That is what my real mother told me when I asked her later why they had left me behind without a warning. They moved to the Pond Inlet area and lived there until they died.

After the accident my adoptive parents became abusive, and the hatred towards me for killing my younger brother became worse. This hatred was from my mother. My father never changed, he was always good to me, but my mother became very abusive and full of hate. She was ashamed of me – that is why she became abusive. Both of them were old and couldn't do much, so I became their slave. I was their only child at this point. Before the accident I used to sleep between them since they had loved me so dearly, but after the accident my mother started to make me sleep way on the edge of the bed. I felt cold when I slept. It was dark and I was alone. She didn't feed me anymore or make clothes for me. My kamiks were ruined, they had holes in the soles. I played outside for long periods of time wearing those kamiks.

When I played outside, neighbours in the camp would invite me into their homes and feed me. I didn't know how down I was at that time, I didn't know how low I had fallen. I never felt sorry for myself or thought that I was being abused, but the neighbours, they felt sorry for me. When I visited, they made me clothing and combed and washed my hair. Since I had long hair, I had head lice. Since my mother didn't care for me at all, they washed my hair and got rid of my head lice.

Some people took me to the eldest blind woman in the camp. She felt sorry for me and was full of affection for me. She was good to me. She fed me cooked or frozen meat, and she melted ice for me so I would have water to drink and wouldn't go thirsty. After she fed me, I felt warm and cosy. I felt much better. Sometimes I wouldn't have eaten for days and days. This went on through the winter. When spring came, we left the winter camp to go hunt for seals. When the ice melted that summer, we went to hunt caribou. I often woke up in the night to hear my mother crying. She said she had bad nightmares about her son. In her dreams she used to say, "Oh, Alurut wants me to join him!" but she couldn't go to where he was so she would start to cry harder.

I remember one day my father went caribou hunting and came back with four caribou. I ran to him when he arrived, and he said "Utagan-naakulu" – that is what he used to call me, "Utagannaakulu"[9] – he said, "Utagannaakulu, I have been given four caribou." I didn't understand what he meant by "given four caribou." At that time I didn't know anything about hunting or God.

It wasn't too long after my brother died that my mother became sick. She had an infection on her breast. The pus went to her lungs, and she got an infection from it. We were at Akkuniq. She was slowly dying. At that time I was eight years old, and all my relatives were mourning for her. My father didn't want her to die, so he went outside to pray so he could be heard more easily by God. I went with him. It was the middle of the night, and some people from the camp were crying inside of the qarmaq. We went outside to the side of the house, and my father started to pray. We closed our eyes as we were praying, and through my eyelids I saw a bright light. I opened my eyes and looked up, and there was a light so bright I couldn't look at it. The bright light went into the qarmaq, and my father said to me, "Utagannaakulu, it has come for your mother." Then he started to cry, and he went inside. I followed him and listened to everyone crying very hard. Then somebody pulled him over to the bed, and he went to his wife to try and bring her back to life. He couldn't bring her back to life. That light came at the right time. The reason that it came was because my mother used to pray a lot. She used to pray that she would be saved by the faith she had in God. She used to pray to God that she wanted to go to heaven and follow her son.

After she died, they wrapped her in caribou sheets. At that time we couldn't wait for the relatives to come from all over the place. They buried her body right away. After they buried her, the rest of the family left to go to the floe edge to hunt seals. We were alone, just my father and me. He didn't want to leave my mother's body. The floe edge was where the food was, but he wouldn't leave her body. He had loved her very much. Since I was too young to be left alone in our old sod-house, I used to go with my father everywhere. We would go out hunting and would return to a very cold home. There was no one to keep the house warm with the qulliq while we were away. Every day we went to her grave and prayed beside her. Sometimes I wondered why he was doing that. Sometimes he prayed in our house in the middle of the floor. We stayed by her body for a month. Then we moved to the camp my grandparents Kaukjak and Nutarariaq were at. We lived with them until I got married.

❈ ❈ ❈

After that incident, when I was a little older, there were people who used to tell me, "You should be a Christian because you are a murderer. Be a Christian, pray a lot, and you will see your baby brother in heaven." People were trying so hard to make us become Christians, my father and me, because we were both murderers. My father had killed a person too. He had killed somebody before, but it had been a long, long time ago. He had done it to protect people because that person who he had killed was killing innocent people. So he killed that person. It was the old Inuit law and order.

Those people who called me a murderer for a lot of my life, they were people who didn't like me at all. They were blaming me for what happened to my little brother, but they didn't know the whole story. They were just being mean and nasty. I think that those people who tried to make me feel guilty, those people were probably related to the man who had gone insane, who my father, Arvaarluk, had killed. They were probably the relatives of that person. They had been trying to get revenge, to get at Arvaarluk any way they could. They couldn't get him, though, because each time they tried, he was probably running too fast. He learned to run fast so he could defend himself against those people. They couldn't keep up with him so they were mean to me instead, by calling me a murderer. My mother told me that Arvaarluk had killed that person when he was very young. He was maybe eighteen or twenty, and he always had nightmares after that about what he had been appointed to do. He had a hard time sleeping, and he had nightmares because he was always anxious that someone from the family of the person he killed would take revenge.

Since we were both murderers, my father and I, the people in the camp wanted us to believe in God. They wanted us to follow God's

word. My father always prayed, every day. He used to have nightmares. When he had nightmares he would start to moan, then he
would sit up and scream, "Satan, keep away from me!" He would grab
his knife and start stabbing at nowhere, trying to get rid of Satan. I
used to call my stepsister when he did that at night. She told me that
our father had been really scared after he killed that man. He was
afraid that people would go after him for revenge. At that time he had
been able to run very fast. He could run as fast as caribou. He had
exercised a lot and practised running so that he could protect himself.
After I learned that about him, I didn't mind so much when he did
things like scream at Satan. When he had nightmares I would wake up
and pray right beside him. Then, as we were praying, he would fall
asleep again.

GROWING UP, WE STAYED WITH OUR MOTHERS

I didn't go to school when I was a child. We didn't have schools. Young
girls stayed with their mothers. We stayed with our mothers all the
time. When we were growing up, we stayed with our mothers, and our
mothers would ask us to do things for them, like go and get ice or take
the bucket out. Also, we learned to sew. Our mothers taught us how to
sew and clean skins. We were always helping our mothers, cleaning the
skins, sewing, taking the bucket out, getting ice, making oil for the
lamps, and chewing sealskins. Working like this, it was like going to
school, because we would be woken up early in the morning to start
our daily work. They would wake us up and tell us to get up and get
ready because we were going out hunting or we were going out
camping. It was like going to school.

Towards the evening we would finish our work. We went to bed
early because we had to get up early in the morning. We went to bed
at around seven or eight at night, and we would wake up around five
or six in the morning. All of us in the camp would wake up early in the
morning. It wasn't like it is today with some people sleeping and some
awake – it wasn't like that. Our parents weren't like this. We all had to
get up early in the morning. We all got up at the same time.

Often in the middle of the night they would wake us up. They would
wake up the boys every time the dogs had a fight. They would ask
them to get up and stop the dogs. The boys, they would get up in the
middle of the night and go out and stop the dogs and then come back
inside and go back to bed. Sometimes they would wake us up and tell
us that there was a polar bear outside. We would have to get up in a
hurry. We didn't stop to have tea every time they woke us. No, we
would get up right away and put on all of our clothes and go outside.

28

We were taught, like soldiers, that we had to be on guard all the time. They taught us how to get up and put on our clothes in a hurry. If there was a polar bear outside, the men would go out and hunt the polar bear. We were always on guard.

Even those nights when we were up in the middle of the night, they would still wake us up again early in the morning. We had a lot of things to do between the time we got up and the time we went to bed. The men always had to make sure the gear was ready in case we had to go hunting or change camps in a hurry and the women always had to make sure they were ready to go. The teenage girls were always chewing sealskins. I chewed on skins all through my childhood – I always had skin in my mouth. Every single day we would work, and then towards the evenings we would relax and play games. In the springtime the little ones would go out and practise hunting with targets and birds. They would hunt birds and take them home, and the rest of the family would eat them. Even the teenagers ate what the family ate. We ate every type of food, and everything was useful.

That was the way it was for us. We were asked to do a lot of things, and we would listen to our parents. It wasn't that our parents were mean – they did this so that we could learn to be strong to help others and help ourselves. They did this so that we could learn to survive. In the future, when we were adults, we would have to know how to look after our own children. They did this to teach us the way.

EIGHT YEARS OLD WHEN MY ADOPTIVE MOTHER DIED

I was eight years old when my adoptive mother died of an abscess in her breast. The abscess grew inside instead of outside. After she died she was buried. We wrapped her in caribou skin, a really clean caribou skin. We wrapped her in the caribou skin and put her in a wooden box we made from wood from the trading post. We left it on top of the ground near Akkuniq, where she died. We didn't dig a grave for her. The ground was too frozen, so we just put her in the box on top of the ground. My father and I used to go visit her grave and pray beside her. Every time my father would go to her grave, I would go with him.

The grave is still there, but there is nothing inside the box anymore. It was a long time ago that she died. My father, I remember he used to travel to that camp where she was buried as much as he could. Since he was very old, he couldn't marry or live with another woman after my mother, so he would go up to her grave and pray. When I look back, I can still see my father going up the hill and looking at his wife's grave.

We were grieving more back then because we didn't believe in Jesus. We didn't know that if a person died they went to heaven. We thought that if a person died, they died forever. People would grieve for a year, and once a year they would visit the grave and cry. It is really different from the way things are today. In the old days people were alone in the camps, and when someone died, they would have to look after the body themselves. They would take the body out of the house and put the body into a grave. Even though they were grieving, they still had to look after the body. They grieved so much because they weren't taught that when they die they go to heaven to be with Jesus. Today we hear these things. In the old days we believed that we were going to lose that person forever and never see them again. We would cry. We weren't thinking about their spirit.

Today we live in a big community. We know that when someone dies, they are not lost to us. They go to heaven and we will see them later. In the old days, nobody would visit a grieving family. There were no radios or telephones to announce that someone had died. The only sound we heard back then was the sound of dogs howling. I think that is one of the reasons why it is different today, because today people visit people who are grieving, and we know for sure that when a person dies they go to heaven and they are not in pain any more. We were told that if we are Christians, we must have patience and believe that we will see our dead relatives again in the future, not on earth but in heaven. I think that is why we don't grieve as much as we did before.

MY FATHER, ARVAARLUK

I used to see people running really fast when I was a child, even faster than dog teams. My father, my son Arvaluk's atiq,[10] he was really healthy and he was a really fast runner. Some people, like Arvaarluk, when they were really energetic and strong, they didn't show it in public. They showed it only when nobody was looking at them. When they were around people, they acted really embarrassed or humble and shy.

My son Arvaluk's grandfather was a really fast runner. He lived in a camp where people looked down on him. People didn't know him very, very well, and they blamed him for something he had done a long time ago. It was this incident that had happened before I was born. My father, Arvaarluk, used to tell me about it. There was this man – I don't know his name – he was living in the settlement and he started killing people. The people in the settlement started to become scared. They wanted to do something. They wanted to protect themselves. My father was asked to do something because he was the bravest and wisest man in the camp, and he could move faster than other men. My father was asked to meet this man and kill him. Even though he was young, he was asked to kill that person. That is what he did – the people in the camp asked him to kill that person and he did. It wasn't his idea. This was before there were any RCMP. This was a long, long time ago.

My father, he told me how he was always afraid of revenge from that incident. He was afraid that the relatives of the man who he had murdered would seek revenge. He learned how to run very fast because of this. He did it to defend himself. When he was out hunting, he would run really fast. One day a person from his camp was watching him while he was hunting. He was hunting caribou, and a group of caribou were running away from him. Once caribou start to run, they are really fast and you can not catch up to them. My father, he was running towards the caribou, and the caribou were ahead of him. The person said that my father ran like the caribou and he was really fast. The caribou were quite fast, but he was faster. The caribou turned to run in another direction, and the man who was watching said that Arvaarluk was right behind the caribou. He looked away for a minute when Arvaarluk was close by, and when he looked back he couldn't see him anymore. Then he saw Arvaarluk and the caribou far, far away, in the dirt of the wet area of the lake. Arvaarluk was running so fast over there the man could barely see his legs move.

When this man went back and told this story, the people in the camp started teasing Arvaarluk, my father. They told him that he looked so old and weak. They said that every time he walked, he walked very slowly and carefully, yet he was so strong and fast. They said they knew about him now. They knew how fast he was. Because his secret was found out by the people in the camp, he started losing his energy and his speed. I think it was because of his shyness. The people in the camp found out that Arvaarluk was really strong and that he could run really fast, and he lost his confidence. I don't know why he lost his speed, but maybe it was because he was always happier when he kept things to himself.

IT WAS GOING TO BE SUNDAY AND WE HAD TO STOP

My father and I were alone, and I was about ten. When my father and I were alone, when my mother died, we lived in Kapuivik. That is the name of the camp we were going to, Kapuivik. We were travelling on open ice, and we were travelling by dog team. We stopped to have a rest, to put up our tent, and we found out that it was Saturday. We found out that we had to stop, because the next day was Sunday and we were supposed to rest. That is what the missionaries said. It was wintertime and we were out of fuel for our qulliq and we didn't have any matches. It was going to be Sunday and we had to stop. I was really thirsty. We didn't have any tea.

My father didn't drink tea. He couldn't drink tea, even if he put sugar in it. We drank caribou broth – that was our tea. When I started living in my father-in-law's camp, that is when I started drinking tea. I don't drink tea that often, only sometimes, even today. While I was growing up, if I was out visiting and if I was asked if I wanted any tea, I wouldn't have any. That is what I was like.

So we stayed on the open ice to rest, but I was really thirsty. We didn't have any fuel, so we couldn't melt ice to make water. There were some people in the camp where we were going, and we knew that they had fuel. We had to stop to rest, though, because it was Sunday. We had no tea and no heat and no water, and we weren't supposed to travel. I was really mad at the people who told us that we weren't supposed to travel on Sunday. I remember it started storming. It was really stormy and I started crying. I was cold and really, really thirsty. My father took out a piece of sealskin and cut a piece from it. He put snow in it and put it next to his body where it started melting. That is how I got some water to drink.

So we stopped that Sunday and the next day was Monday so we started travelling again. We started to untangle the dogs – they were all tangled up. I helped with the dogs, and then we headed for the camp. When I got to the sod-house where everyone was, I was offered a hot-water tea. I was really cold, and I was really thirsty. They knew I was cold and thirsty, so they offered me tea so that I could get warmer quickly. I asked for water instead of tea. I asked for water. The water was quite warm. They knew that I was really cold, so they offered me a cup of warm water. I asked for really cold water even though I was really cold. I went to the porch and I got some really cold water and drank it until I was filled with water. I didn't have any tea. After I drank really cold water, I got warmed up. Just because it was Sunday, I almost died of thirst.

❖ ❖ ❖

Sundays were really important to us. In the future we won't look at Sunday as such an important day. Even today I see people going out hunting on Sunday mornings. I don't really mind people travelling on Sundays, coming home from a trip when they have to work on Monday. I don't mind those people, but it still bothers me when I see people hunting on a Sunday. That is because I still believe what I was taught in the old days. I still believe that we shouldn't travel or hunt on Sundays. We were taught about Jesus. We were taught that Jesus died for us, and there are rules that we should obey that were given to us by Moses in the old days. We were taught not to totally disregard the rules but to make them fit with our lives. We were told that we should love one another. Today we are starting to hear preachers say that it is all right to do these kinds of things on Sundays. Nowadays, if we have something to do on Sundays, we can do it without worrying. Even if we have to sew, we can sew on Sundays and not worry about it. We are losing Sunday as an important day and I am sad about that ...

I am talking about Sundays. If I remember some more about Sundays, I'll talk about it again. As I understand from the Bible, Jesus is the king of Sundays. That is how I understand it ...

THIS IS HOW WE SPENT OUR YEAR

January is the time for light. February is the time for bright. Animals deliver in March, and April is the month of baby seals. May is for putting up tents. June is time for eggs, birds' eggs. July is for calves of caribou, they start delivering in July. August is the middle of the year and September, halfway through the year. October and November are fall. November is for hard times and December is the dark season. That is how the year was described.

This is how we spent our year, this is what we did. I will start with the spring. Seal-hunting season, out on top of the ice, it would be in early spring, April, May, June, no, not June ... April and May would be seal-hunting season out on the ice. We would live in igloos. Then in June the sea ice would start to get thin, so we would move to the camp on the shore, the camp with the sod-houses. We would go back to the shore because in June we started walrus-hunting. We didn't use the sod-houses in this season, we would put up our tents right beside the sod-houses. We just left the sod-houses where they were. Everyone would put up their tents right next to the sod-houses. We would walrus-hunt with boats. We would use boats to hunt because in Igloo-lik in June the ice would be all gone in the area where we walrus-hunted. It was that particular season that we would go out on the boat and hunt for walrus meat. We would use the walrus meat for the dog-meat cache, and we would eat some of it too. Some of it we also used to age. We would let it sit in rock caches over the spring and summer and eat it in the fall.

In August we would start caribou-hunting. We would start working to get skins to make caribou clothing for the winter. It was the younger people who would do this. It was like we had a job – we worked for the elders. The first week of August the elders would take us to the inlets by boat. At this time the ice would be broken up. We would start walking inland from there. Since the caribou were way up there on the land at that time, we would walk quite a ways. The elders would leave us in the inlets and go back to the camp so they could hunt walrus for food for the winter. The walrus meat would be used in the winter, for the dogs and for us to eat. We cached that meat. When the weather was good, like better than it is today, calm and flat on the water, we couldn't travel. We didn't have outboard motors, so we would have to use sails if we wanted to travel. We would have to wait for a windy day to travel.

The elders would drop us off in the inlets, and we would leave all of our things back at the camp with the sod-houses. I grew up going caribou-hunting with my father, Arvaarluk. He wasn't too old to go. He stopped going up to the inlets by the time I was twelve years old. That is when he became old. I got married after that and started going with my husband.

In August we would walk inland from the shore. We would walk for days, looking for caribou. We would take our dogs. We would leave our sleds in the elders' camp, and we would carry everything on our backs. Even the dogs would be carrying supplies on their backs. We would walk for four days, five days, or a week. We would walk with our dogs and our supplies until we reached where the caribou were. Then we would settle down with the caribou. We would spend the whole summer trying to get enough skins for the year, and we would cache meat at certain points to pick up later on in the winter.

In the fall the lakes would become covered with a thin coat of ice. We would still be out caribou-hunting, but the elders at the camp would go looking for fish. We would fish in the fall, spring, and summer – that is when we fished for char.

Then in early fall, about the first week in October, we would wait for the first snowfall to start travelling by dog team back to the shore, back to the sod-house camp. We would wait for the snow to come, and then we would start travelling. We would use polar-bear skins and caribou skins as qamutiks. We would be waiting for the first snow, and when the snow came, that is when we would fill up the caribou skins we had brought with us and use them as qamutiks. We would fill them up with all the supplies and all the caribou skins we had prepared. We would take everything off that we had on our backs, make a makeshift qamutik with the skins, and start travelling to the shore. We would start travelling and caribou-hunting at the same time. We would leave the caribou meat behind and bring only the skins so that they could be used for bedding and for clothing. We would come home when the snow was really hard and good. We would use our qamutiks later on to get the meat that we cached along the way.

On our way back to the camp from caribou-hunting, we would build an igloo and use the caribou fat as qulliq oil. We would walk into the tents and they would be so warm and smelly. Seal and caribou fat, they smell different. Caribou smells so much better than seal! ... We would come back to the shore with all the caribou furs, and people would like our smell, the way we smelled. We smelled like caribou. When we reached the camp, the people in the camp would have been using seal blubber as oil for the qulliq. To me, after coming from inland, it was a different smell in the tents. It didn't smell very good to me. It smelled like old blubber. I would notice the smell right away, and I didn't like the smell of the seal fat. During different seasons there would be different smells in the sod-houses. In the summer we would burn moss and heather and different plants in the qulliq. They would make the tent smell really nice ...

When we reached the camp after hunting inland, the elders would take the caribou skins. We would have nothing to do with the skins after this, because we were young. The young people would do the hunting inland, and then the elders would take over and distribute the skins. This would be in mid November. Once we were back in the camp, we would start trapping foxes for a while. In the late fall, foxes get fresh fur on the outside.

We would stay in our sod-house camp over the winter, during the dark season. We would stay there until the days started coming back. We would eat meat from the caches. We would hunt seals through breathing holes. We would hunt narwhals, sea mammals, anything we could find. We would stay there until March. It is always different every year. If we didn't have enough in our caches, even if it was really cold, we would move from our winter camp early. We would start moving when the caches ran out. March, that is when the caches of walrus meat would go down, and we would have to go to another camp closer to the floe edge to get seal meat.

The birds arrived in the spring. We hunted them as long as they stayed around, all summer long, and then they went back down South. As soon as they arrived, we started hunting the birds. Birds were really useful. We would use their feathers and their skins. The birds would start arriving in the spring. They would arrive during seal hunting seasons when we were out on the ice, April and May ...

Yes, that was our year. As Inuit, we did lots of different things to survive. Since it is a very long story, I have just mentioned the important things. That is all I have told you.

I WAS VISITING AN OLD WOMAN WHOSE DAUGHTER WAS DYING

There was the time when we were in a camp with a group of Inuit. I was with my father, Arvaarluk, I was just a child. I was very young and

I was out visiting. I was visiting an old woman whose daughter was dying. This woman who was dying was my husband's first wife. She was a lot older than me. She was the same age as my husband, and she had been sick for a while. She had been sick off and on. She kept getting pregnant but she kept on having miscarriages. Every time she miscarried, pieces of the fetus would be left behind in her uterus, and these pieces were making her sick. She was bleeding to death. That is what was happening to her.

She was sick when they were travelling in the springtime. We heard that from some other people, that she was very sick. In the summer she got a bit better. She was well enough to walk around. They had a sod-house near the beach, and one day in the late summer a narwhal went by. When she rushed out to see the narwhal, she fell and got sick again – that is what we heard. I met her when she was really sick. She never got up, and she was really skinny. I never thought that her husband would be my husband in the future.

I was visiting this woman's mother when I was just a child. She was my husband's first mother-in-law, and she asked me to pray for her daughter. My husband's first wife was the only daughter and an only child, so the mother was really grieving for her dying daughter. She really wanted her daughter to live. When I was visiting the house, her mother told me to pray for her, to pray that she would get better. I was a child and I didn't know how to pray that well. Even though I was a child, she asked me to pray. I think that she was hoping that the faith of a child would make her daughter better. I was really young. I never knew that her husband would be my husband in the future.

At that time I didn't know how to say prayers on my own. I used to watch my father pray, so I could recite the Lord's Prayer and the Grace of Our Lord Jesus Christ prayer. My father used to pray from his heart all the time. I could say these two prayers along with my father, but I had never prayed a prayer on my own. I remember being a little child and praying for that woman. My father used to say, "Oh God, my Father," when he was praying. I didn't know what "Oh God" meant, but I used to say that too, just like my father. I didn't understand what I was saying, but I prayed as hard as I could for this dying woman.

In the fall after that my father and I moved. We went to live in another camp. That fall we all heard that she had died, she died of her sickness. I am remembering this because I know.

MARRIAGE AND FAMILY: WE WERE FULL OF CHILDREN

I WILL TELL YOU ABOUT MY MARRIAGE

Arranged marriages, they aren't done any more. We used to live with a man really, really young. Sometimes it was right after we had our first period – that was when we were seen as an adult. Sometimes it was even before that. My mother got married when she was twelve years old ... no, maybe she was fourteen. I was born in 1936. No, it was 1931. Maybe she got married a year or two before that, when she was twelve or fourteen. That was a long time ago – I cannot remember. It was before I was even born. I was born in 1931.

This story isn't about my mother, it is about my own arranged marriage. I am a little worried talking about this ... I am a little worried about saying this on tape. If these tapes become a book, I would worry about people becoming shocked, people becoming upset when they read it ... I would worry about that, people being shocked ... My marriage, it isn't a nice story, it doesn't sound nice. I don't want people to be shocked. At first I didn't like my husband, I didn't like him at all. But as I grew up, I began to realize what a good husband I have and how lucky I am. He is a good man. I will tell you about my marriage. I will tell you anyways – that way younger people will learn.

I think my mother was fourteen or fifteen when she had me. I asked her once, and she couldn't quite figure it out how old she was when she had me. Her husband, Kublu, he was a man a lot older than her. It was arranged that she live with him, so she moved in with him when she was really young. He already had children of his own, they were about the same age as my mother. He was a lot older than her. His oldest daughter was a little bit younger than my mother, maybe just a year younger. It was an arranged marriage.

In the old days even if women didn't want to live with the man, the elders would arrange the marriage. They thought they were helping the woman. If the woman was an orphan, she would probably get married very, very young. If a woman didn't have a mother or father, she would need someone to look after her. She would move in with a man at an early age so that her in-laws would look after her. That is how it was in the old days with Inuit.

Not all women were married so young. Some of them would turn seventeen, eighteen or even nineteen before they started living with someone. They would learn how to sew, and they would learn a lot of things before they got married. Sometimes parents and adopted parents wouldn't let their daughter marry early. If they were older people and they couldn't look after themselves, they would want their daughter around to look after them. Daughters would stay at home and look after the parents. They might let their daughter marry if the man who wanted to marry their daughter agreed to stay with that family. That is the only way that they would give the woman to the man to be married. Sometimes it was the man's parents who were old and needed help. Then a woman would be given to that family so that she could look after the parents-in-law. Back then every human being was useful. We would help each other in any way we could.

Yes, the time when I first got married was a really unhappy time for me. I remember it quite well. When I got married, I had no idea what marriage was all about. I didn't know how to treat a husband. I didn't even know about sex. My husband and I, we weren't like the young people today. We weren't lovers when we moved in together. I was very young and I was forced to marry him – my family and his family, they forced me. He was a lot older than me and he was a widower. He had been married to a woman before me. I hadn't finished growing yet. I hadn't even started to menstruate. That is how young I was. I was just a child.

My whole life I had been promised to someone else. We had been promised to each other by our mothers when I was just a baby. I grew up thinking I was going to marry this other man, but he got tired of waiting for me to grow up so he married another woman.

My father, Arvaarluk, and my in-laws were from different camps. We met in a big group once in a while. I lived alone with my father because I didn't have a mother. We lived in a small camp. He wasn't my real father, he was my adoptive father, and he was very, very old. I loved him dearly and I used to help him. He was half deaf, so I would interpret for him every time somebody was talking. I even used to sleep in the same bed as my father. I did this until I was a teenager, until I grew breasts. I remember I used to get really cold in bed when I started sleeping alone.

My father, Arvaarluk, he was getting old when I got married. He knew that he wouldn't be living on the earth for many more years. He knew he was going to die early, and he wanted me taken care of. I had no mother, and my father was afraid of me being an orphan, so he asked my husband's family if they would take me as their daughter-in-law. He knew that when he died I wouldn't be able to live alone, so he arranged a marriage for me. He arranged it out of love. Even though I was his only daughter and the only one around to look after him, my father gave me to this man and his family. At the time my husband and I got married, there were other teenage women in the camp who had their periods and were ready for marriage, but I was the one who got married. I was so young I had never thought about falling in love or marriage. They took me away and we travelled to the Arctic Bay region from around Igloolik. I was maybe thirteen or fourteen years old.

My husband, he was a really shy person. When we got married it was his father who told him to come and take me away from my father. My husband, he was a lot older than me, and he had already been married, but he was still really scared. I remember that day. We were at Akkuniq. I was with my father and there were people camped together there. My future husband came to my house while I was playing outside with a friend. He had a blanket with him and he covered himself. I was running around with my friend, visiting people, and he started following me. I noticed that he was following me, and I started running away, trying to get away from him. The friend who I was with, she had her period already, she looked older than me, but he wasn't after her. He was after me.

We went into a house beside the beach, and in the house there was an old lady. It was night-time. She asked me what I was doing there, and I said Awa was looking for me. As soon as I told her that, she told me not to be scared. She said she had already heard what was going on. I was still scared. Her whole family was in the sod-house, they were all on the bed together. The older people were not concerned with what was going on. They thought I was being silly, so I walked over all the people on the bed to where the young people were. I was desperate, and I figured the young people might understand. I walked on top of the people who were in bed and put myself between the young people and tried to hide. My husband, he looked in, but he didn't see me. He just came in and took off again. As soon as I noticed that he had gone, I got out of the bed and left the sod-house. As I was walking out, he grabbed me, and I started crying. I was so scared. I wondered why he was after me. I was so scared of him. I was wondering what he was going to do. I had never thought about falling in love or going to bed with a man.

My future husband, he took me to his parents' house. I was crying and struggling so hard he let me go. As soon as he let me go I started running. I ran over to my friends' sod-house, and when I reached the entrance-way I hid myself underneath all the caribou clothing. My future husband followed me. When he entered the house I ran out. I was really young. I went and hid somewhere else in the entrance-way, and when my future husband came out again – when I heard him leave – I went back outside to where my friends were. He wasn't around, but I stayed close to the other teenagers playing outside for the next little while, and when he came outside again, I started running. He grabbed me. He took me over to his house again. I was fighting and struggling, so he had a hard time taking me into the house. I was still crying when he brought me in, but he held on to me so hard that I couldn't move. I didn't want to stay in the house, I wanted to go back to my father, so I started kicking the door and the wall and crying. He still held on to me. There was an axe close by and as soon as he let me go, I grabbed the axe and I tried to kill him. Since I was weak and he was strong, he grabbed the axe from me. My in-laws were in the same bed as us. They didn't care what we were doing. They were laughing at me. I felt so alone. He kept me in that house all night long. Since I couldn't leave the house, I slept inside.

The next morning when I woke up, my future husband left the house, so I ran home. I told my father what happened. He didn't care, he just laughed. My stepsisters, they heard what I said and they all started working together, making new caribou clothing for me. They told me that I was going to need new caribou clothing because I was leaving the camp. They didn't want to worry me, so they told me that I was leaving my future husband behind to go out travelling. I was so happy!

They put the new clothes on me. They were beautiful clothes, and I went out to the entrance-way to get oil for the qulliq. While I was there, I heard my future husband and my father talking about me becoming his wife. My father was telling him how he was getting old and how he couldn't look after me anymore. "As long as she is well looked after," my father said, my husband could take me.

When I heard this, I went back inside in the house and started screaming. I was screaming that there was no way that I was going to go with my husband. I asked my future husband to leave the house, so he left. I started crying and talking back to my father. I was screaming at him, telling him that I didn't want to leave him, I didn't want to get married. That night when I went to sleep, my future husband came in and got into the bed with me. I was crying and screaming, but no one did anything.

The next morning I woke up. My family had told me that I was going out travelling that day. My sister Qajaaq and some others had made me a new caribou parka, and I remember putting on the new clothing that they had made for me. I was really happy knowing that I would be leaving my future husband in the camp, leaving him behind. We left the camp and I remember travelling on the qamutik across the ice. My stepbrother Kuutiq and his wife, Niaquttiaq, were travelling with me that time. We stopped to have tea and I remember seeing a dog team coming. They were moving very fast. Then the dog team got close to us, and I recognized him. It was my future husband. We were out on the ice having tea, we were drinking tea at that time, so when he pulled up they offered him tea. I found out later that my family and the people in the camp had fooled me. They knew about him coming to pick me up. They had all planned it together without me knowing.

After our tea I went to get back on my brother's qamutik, but before I could get on, my brother took off really fast. He left me behind. My future husband grabbed me. I was kicking and screaming. He put me on his qamutik and tied me up. I remember he was very careful tying me up. He took me to his parents' camp. It was getting dark when we arrived and the house was dark. My eyes were swollen from crying. I was embarrassed and sorry to be sleeping in my father-in-law's house.

The next day I went out visiting. I went to go see other people in the camp who I knew. I was trying to get away from him. That is how badly I didn't want to be married to him. I had never grown up with him. He looked a lot older than I was, and I was very young. I had never been told about men. I had never been touched by a man before. I hadn't even had my first menstruation. Every time I left, he went to get me from the neighbour's house. I was trying to hide from him, but the people who I was visiting always told him where I was.

We used to go to bed, but we never had sex for a long time. I would be in bed with him and stay with him in bed, and I thought this was the way married life was. Apparently I was wrong. I guess he was waiting for me to grow up. He wanted to be with me and be my husband, but he thought I was too young. He was waiting for my body to develop into adulthood. I was small and he waited for a long time. He never bothered me or tried to have sex with me.

When I started menstruating, that is when I found out about sex ... If it was today, with the RCMP and Social Services here, I would report that I was raped by my husband, and they would take him away from me ... I remember being so upset after it happened to me. I remember telling my mother-in-law about this bad thing that had happened to me. She scolded me. She screamed at me, saying, "Don't say things like that!" and I remember telling her, "But it hurt!" Sometimes I wasn't too truthful.

When I saw other women, they were treated differently. I remember seeing women who went to bed without fighting their husband. I fought with my husband lots of times. I know a woman, she and her husband started living together in springtime and she fought so much that they didn't have sex until that fall. She would run away from him, and he would follow. He would chase her and she would get angrier. That is how life was for us.

In these new camps girls wouldn't know what to do, what to say. It was like that for me and my in-laws. I didn't want to be married at all. My husband just picked me up from my father's camp and moved me to another camp. I had to live with people I had never met before, people who were strangers to me. I didn't know what to do, what to say around them. It was very confusing for me. I missed my father and I was very homesick. Slowly, though, we young wives learned the way things worked in the new camps. We would learn about married life. Looking back, when I think about how it was for me, I feel sorry for myself. It was terrible ...

It took almost a year, maybe two years for me to stop being homesick all the time. It took that long for me to learn how my husband behaved and what kind of things he liked. That was how it was.

BACK THEN, GETTING MARRIED

Back then, getting married wasn't the same as it is today. Marriages were often arranged at birth. As soon as a baby was born, it would be promised to someone. If a baby girl was born and if there was a boy born at the same time, then often it would be arranged that when they grew up they would be married to each other. That actually happened – the two sets of parents would make the decision together, and babies would grow up promised to each other. The parents would arrange it when the babies were first born.

In the old days men could only get married if they were ready. If a man couldn't hunt, if he didn't have dogs of his own, and if he couldn't support his family by himself, then he couldn't get married. Today, it is different. Today nobody has a job all the time. Today even if a man doesn't have a job, he can still get married.

Back then if a man was ready for a wife, he would start visiting the family of the woman he was promised to and start living with her. The man would start staying over at the woman's house. He would stay in the house often enough so that the woman would know that she was going to marry this man. In the end she didn't have any choice but to marry him. She would leave her family to go live with him and with his parents. That is how marriages were. They didn't go out together or fall in love before they started to live together – they just moved in. That was how it happened.

If it was an arranged marriage and if the couple was old enough, they would get married even if they didn't know each other. Sometimes couples who had never talked or slept together would get married. Women were just taken from their camps one day. We were taken away – we had no say. Once we got married, we would start sleeping with our husbands. It was really terrible that way. I had never slept with a man before I got married. When we got married, I had to open up and fall in love with my husband. That is how it was done in the old days.

When we started living with a man, we left our families. We wouldn't see them for a year or so, and we couldn't call them on the telephone. Parents, when it came time for their daughters to get married, they would worry about them. Sometimes the elders would worry about the women in their families who were taken away. Sometimes there were men who would beat up their wives. The elders would worry about their daughters. It was like that in the old days.

Getting married, it was fun, part of it, but part of it would build up anger in us. We had to agree, when we went to live with our in-laws, we were supposed to keep quiet and not talk about ourselves or the problems we were having with other people. When we were living in it, when we were doing it, it was all right. Happiness was around us. There didn't seem to be all that many stressful situations ... But looking back, it was a very difficult lifestyle. It was a terrible thing we went through as women, as teenagers. The struggles we went through, we don't forget.

THAT WOMAN'S HUSBAND HAD A BOIL

I remember my husband and I were alone with another couple and their two children. My sister-in-law, she was a young girl and she came with us to go fishing. People took us there by boat and dropped us off. We stayed there. We stayed a long time out there in a camp. That is when I had my first menstruation, even though I had been married for some time. I was ashamed. I was shy, I was scared of my husband. He had been married before, and he already knew everything that I was ashamed of. That is when I was quite young.

We were in one tent. Since we were all young people, we would play around in the tent. We would play around and laugh and talk. We were so young then ...

Her husband was Kunuk, and she was Qaaqiuq. The children were Ittukusuk and Aula and Ulaayuk. We were camped with them for a long time, the whole summer, looking for caribou. We would go out walking during the days looking for caribou.

At that time people used to get big boils inside their skin. You would put a lemming skin on top to get the boil out. If there was tobacco around, we would use the tobacco pouch. They used to have hard covers on them. Even if there was a lot of pus inside, the boils wouldn't always burst by themselves. They would have to be cut to get the pus out, and there would be a lot of pus. That was how the boils were dealt with. That was our way of doing medicine.

That woman's husband, he had this boil on his shoulder. Even though we tried to do those medical things to it, the pus wouldn't come out. He became sick and he was sick for a week. We had been camped with that couple for two weeks before that happened. We had caught a lot of fish the first two weeks we were there. We filled up all the caches in the area with fish. There were so many fish, we didn't even use our spears, we would just use our knives and kill them like that. We had so many fish we even fed some to the dogs.

We had long boots that time. They were made out of sealskin. We would use one whole seal and sew the boot right up to the thighs. For both legs we would use two sealskins. Those boots, they would keep us from getting wet when we were fishing.

We were very happy that time. We were having a great time – all of the fishing we were doing didn't seem to make us tired at all! When we were finished we would play dolls. That woman and I, we would play dolls with the children. Sometimes my husband would play with us. He would pretend to go to the trading store or something.

There is this one incident that I really laugh about, I laugh when I remember. It was night-time and we were in the tent. My husband was playing with the dolls and pretending to go to the trading store. Then he pretended to come back to the camp. The other man asked him, "Did you get any oatmeal?" He was playing with English words. My husband said, "No, it is very expensive!" We were all laughing. We laughed very hard. That woman, she was sleeping, so we were trying not to wake her up with our laughing. We were trying to be very quiet. It was hard not to laugh loudly. We would say the word "oatmeal" over and over again. We would repeat what my husband had replied about the oatmeal, and we would laugh and laugh.

That woman's husband, he had a boil. We were trying to take off the boil with the lemming skin, but it wouldn't come out, it wasn't rising to the surface. The man with the boil thought that if we moved our camp to another site, if we moved the tent, it would help his boil to get better. We cared for him and wanted him to get better, so we all got together to move that tent. I had been helping that family out at that time, helping dry the caribou skins when the children peed on them and helping dry everyone's kamiks. The husband, he helped a lot and did a lot of the work too. We figured that perhaps if we moved to a cleaner place, a better place, it would be easier for us.

After we moved, during the moving, the man who wanted to move just sat there and put his hands together and watched. He looked really weak. Apparently he was on his last breath. The dogs were hanging around him and he was playing with the dogs. He was sitting there for a long time while we were moving the tent. After we had moved the tent, I asked the wife what was wrong with him. She didn't know. We finished moving the tent, and my husband went and told the man that the tent was ready for him to move into. Apparently that man was crying, saying that he couldn't do anything any more. When we went into the tent, he went straight into bed and didn't get up at all.

Apparently the boil went inwards, right into his ribs and into his lungs. That is where the infection went. That is what the elders said at the time. We had no idea. He was vomiting really black stuff, and he wasn't eating at all. He didn't want to eat any more.

I was really young at the time, I was maybe fourteen years old. I was trying to help this sick person, and I didn't know anything about sick people. There were no elders around, just us young people. The wife was scared. She kept running away. Her husband had asked her to move into the bed and lie beside him so that he could sleep. She didn't want to move closer to him. She was scared of him and she didn't know what to do, so I went beside the husband.

When he tried to sit up, his teeth would chatter. He would start talking, saying things that didn't make sense, so I would make him lie down again. Even though he wanted to sit up, I told him that each time he sat up his teeth chattered. He agreed and stayed lying down. Apparently he was losing his mind. When he talked, I would talk to him. I didn't know then that he had lost his mind. My husband was going to go by dog team to get some seal fat. He went seal hunting because we were getting low on fuel for our lamps. By that time it was early fall and there was fresh snow on the ground. The ground had frozen, so my husband hooked up the dog teams. He was gone for a long time, he was taking a long time to come back. The man kept saying, "Isn't he back yet? Will he ever come back?" I would answer, "Yes, he is coming back." After asking that same question over and over again, he stopped.

He stopped asking questions and lay with his back facing me, so I couldn't see him. I thought that he might be tired of being in the same position on his side so I lay him down on his back, but he didn't move. He was sleeping all night and I wasn't sleeping soundly so I picked up my sewing and sewed for the longest time. He never asked me anything. He barely moved.

I heard my husband returning so I went out to help him out with the dogs. When my husband came into the tent, he asked me how Kunuk was. I said that he had been sleeping for long, long time. Apparently he was dead, and the body had become hard. My husband went over to Kunuk. Kunuk's eyes were wide open. My husband said, "I think that he is dead now." He was shouting at him, "Kunuk! Kunuk! Wake up! Wake up!" We couldn't wake him up. He was dead. The wife was crying. I wasn't crying. I didn't feel like crying. I was told later that I wasn't crying because I had no energy left. That is what the people told me later.

After we found out he was dead, we tried to dress him but the body had stiffened up so much he was crooked. It was really hard to put his clothes back on. I hadn't realized that he had died. That is when I got scared of him. His eyes were wide open. It looked like he was going to speak at any moment. We couldn't put on his clothing. I was trying to hold him, trying to help dress him, but I was really getting scared of him. I was crying and crying. I didn't want to touch him anymore. My husband scolded me. He had never scolded me before at all. I think he really felt sorry for me. He said, "Look, you know that animals die. When they die, they never live again. They don't breathe again at all. You should know that. This is how it is with this person. He is not going to breath again. He is not going to be alive again. He is dead!"

He told me that Kunuk was not going to say anything anymore, that he was not breathing anymore, and that he wasn't looking at me. When I finally got my senses back, we put his clothes on and wrapped him up in the only blanket that we had to take him out of the tent. We were trying to take him out of the tent, but his wife didn't want him to leave. We got scared of his wife and put him back inside the tent on his bed. It felt like the tent was really large. Even though the tent was made of skin, we scrunched it down a bit and put some rocks on it to make the tent smaller. We fell asleep that night.

Early the next morning we tried to bury him. As we were putting the harnesses on our dogs, Kunuk's dogs were lying down. His dogs were lying down on the ground. They didn't even try to stand up. We put him on the qamutik and left. We took him a little ways by dog team. I was on the qamutik with him, and my husband was walking. It was still summer, maybe early fall, and there was just a little snow on the ground. His own dogs started howling as we were leaving. They were howling so loud. I asked my husband why, even though they were lying down, why the dogs were howling. He told me that they were mourning for their dead owner. Earlier that spring, before this had all happened, when we were seal-hunting on the land, the dogs had already begun howling because they were mourning him already.

We went to that place where there were flat rocks. We cut a box that we had picked up from the trading post when we had gone to buy supplies. We cut that box in half and placed half on his head and half on his feet. There was no other wood around. We put these flat rocks on top of him and that is how we buried him.

When we got back to our tent, we started getting prepared to go back home, to go to the place where our relatives would pick us up by boat. It was time for the boat to come pick us up, so we left to travel to the place where we were supposed to meet the boat. I kept on looking behind me as we were leaving, thinking that Kunuk would come and follow us. He didn't follow us. "He is not here yet," that is what I kept on thinking, "he is not here yet."

The wife was crying. She didn't want to leave, she was grieving so much. She was grieving for her husband. We went to the beach and it was dark. We pitched our tent to wait for the boat. When we put up the tent, it was too big, so we fixed it so that it was much smaller and that is how we slept. We heard the boat coming. It came the next day. It was an outboard motor. There were a lot of people in the boat, my in-laws as well. The water was calm that day and you could hear it really well. We were crying. We could hear the motor cutting off. It was low tide so they beached a long ways away. They didn't come towards us right away, so we fell asleep.

We could see them when we woke up but they wouldn't come. We didn't try to go to them so they walked to us. We were just inside the tent, and how scary that was at the time! I thought that they were going to blame us for letting that person die. It was like killing him, like the wife had killed him. The man's older brothers were there but their father wasn't. They had dropped him off at a camp along the way. I don't know why he stopped in a middle camp. Maybe he didn't want to meet his son right away.

Apparently when they stopped at that camp along the way, the father started looking around with his telescope. He had sat on a piece of rock where there was nothing around, and he was twirling his pipe around and around. He put his pipe down after he had lit it and he went to retrieve his telescope but he couldn't find it. He couldn't find his telescope at all. That is when he knew that he had lost a relative. That is when he knew that there was something wrong. The man who died was his son and he really loved him. He loved him like you love your family.

Mamatiaq, he was the one who came to pick us up. Mamatiaq was Kunuk's real brother and Uuyukuluk was his stepbrother. They came to pick us up. When they came into the camp, I wouldn't leave the tent. It was really scary. I was so scared I didn't want to go outside. I had a lot of fear when I was young. Fear went with me wherever I went. When they came over and peeked inside the tent, we all started crying. Of course they didn't see him inside the tent. Even though my husband told them what had happenned, they didn't understand him. He was telling them that Kunuk left us. Uuyukuluk was so shocked he was saying, "What? Did somebody kill him? Did he shoot himself?" My husband said no, but he couldn't explain further, he was too upset. Finally they understood us when I told them that he had died from a boil. People don't die from boils, but that is what I told them.

They prepared to get us ready to leave. We couldn't do anything by ourselves at that time so they took us by boat. We went to a camp where Kunuk's father, Attitaaq, was. We beached at that place. We didn't get out of the little cabin on the boat. I didn't get out, perhaps because I was so tired or scared. You could hear the dogs howling. We took Attitaaq on board and kept on travelling.

We went to my in-laws' place at another camp. It was rough water on the way there. When we beached, I saw another person who was crying. It was my sister-in-law. The man who died was her other brother. She was rolling around on the ground even though it was raining. She was rolling around on the ground and crying. I was so scared of her.

Apparently we were wrong to be so scared. Apparently everyone was really grateful for how we had taken care of that person who had died. Everyone was happy that we had buried him properly. We were really scared when they said that. I thought that they were trying to scare us. Later on, though, Attitaaq came to us, he came to talk to my husband and myself. He talked in a calm voice. We didn't talk back to him. We were young and he was our elder. We never answered back to him, we just listened. He was thanking us and crying. He was crying a little.

Because it was fall, we had to start travelling back to the place where we were going to spend the winter. We had to travel before the ice moved in. We left that camp behind. We didn't move anywhere else. We left as soon as we could and went with my in-laws to camp in the sod-houses.

That fall I was pregnant, I was pregnant with my first child. I started feeling really creepy. I had never felt creepy like that. I had never felt haunted before. I used to really feel haunted. Apparently the man who had died, he wanted to be named in someone else. I wouldn't take out the pee-pots by myself or pick up ice. I wouldn't go anywhere by myself. I thought that ghosts were going to come after me. Because I was so scared at that time, I would wake up with a very heavy body. I would know everything that was going on around me, but I couldn't move. That is how it was for me at that time. I wouldn't be able to move even though I was awake. It was because I was so scared ...

When my husband and father-in-law went out hunting, only the women were left in the sod-house. Because I was so afraid to be alone, I would go to bed with my mother-in-law. I don't know how many of us were under the same blanket. There was my mother-in-law, her three daughters, and myself. There were five of us under one blanket – yes, five. I would put myself in between the children. Nobody at that time ever thought of helping me or protecting me. I told them how scared I was. I was really scared. When I talked to my mother-in-law about it later, she told me that she had been scared too.

My mother-in-law had a baby daughter at that time. We weren't supposed to use old names, Inuktitut names, the Qallunaat told us so. We gave her a name from the Bible. We were scared to give her Kunuk's name because we were afraid she would get sick and die the way Kunuk had. Since we didn't have any small babies with us that time, we really liked that baby. We were scared she would die, so we gave her Kunuk only as a second name. It wasn't until much later when I had Oopah – I had Oopah and I gave her away for adoption – only when Oopah had grown, when I took her back, that is when we had named her after Kunuk. That is how it was at that time.

WHEN I FIRST FOUND OUT I WAS PREGNANT

I am going to talk about how pregnancy was taken care of in the old days. When we were children we weren't told about pregnancies. I was told by my parents that I wouldn't get pregnant unless I slept with a man. When I met my husband, after we had sex, that is when I got pregnant. I didn't know that I was pregnant. That was after the first time I had sex.

I had my first period when I was already with my husband. I had my first period, I had my second period, and then I got pregnant. I was only fourteen years old when I got pregnant. By the time I was fifteen years old, I had a baby. I didn't know anything about pregnancy at that time. I didn't know that I was pregnant. I wasn't worried about my periods. I tricked my body and I played outside and did a lot of heavy work, not knowing that I was pregnant. I wasn't worried about losing the baby either.

I remember when I first found out I was pregnant, I didn't know anything about having babies at that time. I was so young back then. My mother-in-law, she noticed something was happening to me. She noticed by my face that I was pregnant. My face looked like I was pregnant. Women, you can tell by their faces when they are pregnant, and they get cold very quickly. They are pale and tired-looking when they are pregnant. My face was like that, and I felt tired all the time. One day when I was sewing, I was working on a caribou amautik, she turned to me and asked me to sit down in front of her. I didn't know what she was doing so I sat down. I was holding the amautik in my hands. She reached out her hand and touched my belly. She said, "There it is," and I asked her, "What is it?" And she said, "You are pregnant!"

I got really scared when I found out I was pregnant. I became really frightened. I didn't know I was pregnant until then, and I told her,

"Don't tell anybody!" I told her, "Don't tell your aniannuk!" She called my husband her aniannuk.[11] She said, "I won't tell anybody." I was really happy knowing that she wouldn't tell anybody. I was scared of my husband finding out. I was scared of him still. She said that she wouldn't tell him. It was a big thing that I was pregnant!

When my husband came in from hunting, I helped him undress. I went out into the entrance-way to hang his caribou clothing. He was putting on his indoor clothing, and while I was outside in the entrance-way, she told him. She said, "Aniannuk, you are going to be a father!"

That night when we went to bed, he reached out his hand and started rubbing my belly. I used to be so scared of him at that time that I would wake up my parents-in-law every time he would try and have sex with me. I would scream out in pain and my father-in-law would save me. I was so stupid at that time ... That night, though, I asked him, "What are you doing? Why are you rubbing my belly?" He said, "You are going to have a baby!" I started crying, I was so scared. I asked him, "You found out?" Of course he found out ... He was going to find out anyway.

IT SEEMED AS IF WE WERE REALLY POOR

We have a lot of things in our house now. We have a lot of things. Looking back, when you look at how things were back then, it seemed as if we were really poor. But living in it, it was all right, it was fine. All those things that you see today, we never had. Just a needle, thread, ulu, scraping board, cup and teapot and our qulliq, that is what we had. If we had these things, we would feel like we had lots of things. If we had those things we would be happy. We would feel rich.

My husband and I when we first met each other that spring, we didn't have much. We didn't even have a tent. We moved to the land around Arctic Bay when I was taken away from my family to live with my husband. It was springtime and we didn't have any tent. That is how we lived. We were on our way to Arctic Bay, and every time we stopped to sleep, we would make an iqluvigaq, just big enough for two of us. We would cover it with sealskin and we would take off our outdoor clothing, our caribou clothing. Once we took off our caribou clothing, we would go into the little iqluvigaq. We could only have a tiny iqluvigaq because it was springtime, and the snow was melting fast.

When the snow melted in the summer and we were out hunting, we slept using one caribou mattress on the ground, beside the rock in the open air. That is how poor we were. It didn't matter to us at that time. We weren't cold. It was all right. We slept well. We would travel along and be happy. If it was today, we would feel upset about the way it was for us. We had enough to eat and drink and that was okay. Living that kind of life didn't bother us. It was fine and we were happy.

In the old days there were some very poor people around. I once saw a family that was so poor all they had was a mattress made out of a polar-bear skin. The husband didn't have a dog team, he had no dogs, so he couldn't hunt. They didn't have any caribou skins. They would use their polar-bear skin to sleep on, even though it was a tiny skin. They had nothing to put on top of it. They had no blankets, they had no caribou skins. It was really cold in the wintertime, especially in igluvigait. They would sleep on this polar-bear skin, and they had children. The husband would sleep using a dog skin as a blanket. The wife had a baby, and the amautik that she used always had pee at the back. She didn't clean it properly and she didn't have any needle to sew with. I gave her one of my needles so she could sew and make things for herself and the family. That is how we shared and helped each other. Even though there were really hard times that we went through, we shared and helped each other. That is the only way that we could survive in our camps.

Back then if we had sinew and a needle, we thought ourselves rich people. We would use caribou sinew to sew. We didn't have any thread, like cotton thread today and we didn't have any sewing machines. We didn't have any of that. We would use caribou sinew. If we had sinew, everything was all right. One time we couldn't even find any sinew to use as thread. There were no caribou where we were at. The caribou were a long way away that year so we had to use seal intestines for our sinew. We dried it up and took the skin off, and when it was dry we used scissors and cut it in strips until there was enough thread to sew. We used it to sew our kamiks. We would also use narwhal sinew sometimes. We would take off the meat and dry the sinew. Also, old things, old clothes, we would take them apart and use them for thread. That is how I sewed a parka once, with thread from old clothes. Caribou sinew we used the most. It was really nice to make kamiks and parkas and socks and pants out of caribou sinew and caribou skin. It was really fun. We made a lot of our clothing out of caribou.

SUNDAYS WERE REALLY IMPORTANT TO US

Sundays were really important to us. They were our resting days. We weren't supposed to do anything important on Sundays. It was really scary to do anything on a Sunday.

We once went out on Saturday, just the two of us, my husband and I. I didn't have any children that time. We were alone. It was in the springtime and the snow was melting really fast. It was getting really difficult to travel. It became Sunday, and we knew that we had to stop and stay overnight. We knew that we were not supposed to travel on Sunday. My husband and I talked about it that night. We talked about it. We had to travel before the ice melted ... We were in a big hurry to get out of that camp because the snow was melting really fast. We travelled that night. My husband said that we would pretend that it was Monday so that we wouldn't feel guilty that we were travelling on a Sunday. We pretended it was Monday. We never told my in-laws that we travelled on a Sunday. We knew that if we told them, we would get a lecture from them about travelling on a Sunday.

❈ ❈ ❈

I remember that not long before that, we were out hunting in the summertime and there were fresh grass and blueberries around. I was with my in-laws and their family. We knew that it was Sunday and we weren't supposed to pick anything. We were allowed to walk around on Sunday, but we weren't allowed to pick anything or hunt. If seals or narwhals came around, we weren't supposed to shoot them. We were walking around on the land and my in-laws' youngest children, they asked if they could pick blueberries. They wanted to pick them just to eat them, not to keep them. My mother-in-law said, yes, but only if they ate them right away. I was the oldest of these children. Even though I was already married, I went with the children to pick and eat blueberries. We ate all the blueberries on the ground and also the fresh grass and the leaves. The rule was that we were not supposed to pick things to keep but we could pick berries and eat them on Sundays. These are the things that I remember we weren't supposed to do on Sundays. These are the important things that we were told.

NO MORE SNOW TO TRAVEL ON

We got stranded because there was no more snow to travel on. That was a difficult time. It was a difficult time and we were not happy. This was when I was quite young. I had no children at the time, but I had a husband. We were going to the Igloolik area from Arctic Bay, from Ikpiaqjuk. We had gone to Arctic Bay to trade. There was no trading post at Igloolik then. And while we were over there that spring, it seemed like there would be no spring at all. It was colder than usual, and the snow was still everywhere. We thought spring was never going to come, and then all of a sudden it got really warm. We were with my brother-in-law Qayaarjuaq, his wife, Ipiksaut, and their children,

Naktaan and Hanna. Their other children, Isigaittuq and Inuaraq, they
were with their grandparents, so they were not there. Qaataniq and
Pilakapsik were there, and so were Amiimiarjuk and his wife and his
children, Taapittiaq, Joanna, and Auqsaaq. This was the group.

There was me, my husband, and a whole bunch of us travelling. We
were coming back from trading. When we arrived in the middle of the
land, we over-nighted. We were okay, we weren't worried about anything. We cooked caribou outside and it was a really nice time. The
caribou were losing their fur because it was spring. There was no fat
on the caribou, but the meat was still really, really delicious. We were
having a nice and easy time just settling in for the night. We went to
sleep and when we got up, it was warm. It was snowing just a little bit.
The whole land was wet, really, really wet. It was like the ice and snow
had thawed overnight. There was water everywhere. We had been
planning to travel along a particular route, but the land where we were
going to travel was all filled with water. We had a lot of things on our
qamutik, supplies that we needed for the whole spring and summer. We
wouldn't be going trading again. That was our last time, so we had lots
of stuff on our qamutiks to use for the year. There were no Qallunaat
in Igloolik at that time, so we weren't going to be able to trade there.
And it was really, really wet.

We started travelling as soon as we woke up. We were trying to get
back home. The runners on the qamutiks, they were brand new pieces
of whalebone. We didn't want to wear them out travelling with no
snow on the ground. They were quite thick bones, very pretty-looking,
good bones, and the men didn't want to wear them out. We started
travelling anyway, on the bare ground. We tried to find bits of snow to
go on and after a while we set up camp for the night. We started trying
to travel again the next day but it had thawed even more.

It had become really warm, and the ground, it was really hard to
travel on. We came to a river that was flowing already. The top part of
the river was flowing even though underneath it was still frozen. We
kept travelling straight through the night without getting any sleep. We
were tired, and we walked ahead of the dogs just to keep them going.
We put the supplies we had bought on the qamutik. We moved them
ahead, and then we came back for the people. We would pick up the
people, start travelling again, drop them off and pick up the supplies,
travel with them forward and then come back again for the people.

We didn't sleep at all that time. I don't know how many days we
travelled for, but we stayed up late into the night and we travelled all
day. We were trying to get to our camp before all the snow thawed. I
remember there was an old man and woman who were shouting at the
dogs, telling them to go. "Just keep going, keep going!" – that is what

they kept telling the dogs to do. They were a white-haired old couple. They were even older than elders today, but they were quite capable of travelling during such a difficult time. They were strong and energetic. They would get ready quickly in the mornings and start travelling ahead.

We would walk ahead of the dogs, we would walk and walk, and we would get really tired and sleepy. There were times when we would suddenly trip and fall forward. We would lie down on the ground and fall asleep. After a little bit of sleep someone would eventually wake us up and say, "You are being left behind!" so we would get up and start walking again. We would pick up the supplies, move them forward, take them off and go back again.

At one point when they were getting the qamutiks ready, packing them up, I started walking ahead. The men were helping the dogs pull the qamutiks. We put our dogs together with Qayaarjuaq's dogs, and Amiimiarjuk and his father, Pilakapsik, put their dogs together too. My sister-in-law, Qayarjuaq's wife, was quite a fussy lady and she would scold people often. She was quite tired by then. She had nobody to scold so she was quite silent. She was exhausted and she had a baby on her back. At one point when we were travelling, we were slanted to one side, travelling on a slope on a very little bit of snow and she slowly, slowly, slowly, fell off the qamutik, right into the middle of a puddle. Her husband didn't realize what had happened. He was shouting at the dogs and getting the dogs to go, and he didn't realize that his wife had fallen off. Even to this day I can hear her husband telling the dogs to keep going. The way he was screaming at those dogs, I will always remember that. Ipiksaut, the wife, she fell into the puddle and was being left behind.

I told my brother-in-law, "Your wife, my angajurnguqtaara,[12] she fell down, she fell down on the ground!" And Qayarjuaq said, "Never mind, I want to get to steady ground before I go back to deal with her." She didn't get up. She just lay down on the ground and fell asleep. Even though she was on a wet area, she didn't seem to care. Even though she fell off the qamutik, she just kept on sleeping. We were so tired at that time.

We didn't carry a boat with us that particular time, just the supplies that we had bought. We went to the lake that was used for fishing, it is called Iqalugasugvik. That is what we called it at that time. And there were some people fishing there. We met with them, the man's name was Siqujjutt. He had caught a lot of fish. We stopped to jig for fish there, and we had lots of fun jigging for fish. I was doing well, catching lots of fish, and my husband said, "Don't catch any fish!" I asked why, and he said, "Because they are too heavy and we can't carry any more on our load!" We started crossing a river then, and the men were shouting instructions to the dogs, and I was the only one on top of the qamutik. If the river had pushed the qamutik on its side, I would have fallen into the water. We were crossing the river that time, and the dogs were really hard to control. Even if we told the dogs to go a certain way, if they decided that they didn't want to go that way, they would turn. I really, really wanted the dogs to listen. We finally crossed the river, and then the rest of the other qamutiks crossed the river. We finally all crossed, and then we arrived at the sea ice. We didn't want to leave anything behind so we went back and forth, picking up the supplies and then picking up the people.

We finally arrived at the beach, and we slept overnight there. We really slept a lot that time. I don't remember much about what happened after that, after my good night's sleep. There were no more tragedies or heavy problems that I can remember. I don't even remember packing up the next day. The next day we travelled on the ice and stopped on a little island and started picking up birds' eggs. There were sea birds there. And then our big group split up, and we started going in different directions. We were going to Aggu and then to our home camp Naujaaruluk, and the rest of the group were going to Kapuivik and Qaiqsut. We separated and started travelling. My husband and I were alone then, we had no children.

When we got close to our camp, the snow started getting soft again. We were having trouble travelling, so we set up camp for the night, and we began travelling again the next morning. We were less exhausted and we had lots of supplies with us on the sled. We knew that my in-laws were travelling the far route past Arctic Bay through to Aggu. They were going to travel that particular way. We were supposed to meet in our home camp, Naujaaruluk. We settled in for the night and we got into bed. Then, all of the sudden, we heard a bee. I got really scared. I jumped up and started running. I had just bought a new skirt at the trading post. We were running around and the bee was flying around. I just had my skirt on, and my husband just had his long underwear on. I was crying and screaming, I didn't like bees at all. My husband was scary the way he played with the bee. He would pretend to hang onto the bee and throw it at me. We were just playing around. How young we were then, just playing outside ...

We fell asleep, and I woke up watching my husband putting little kamiks on the dogs' feet. Our dogs had sore feet, so he was putting little sealskin kamiks on them that he had made. He would cut a small thin strip of sealskin, and he would make the holes in the skin fit with the nails of the dogs' feet. The nails would stick out of these holes and it would be sort of like a Bandaid on the pad of the foot to keep it from bleeding. And that is how we put booties on the dogs.

Finally we started moving again. We travelled on the sea ice, on pieces of ice floes, and we finally got to the land close to the camp. I was scared travelling on the floes. When our dogs were well-trained, they would know what to do. They would listen to my husband telling them where to go, and they would go exactly where they were told. They jumped from floe to floe. The dogs followed the lead dog, the one in the front. Finally, without falling into the water, we got on dry land. My husband was screaming at the dogs that time, shouting at them and telling them what to do. This was not the way he usually instructed the dogs. Usually he wanted them to be good listeners so he talked to them really quietly, almost in a whisper. This time he was shouting at them, and the dogs handled themselves perfectly getting us onto the land.

When we finally got to the land we looked back at what we had just travelled on. There was so much water it seemed really amazing to us that we had travelled across it. It seemed as if we had not touched any water at all, because we had been jumping from floe to floe. When we finally got to dry land we were wet from the splashing, and we were tired after all that shouting and screaming at the dogs to get them going. We wrung out our clothes and then we put them back on. Then we walked across the land and up a hill so that we could see the land around us. There were lots of snow geese there that couldn't fly. We started running around again, trying to catch them. We would catch them and wring their necks to kill them. We got a lot of geese that way, without using any guns. We ran and ran. Oh, how fast we were at running! ... Just thinking about how my life is now, I will never be able to do that again, what I did back then ...

So we were eating geese and geese stomachs, and we had lots of supplies from the trading post with us. We never gorged ourselves with that food. My husband told me that we would travel to a point a little ways away on the land, and that was where we would wait for my in-laws. We would walk across the land. We were quite full and I was pregnant at this time, my first pregnancy. I never thought about taking care of myself, I never thought of being delicate. I was running around, thinking that there was nothing wrong with me.

We started walking towards the spot on the land where we were going to meet my in-laws. It was probably because I was quite full, but I was feeling like I had cramps. I was falling behind, trying to walk with my husband and eating plants on the ground along the way. My husband was quite a ways in front of me and I ran to him. I caught up with him. I wanted him to hold my hand, so he held my hand. He had been leaving me behind, and I was scared of bees.

My husband said he had to take a shit, and he had sealskin wind-pants on and kamiks. They are the ones that kept you from getting wet. They weren't totally waterproof like the Qallunaat ones we have today, but they were good at keeping you from getting wet inside. He was carrying his gun and he gave his gun to me to hold. I put it on my back and he was trying to pull his pants down. I continued to walk while he squatted on the ground. I thought he would catch up to me really fast anyway, so I started walking. I was walking on the beach. I thought I was seeing things. I saw something on the beach. I thought I saw antlers. We didn't expect any caribou in that particular area, but all of the sudden I saw this set of antlers and they were moving.

My husband was quite a ways behind by then so I ran back and I told him, "Look! Look over there! There is a caribou!" He said, "Oh, you are kidding, you are lying." And I said, "No! Look! Look there, there is a caribou!" I don't remember him taking the gun off my back but apparently he took the gun off my back and he took off his sealskin wind-pants. I saw him start crawling on the ground with no pants on, trying to approach the caribou. I was walking and crouching low behind him. The caribou didn't even realize we were there, even though we had really been playing around before and being loud, running around on the land. It was a big caribou with lots of caribou fat, and when he shot at it he didn't think he had hit it. Apparently he had wounded it. The caribou charged. He started running towards us so I wrapped my hands around my head. I thought I was going to be trampled and I started screaming. I was really terrified – this was really serious business! I was really scared. The caribou ran close to me and then he fell down. My husband started walking towards the caribou, and I said, "Oh boy, we got a caribou! How amazing!" – things like that. After we cut up the caribou we didn't eat anything. We had already had all those geese to eat. We were full.

We started walking again to the place we wanted to go. We left the caribou there. We were planning to pick it up on the way back. We left our dogs and our stuff there as well. We would be coming back for all of it. My husband wanted to climb up on a hill so he could look around for my in-laws with his telescope to see if they were coming in. We had not seen them for all of the spring, and he wanted to see if they were anywhere close by. They were travelling from a place quite far away. We got up on the hill, and there was a dog team out on the ice! It was right in front of the land we were on, and it was headed for our campsite. We started running back to our camp, and we were really happy, because we had been alone for a long time, just the two of us. We were so happy to see people again. We got back to our camp to where we left our dogs and we started waving a white flag to get their attention. When they saw us we took the seal meat off the qamutik and put the caribou on top.

They were coming towards us, and we were looking at how much the ice had broken up along the seashore. We were wondering how they were going to get onto the land. It was all water. The ice was far from the shore. They started trying to find a place on the shore where there was still a bit of ice, a place where they could get on the land. When they got to a place where the ice was close enough, they walked to the edge of the ice and told their dogs to swim to the shore. Then they made a boat out of their qamutik and floated to shore. When we finally met up with them we cried and hugged them. My father-in-law was praying and saying thanks, and we were singing, "Thank you for the food," that song, that Christian song. And then after that we went back to the camp and cooked the caribou. Oh, how happy I was.

ON TOP OF THE HILL THERE WAS A GRAVE

This was when I was fifteen. I was pregnant with Oopah, and we were living in a camp, one of the fishing camps not far from Igloolik. It was spring and we were going to hunt seals. My in-laws weren't there at that time – they were in Arctic Bay – but we had planned earlier on in the season to meet them at that camp at a certain time. We didn't have much of a dog team then, only puppies with us. It was springtime and my husband was going to go out and meet my father-in-law on the ice. He went looking for them on the trail that day, but he came back early because he kept on getting snow-blind. He was having problems with his eyes from the sun and the snow. He went out again the next day to meet my in-laws. He didn't find them but he caught a seal, so he came back. He tried to go out again the day after that, hunting and looking for his parents, but it was very bright and he kept on having trouble with his eyes.

My husband left us alone during the days, just the three of us, me, my sister-in-law Amarualik, and her husband, Kallirraq. We were alone with one dog, a pup. It was springtime so we had tents, we were not in igluvigait. There was a hill behind our tents, and on top of the hill there was a grave. The dog kept barking and growling at the grave. He would run towards it, bark, and then run away. The dog was scared of something. He was only a pup.

I was very young at that time, and I got scared easily. Amarualik and her husband were teasing me because the dog was making me scared. They took me up the hill to look at the grave. They were trying to show off how they weren't afraid like me. We didn't see much of the body, but we could see black hair. I remember we were spooking each other, and we started racing. I was the first one down the hill, even though I was very pregnant. We couldn't sleep at night because of the dog's howling and barking, so we started taking the dog inside the tent so we would be able to sleep at night. He would stop barking and howling when he was inside. We would close the wooden door to our tent and lock it.

My husband came home and after a few days when his snow-blindness had healed, he decided to go back out looking for his parents. I didn't want to stay in that camp with the haunted grave anymore but he told me to stay. I wanted to go with him very badly so I started crying and crying, I cried really loud. And after awhile he asked me to go with him, he changed his mind, so we left the camp together, leaving the couple behind with the puppy. We were riding on the qamutik across the sea ice and when we looked behind us, the puppy was following us. He didn't want to be left behind with the grave either.

While we were riding we both started getting nosebleeds. I was bleeding so badly that I started losing my strength. We stopped to pitch our tent, and I was really tired and I was really thirsty. I was losing too much blood. I didn't have the strength to go on, so my husband melted some ice and heated up some water for me. He made some tea. It was springtime and we had just bought tea in Arctic Bay. We never used to drink too much tea at that time. We had some tea and then went to sleep on the qamutik. We slept there without a tent, just on the qamutik.

When my husband woke me up the next day, the nosebleed was gone. We travelled the next day and found my in-laws, so we turned to go back to our camp. We had left most of our supplies back at the camp, so we took half of their supplies to help them out with their loads. I told my in-laws about the incident with the grave, and they just laughed at me, they didn't believe what I was talking about. They told me that the grave had a cross on it, a huge cross, so the body had gone to heaven. The body was named Qiluqisaaq, the person who died.

When we got back to the camp the couple we left behind, the husband, Kalirraq, he had become really sick and he was unconscious. It was scary. I guess we hadn't realized that we had left them alone long enough for him to get so sick. We didn't have any radios or telephones, and they had been alone in that camp almost a week. He was really skinny, very skinny. He hadn't eaten for a long time. Later on we found out that he had a problem with his lungs. He was coughing up blood and he almost died. He had stopped breathing for a while, and Amarualik had blown air into his mouth with hers and revived him. It was really frightening to see him that way. He looked like he was going to die. We stayed in that camp with them as a family until he got better.

GONE OUT TO TRADE IN IGLOOLIK

We had gone out to trade in Igloolik. Coming back it was really hard to travel. It was February, and I was pregnant for the first time and hungry for meat. All we had were the biscuits that we had brought with us, our Qallunaat food. Even though we had some meat for the dogs, seal meat, there wasn't enough for us to have some too. There wasn't enough to go around.

We were hungry and cold on that trip. It was hard to travel, so we made a house out of the boxes that we had with us, sugar boxes and biscuit boxes. We had those boxes with us because my husband was going to build a new qamutik. We put duffle material on top of the boxes, and we were quite warm.

We trapped a whole bunch of foxes on that trip. My husband left a big fish beside each fox trap to draw them in. We were checking our fox traps on the way home. We had a big qamutik at that time, and when we got back home, my husband had trapped so many foxes he filled the qamutik. We got back to the camp and spent the whole night skinning the foxes. We worked all night, and we still didn't finish them all. That was the first time that I had ever skinned foxes, and it took me a long time to remove the skins.

There were lots of fox skins. I was trying to remove the bone from the ears, I was removing them in the same way I removed caribou ears. My mother-in-law was allowed to say anything to me at that time because she was older than me. She was Uyarak's second wife and she was just a bit older, but she was still older. My mother-in-law, she scolded me for skinning foxes that way. We were still young people at that time, and my father-in-law, he loved me very much. He was always very nice to me because he had looked after my mother, Suula, when she was a small child. He had looked after her when she was a child, so he included me in his circle of love. He talked to me like I was his daughter. He taught me how to skin foxes. He told me that I was not supposed to remove the whole ear but to try and leave a little dent inside the ear. They were not like caribou ears, he told me. I learned from my father-in-law that time how to skin foxes. I skinned the foxes, and then my husband would remove the fat.

We placed the skins on wood to dry, and then we filled a whole bunch of boxes with the fox skins and brought them to the trading post. We bought a boat with those foxes, and we bought a whole bunch of supplies. We were like millionaires that time. Qallunaat things were cheap that time so we bought a whole bunch of supplies.

We came back from trading, and I had bought a lot of little things for my new little sister-in-law, little dresses and perfumes. I gave her all these things when we got back, but it seemed like she wasn't going to keep them. It was the first night that we were back, and somebody woke us up. They told us that my little sister-in-law, the baby that had been born recently, had died in the night. We were crying. We got up. My husband wanted to hold the baby and told his stepmother this but she wouldn't let the baby go. Her husband, my father-in-law, was trying to take the baby from her, and they started fighting over the baby. He was trying to get the baby away from the mother.

Apparently her lungs had been full of water, and she had not been coughing. Perhaps if she had been named after the right person she would have lived, but she died. Because she was a little baby I had no problems getting her dressed and getting her ready for burial. I went to bury that little baby. It felt like we were burying everybody, left, right, and centre at that time. So many people were dying.

After the baby died, we joined some other people and travelled to Igloolik. It was springtime. We stayed at Igloolik for awhile, and then we left and went further on to Hall Beach. I had lost my father before that – no, I still had my father – he was still living. We went there to see him, but my father was not there. Apparently after I left him to be married, he had met up with his nephew Aaluluuq and his wife, and they had moved him to a camp called Siuraarjuk. They asked him to stay with them, to be the elder in their family, so he was living with them there. He wasn't living in Hall Beach any more. He was such an old man.

THE FALL THAT I HAD MY FIRST BABY

We had just built a new sod-house the fall that I had my first baby. We were in Qaqqalik, we were in the sod-house, and it was covered with snow. That was a scary time! Those scary times, there have been lots of them for me. I was scared of a lot of things in my teenage years. I carried fear with me all of my life. I used to be scared of everything.

Giving birth is not a scary thing, but for me, I thought it was scary. I remember when I went into labour that first time. I was just fifteen, and my husband had gone out hunting for the day. It was October, and the ice hadn't come back in yet. My husband had taken the rifle, the one we used for seals. He took that with him and left the bigger narwhal rifle behind. I remember I was outside the sod-house by the shore. I looked up and saw a seal in the water not far from the camp. I was quite small that time when I was pregnant. I had a big stomach, but I was still growing myself. I grabbed the narwhal gun and shot the seal. When the gun went off, it tipped me over on my back. I fell down, and then I had trouble standing up again, I was so pregnant! I had a pain in my stomach and my back, and I had trouble standing up. I went into labour right after that and stayed in labour for quite a while. My husband came home from hunting, and when it came time for me to deliver, he made a bed for me to lie on. He took the skin mattress out and he dug up the rocks on the floor of the tent and made a ditch. He put a nice blanket on it, and right there I delivered.

When I was having that first baby I was really frightened. I was in that ditch and I had someone behind me, behind my back, holding me up. Everyone around me was telling me, "Try and break the water! Try and break the water! If the water is broken, then the baby will come out!" I kept looking for water, I was looking around the tent. I couldn't find any water! They told me it was a hard thing between my legs, something I had to burst. I tried to reach it but I didn't know what I was doing. I tried to scratch between my legs. I was scratching, looking for this hard spot that I would have to burst. Apparently I was scratching at the poor baby's head, pinching the baby's head and scratching the skin off! There was no water, I couldn't find any water, and I was really, really sore. When the woman helping me finally checked to see what I was doing, she said it was the head that I had been scratching and told me to push. I tried to push. I pushed so hard my ears were ringing and I fainted.

Afterwards I woke up and found out I had a baby daughter, I had a baby girl. Poor Oopah, she was born with sores on her head because I didn't know what I was doing. I felt so horrible looking at her head, thinking about how I had scratched the skin off. It wasn't that I was dumb – if I had been told what was going to happen, at least I would have known better. That is how it was that particular time. That is how I had my first baby.

TOLD THAT MY FATHER HAD DIED

When I gave birth to Oopah it was in 1946. She was my first baby. When I gave birth to her, when the baby came out, I didn't really care about her. I was just fifteen years old. My family really liked her, though. They were really happy I had a child.

That spring after I had Oopah I heard that my father, Arvaarluk, had gotten sick. It was April. We wanted to go over to the camp he was at and see him. It was almost Eastertime. Oopah was born in October, and it came to be April when we started travelling ... November, December, January, I don't know how many months old she was. She was crawling around, crawling a little bit. We started travelling to go see my father. She was my first baby, and I couldn't put her on my back by myself. We got close to this camp, Aukarnaarjuk, and when we stopped there for a while I took the baby out of my amautik to let her pee. I pulled her out into the very cold air. The baby didn't have any clothes on, no pants. Then she needed to eat, so I put her on my breast under my amautik. I didn't know how to get her back into the back of my amautik, so my husband took her out into the cold air and put her on my back. I remember her body in the cold air.

We stopped at Arctic Bay on the way to go see my father, and they were having a spring festival there. There were games there – the Roman Catholic mission people, they were the ones who were throwing the games. We were playing a game with beans and rice, and our prizes were used clothing. The missonaries threw lots of things on the ground outside, like tobacco and gum, and sometimes there was clothing that they would throw out and we would run for it. We would try to get as much as possible. We were having fun at the festival, we were running around and playing games. Apparently my baby's hands had been stuck outside the amautik during this time. She froze her fingers. That evening she started crying and crying and crying. Her hands were swollen. I started looking at them closely. My husband said, "There is a big blister there." She had a frozen area on her index finger. We were staying with Nattiq, my older sister, and her husband. When I told my older sister about it, she started scolding me, saying, "Oh, what a mother you are, playing outside, having a good time while your baby is freezing!" I had gotten a pair of long johns from the missionaries. I thought they were really nice. There were no holes in them, and they smelled like Roman Catholic mission people, that is how they smelled.

After the festival we started travelling again, and we went to a place called Akunniq. We were told that my family was in Qarmmat, past Hall Beach, and we were told that my father had died. I didn't believe them, I didn't want to believe them. We kept on travelling, and the whole time I thought I was going to see my father, just the same way I had seen him before. We travelled and travelled with our dog team and our qamutik, and when we finally got to Qarmmat, we found the tools and gear that my father had used, but he wasn't there. The only people around were the people who had stayed with him while he died. My cousin Aakuvaapik and Ivaluarjuk's wife, Qaunnaq, and Aakuvaapik's son Avingaq were the ones who were there, and Aakuvaapik's two other children, two children, they were the only ones there. I hadn't seen my father since my marriage. When I married my husband, I left to go to another place, to a place past Arctic Bay with my in-laws, and I never saw him again.

I didn't cry very much. I really didn't believe what had happened. Every time I left the sod-house, I would look around for my father. I would look for him everywhere, all over the place, and when I didn't find him I would start crying. I was crying all by myself. How stupid of them at that time – they didn't even take me to where he was buried!

As we were about to leave to go home, somebody wanted me to give away my baby, Oopah, the little baby on my back. How horrible – my father had just died, and now they wanted my baby! The people at the camp, they told me that before he died my father had said that he thought that I was too young to have children of my own. I was only fifteen. They told me that he had said that he wanted the family to take my daughter. My mother's cousin's wife, Niaquttiaq, was supposed to take her. She was Timoti's namesake. Sometimes they called her Kakkiviaq. I didn't want to give the baby away. I was really happy with my baby. She was at the crawling stage, and I had never had a younger sister. I loved her very much. But since they were all older people and since it was what my father had said right before he died, that was the only thing to do, to give up my baby.

We left Qarmmat, just my husband and I. We travelled all of the next day and finally went to sleep that night. My breasts were swollen from so much milk. I was hurting so much under my arms I was crying and crying. I was screaming for my father, screaming, "Ataata! Ataata!"[13] To help me, my husband would suck the milk out of my breasts and then spit it out into a cup. When the cup got too full he would pour it out and then keep sucking to get rid of the milk. Finally they drained.

Eventually we went home to a place, Qaqqalik. That is where my husband's family was camped. When we got into the camp, I went inside and everybody was expecting to see the baby. Of course they hadn't heard that I had given the baby away. We didn't have radios and phones like we do today. When they saw that the baby was not there, they started crying. My in-laws, they missed the baby so much, they had been hoping to see the baby when we got back.

My mother-in-law was pregnant at that time. It was her sixth pregnancy. She had lost two babies before that, a baby boy and a baby girl. They died from suffocating, from something filling up in their lungs. I remember the older one, the little girl, she lived only two months before she got sick and died. My mother-in-law became pregnant soon after that. She was pregnant with Peter the same time I was pregnant. She had him a few months after I had Oopah. He is still alive. After Peter, the next three pregnancies went well for her, then the fourth one died.

When we came back from giving Oopah away, they asked me about my father. I told them he had died. They wanted to find out whether the baby had died also. So many babies were dying back then. They

really wanted to have a baby in the family. I told them that someone
had wanted the baby, and that I had given her away.

My in-laws were upset at first, but after a while, as time went on, it
didn't seem to matter that much. Since I was quite young and I didn't
have a baby anymore, I played around, sliding down hills on sealskins
with the younger children, trying to clean them. We used to clean sealskins that way, also polar-bear skins which we used as mattresses. Back
then, that time I would climb up to the top of the hill, and that is where
I would cry. I would cry and cry. I would pretend that I was okay by the
time they caught up with me – that is how I eventually got rid of my grief.
I was hiding my grief. I thought they were going to think I was strange if
I cried openly. Finally as time went on it didn't matter too much. I got
used to it. The grief after a while didn't seem to matter too much.

MY SON KNEW THAT HE WANTED TO BE CALLED ARVALUK

I was just telling a story of how Arvaluk was born. This was at Naujaaruluk. I was telling a story about how things were at that time.

When he was a newborn, when he came out of my womb, before my
mother-in-law picked him up, he was facing my mother-in-law and
looking at her very clearly. When newborns are born, they don't see
very clearly, and they don't know which people they are looking at. My
mother-in-law, when she first saw the baby, thought that the baby was
going to smile. She said that felt kind of creepy. Apparently it was
because the baby wanted to be named Arvaluk after my father who
had died. We knew right away what to call the baby that time.

The very moment that he was born, my son knew that he wanted to
be called Arvaluk. Arvaluk remembers being born because he told us
later in his life who was there and that he saw us all there in our home
and that he felt really warm. We were kind of wary of him after he said
this. We knew that he remembered being born because at the time that
he was born, he was warm. He was looking straight up at my mother-
in-law when he came out and she said to never mind and to let him be
like that. He was a little boy, and we didn't have many little boys at the
time.

Arvaluk, when he was a brand new baby, he had just the one name.
At that time people usually named newborns right after they came out.
We wouldn't just name them, we would do a little ceremony to name
them. Arvaluk was given his other names a few weeks after he was
born. The naming ceremony that I know of, they pick the child up and
pray over the child. They say things like, "God bless you and save you
and protect you. Your name is Arvaluk." They would pray over the

babies or the children when they were born. When Arvaluk was named, that day of the naming, even though he was too small, just a baby, he smiled when the praying was done. As soon as the person who prayed over him told him that his name was Arvaluk, he smiled. I felt really creepy then.

Peter Awa, my husband's younger brother, he was the only boy until Arvaluk was born. My mother-in-law named him just a Christian name, just Peter. She wouldn't name him an Inuktitut name because she was scared of the missionaries. There were a lot of Inuktitut names to choose from. Some of her relatives and her older sisters had just died. Even though she was grieving for those members of the family, she wouldn't name her new son any other name other than Peter or Peter-loosie.[14] That is what his name was for a long time. He was really envious of people who had second names or Inuktitut names, so when he got a little older he named himself Nataaq, after my grandfather's older brother.

When Arvaluk thought that he didn't have enough names, he ended up calling himself another name. He called himself Paula. We don't remember that person Paula at all – she was his sister-in-law's step-mother – but Arvaluk called himself Paula. Lucas Ivalu, his uncle, started calling him Paula all the time. Up to this day he calls him Arvaluk Paula and asks "Where is my Paula?" when he sees us.

WHEN THERE WAS A LOT OF SICKNESS IN THE CAMPS

Arvaluk – he was born before Simon – he was my second baby after Oopah. He was the one who was born when there was a lot of sickness in the camps. In each camp, like in Qarmmat or Ikpiarjuk, there were a lot of people who died then. There were a lot of people who had died in our own camp too, but we hadn't heard anything about all the deaths because we had been travelling. My husband and I stopped at a camp not far from our home. We stopped for a rest because we had been travelling, and the whole camp that we were staying at, the whole camp, was getting sick. I had never even had a cold before, I had never been sick before. I was young then and I was envious of people who were sick. I tried to cough sometimes because I was envious of them. I had to try to cough – I didn't have any ciga-rettes at that time.

When we got back to Naujaaruluk, everybody got sick. Everybody in the family was sick but me. Arvaluk was a small baby on my back when the sickness was here. He was born in April, the same month that my husband got really sick. When my husband coughed, he would start vomiting blood. If there had been a pail to spit in he would have filled it with blood, but we had no pail. The blood that he spit spread into the floor of the house. It was getting frozen on the wall.

He was sick for a long time, and when May came it started getting really sunny. Everybody was in bed sick, and I had two children. We had taken Oopah back from the people who had adopted her. She was a toddler and I had Arvaluk on my back. Arvaluk was always crying, he was a cranky baby. He was sick at this time, so it was really hard to get him to quiet down. All my in-laws, men and women, were in bed with all of their children. It got really warm and sunny one day, and our igluvigaq fell down on top of us.

When the igluvigaq fell down on us, at first nobody moved. Everyone was sick in bed and nobody even moved. I was putting Arvaluk on my back and he was crying. I stood up and started throwing snow out of the igluvigaq – I was young at the time and quite energetic, so I didn't get as tired as I do now. The baby I had on my back kept crying and crying, and my husband was vomiting blood and vomiting blood, and I was digging and the baby on my back was crying and crying ... I remember my mother-in-law started screaming at me, "I wish that this baby would die!" She was really serious. There were no medicines then and she was scared that her son, my husband, was going to die. If someone had to die in the camp for everyone to get better, she wanted it to be the baby and not my husband. I didn't want my husband to die either, and I thought that if the baby died, at least things would be better and he would shut up ... So I told her, "Yes, of course, I wish he would die too!" But the baby on my back, the small baby, Arvaluk, he didn't die that time.

When the igluvigaq fell down, I prepared a tent for the rest of the family. I was the only one who wasn't sick. It was kind of a lopsided tent, the tent I made, but I propped it up. It was cold at first but then it became warmer as the sun was absorbed into it, and finally after a while my husband was able to get up. We were hungry – we had dogs with us, and they had been hungry for a long time. My husband's father asked him to go to the nearby camp to find out what was going on. My mother-in-law had been saying, "That is why we are not getting any food from the hunt, because we are going to hear about deaths in our family." Before we heard about something bad, like news of a death in the family, it was always hard to catch wildlife. My husband, he left to go see what was happening in the other camp. He went to see if the sickness had spread. He also wanted to see if they had food to share.

The camp was Qaqqalik. It was close to us, about one night's travel away. It was springtime and the sun wasn't going down, so he travelled all night. He was pretty sick when he went and sick when he got back.

When he came back he told us that a lot of people had died in that camp. So many people died! He told us the names of everyone who was dead. That woman who adopted Oopah died then.

Once we heard about these deaths in Qaqqalik, about all the people who had died, on the same day my husband went out hunting. There was sun all day and night at the time. It was very sunny. Even though he was still sick, he went out seal hunting, and there was a seal on top of the ice waiting for him. The seal was waiting for him, so he shot it to feed the family and the dogs, my in-laws' dogs. He shot two more seals after that. The dogs were really hungry.

He shot the seals, and it was the first food we had eaten in a long time. It was really difficult to figure out how we were going to cut the meat. The dogs were starving, and we had to feed them first. If they died we wouldn't be able to hunt any more, we wouldn't be able to travel. When we brought the meat out, the dogs were trying so hard to get at it I remember I was whipping the dogs to keep them away. We put the qamutik to the side to keep the dogs away from the meat, and since I was the only one who was strong enough to do anything, I was whipping the dogs, waiting for my husband to cut up the meat. My mother-in-law was also strong, but she was taking care of the children.

We cut up the three seals and took what we wanted from them. All the time I was trying to keep the dogs from getting at it. As soon as he said "Go!" the dogs rushed in. The dogs rushed in all together, and since they rushed in so hard, one of the dogs, he bit the other dog's tongue out and ate it. He was trying to lick his tongue, trying to feel whether it was there, but it was bleeding, and the dogs were really, really hungry. He was a brown dog and he was called Nagvaaqtaaq.[15] When he saw the dog with no tongue, my husband started laughing. He had been sick for a long time. He hadn't laughed for a long, long time. Finally he started laughing – all he could manage was a little "Huh, huh" that time. He was so weak all he said was "Huh, huh" ... Then he took his gun and shot the dog who had no tongue. The dog who ate it must have been desperate for food!

When the family started getting better, we started travelling again. It was probably around June, end of May or June, and we started heading inland. We were going across the land. The place where we were headed was our camp, Naujaaruluk. I had Arvaluk then. He was a small baby on my back. We were going to pick up the boat that we had left behind the year before. Because my husband didn't have a younger brother, he went to another camp to pick up a boy to help. We travelled all the way without stopping. We didn't stop travelling and we didn't sleep. We hardly slept. My husband was the one doing all the work. That is how he is today, he doesn't stop working!

We went by boat with some people to the place where we had left our boat. Our boat was a traditional Inuit boat back then. We shovelled it out and put it on our qamutik. We turned to go back to our camp, but by the time we got midway across the land, most of the snow had melted from the ground and the qamutik was starting to drag. The boat was on top of the qamutik, and it was too heavy. My husband, he got a rope and lifted the boat up. It was a big boat. Boats were made out of wood back then, and it was a big boat. He carried it all by himself and we made it to a river. The water in the river was running. We crossed the river in the boat, and it very rough water. There were four of us, my husband and I, the boy, and the baby on my back. When we reached the shore, my husband got back in the boat to travel on the river, and the boy and I kept on travelling on the land with the qamutik. There was no snow left on some parts of the land so we had to carry the qamutik some of the way. When we got to the beach there were birds' eggs already. We got to the beach, and we started travelling by boat towards our land, Naujaaruluk.

When we got close to Naujaaruluk, we saw a dog team. It was my in-laws, they were coming to meet us on the trail. We hadn't brought that many dogs with us on that trip. When we greeted them, my father-in-law prayed for thanks. We gathered seagull eggs there.

ATAGUTTAALUK

That time we went to pick up our boat, we were going towards Igloolik by dog team. When we reached Igloolik, we were told that Ataguttaaluk was really sick. Ataguttaaluk was the oldest elder in the camp. She was Ittuksaarjuat's wife and my grandfather Nutarariaq's sister.

It was a nice springtime day. She was dying, so we travelled to her camp. Kangiq, that is where she was. We pitched our tents at her camp so that we could be with her. All of her relatives, my uncles, my mother's relatives, and my grandfather's nieces and nephews were there. It was 1948 and Arvaluk was just a baby with an older sister, Oopah. In 1948 Ataguttaaluk was a very old woman, she was very old. I was staying with my uncle Angiliq in their tent. They were the youngest of the aunts and uncles, Angiliq and his wife, Ingnirjuk. The old lady, our great-aunt, she was sick. She had no reason to be sick, it was just that she was old. She died in a nice way. She was quite peaceful because this was the end of her life, her life was finished.

Maktaaq's wife, Kupaaq, and I, we were adolescents at that time. We used to warm ourselves with blankets. I remember that time because even though our great-aunt was really sick, even though she was dying, we were playing ball together and having fun. We used to have so much fun! We were young and carefree back then. There was not much else to do but play. When night came and our children went to bed, we would play ball. When we were in the tent, we would rough around with each other, play with each other. It was during one of those times that I heard that my great-aunt had stopped breathing. She was dead.

I went outside. Nobody really cried that she was gone, they didn't mourn much. I was surprised at that. Maybe because she was so old. My uncle, the oldest, Piugaatuk, he was the only one who cried and said goodbye. He was crying out loud, saying that his mother had almost died of starvation. She was so hungry that she had to eat human flesh. If she hadn't, she would have died. Because of that, he was very grateful. She died very old because she was a good woman. She was always kind to people and never gave people a hard time. Because of that, she didn't get sick very often.

※ ※ ※

The story about her that Piugaatuk was talking about, it made her famous. There are people in town that know more of the details than me. All I know is from what my grandmother Kaukjak told me. She used to tell me stories.

I am not sure exactly what happened. I only know what my grandmother told me ... I know that they were out caribou-hunting for the summer, Ataguttaaluk, her husband, and her two children. They were between Pond Inlet and Igloolik. They were inland and there was no caribou. They were hungry and they started getting weak. Their dogs died, and after they ate them the family started starving. The children both died, and her husband told her, "I am going to die soon too, wife of mine. Humans are made to live longer, so you must live to tell other people what has happened. Live with human flesh as long as you can. Make sure you live!"

He said that before he died, so that is what she did. She lived by eating human flesh. Even though she couldn't eat him, she used her little children as food. She was all alone over the summer, fall, winter, and then it became spring again. She would take just a little bite of the flesh. This didn't make her full, but it stopped her from starving.

It became spring, and she was still living that spring when some people from Igloolik came by. The people that found her were my husband's parents, Palluq and his wife. They had only one child at the time who had just died recently. They were the ones who found her. They were on their way to Pond Inlet to trade and they took the same route Ataguttaaluk and her husband had taken. She had been alone all

winter and it was spring. She was almost starving to death by the time
they found her. Whatever human flesh she had to eat over the winter
was all gone. My grandmother told me that she only had two children
when she was stranded on the land. She was very young at the time,
probably close to fourteen years old. I don't know whether they were
boys or girls who died, but my grandmother told me that she ate the
younger one first.

At the time, just before they found her, Palluq and his wife had
been travelling by dog team. They said they heard this strange noise.
They knew that it wasn't a dog noise or a human noise. They couldn't
recognize it. Maybe Ataguttaaluk was trying to say, "I am over here!"
Maybe she was crying because she hadn't heard a dog team for so
long ... They heard it when they were travelling, and that is how they
found her. Palluq heard the noise and realized something was wrong.
He said, "There is something strange going on over there. What is
making that noise?"

His wife wanted to look for where that sound was coming from.
They could only go there by walking because there was hardly any
snow where the voice was coming from. He said to his wife, "Wife of
mine, wait for me. Wait and we will go there together. If it is scary or if
it is not scary, we will find out together." They were anxious to see what
was there, but they were scared of what they would find. They went
there. Palluq was walking behind his wife. They recognized her, Ataguttaaluk. She was making noises from inside of herself. When they went
to her, she couldn't stand up. She had no strength, she was so skinny,
very skinny. There was no meat or flesh on her face and you could see
her teeth and they were really white. Because there was no snow and no
way to make an igloo, she had been outside for a long time. They asked
her if she recognized them. She said yes, she recognized them, and they
felt much better. They carried her down to the place where they were
going to spend the night, and they tried feeding her. They made a separate place for her to stay. That was the only way. They had laws back
then, and there were particular things that you couldn't do. They had
been heading towards Pond Inlet at the time to trade, but they ended up
taking her back to a camp around Igloolik. Later on Ituksaarjuat
married her. He also had another wife but she hadn't made any children
yet, she was quite young. Because he wanted Ataguttaaluk to have
descendants, he married her. He had two wives then.

After almost starving Ataguttaaluk got fat and filled up with flesh.
She ended up having lots of sons and daughters. She had five. Ataguttaaluk ended up with so many children afterwards that her husband
gave away his first wife. He gave her to Arvaarluk, my adopted father.
Arvaarluk ended up raising a few children from that marriage before

he adopted me – Kuutiq and Qajaaq, they are my stepbrother and step-sister. Ataguttaaluk had many more children after that. Now the only living relations of hers who are left are probably the grandchildren, because all of her natural children are dead now. It is only her grand-children who are alive today.

When Ataguttaaluk's second set of children grew up, when her sons grew up, that is when she was an elder and that is when she started taking charge of telling people where the meat should go. She was the one who handed out the meat. If people were hungry, if they didn't have any food, she would split her food with those people and make sure that they had some of whatever she had. She would make up little teas, little sugars, she would share with all the people in her camp and give them each a little something. She didn't want anybody to be poor. If she had not eaten human flesh, she would not have lived, so she didn't want anybody ever to be hungry. If she heard that someone from another camp was poor or hungry, she would tell people to go and bring them meat. If she had extra flour, she would share the flour with the people in her camp. When she had finished feeding her family, if she had any flour left over she would invite the rest of the camp to come over and have some tea and share the bannock. She didn't want anybody to ever be hungry and she made sure that everybody got the food they needed. That is how she became a leader. She would tell all the people to share, to never let anyone go hungry. Being hungry, it is not a good way to be. People should not be hungry.

❊ ❊ ❊

Ataguttaaluk, the whalers called her the Queen of Igloolik. She had a headband that was made out of metal that they gave her. It was like a crown – she wore it on her forehead, and it was very visible. It went under her braid at the back. When I was a young child, I used to try and find out what it was. She was my great-aunt, my other grand-mother, so I used to pick lice from her hair. I would pick lice from her hair and I would try to look at the headband more closely. But when I did, she would hide it with her hair. I used to think it was nailed in, but there was this little clip at the back to hold it onto her head.

When she remarried, Ataguttaaluk and her new husband started travelling between Pond Inlet and Igloolik to trade. Looking back now, maybe it would be almost like a type of business they ran. There was no trading post in the Igloolik area at that time, so people would have to go to Pond Inlet to pick up their supplies. People in Igloolik would give their fox skins to Ataguttaaluk and her family to bring to Pond Inlet and trade for Qallunaaq supplies. They didn't want anyone to be

without supplies, that is why they started doing this business. They
would buy a whole bunch of supplies, like ammunition and tea and
sugar and flour, for people in the Igloolik area. People didn't have
actual money at the time. They just had credit at the Hudson's Bay, so
Ataguttaaluk and her husband would trade and then use whatever they
had left over in the account for themselves. They would get extra for
the fox skins and support themselves that way. She started travelling a
lot when her sons were children. After a while the sons took it over.
Ataguttaaluk and her husband would stay in Igloolik, and the sons
would make the trip, taking foxes with them and trading them. Sometimes she and her husband would go along with them, but only if there
was enough food for another dog team.

People who travel between Igloolik and Pond Inlet, especially her
grandchildren, they always want to visit and take pictures of the place
where she almost starved. Her grandchildren and her children, they are
still thankful to Palluq and his wife for finding her. Her children, they
used to be so thankful when they were alive they used to say to Palluq
and his wife, "If you had not saved our mother, we would not be alive
today." Her children gave a lot of things to Palluq and his wife. They
were so thankful they would give Palluq anything he didn't have. That
is how he was treated because he had found their mother.

When I had two children, Oopah and Arvaluk, that is when she died.
That is how it was then. She was the leader of Igloolik, she was like a
queen. She wanted everybody to live well. She had a good life.[16]

WHEN I FINALLY DID GET MY LITTLE OOPAH BACK

After Ataguttaaluk died, I am not sure why but we started travelling to
Hall Beach by boat. We had two boats then, and it was a lot easier for
us to travel with two. My in-laws travelled a lot. They didn't like to
stay in one place for too long. When we got to Akkuniq, near Hall
Beach, my daughter Oopah was there. It was the first time I had seen
her since I had adopted her out. She had very curly hair and she
couldn't talk yet. I remember she was always hungry, she was never
satisfied with the food that she had. I used to feel the same way Oopah
did – there was never enough food around. I loved her dearly.

We had carried walruses with us that time on the boat to Akkuniq,
huge walruses. We had hunted them for food for our dogs. There was
a lot of cooked meat around, and I remember we were cooking the
meat in pits outside. In Akkuniq there were a lot of cooking pits
outside. We cooked walrus intestines and ribs. We would put the
cooked meat on the ground and call out loudly, "Uujuq! Food is
ready!"[17] I remember Oopah was quite tiny. She would open her legs

wide and sit down. I was really amazed at her. I kept thinking to myself, "This person used to be my child."

While we were there in Akkuniq, we heard that the RCMP people had contacted the Roman Catholic missionaries about Oopah and told the priest to tell us, the original parents, to take her back. We were told that she was being abused. Her little eyes were very intelligent, but she was very wary of strange people. She couldn't talk, but she would always make sure she got approval before she started to eat anything. She was always looking to everybody for approval before she did anything. She was one year old, only a year old, maybe two ... I don't remember ... she was born in 1946 and I got her back in 1948, at the beginning of 1948, when Arvaluk was born.

WE WERE SNOWED OVER

There was this time a long time ago we were with my in-laws and some other relatives, and I had only a few children. We were inland hunting caribou, and we were catching lots of them. There were so many. We would take the skins and scrape the water from them. My husband would stamp on the skins and shake them. When the water is shaken off caribou skins, they dry up, just like that. That was a difficult time then and that is how difficult our life was. When I think about it, I feel sorry for my children, when I think of the life they had. At the time it didn't seem to be hard. It was our way of life. We never thought that it was hard.

We looked after our children carefully at that time. We made sure they didn't freeze and we fed them and made sure that they slept ...

We were in tents on the land, and we were making warm clothing for the winter. I made warm clothing for the children, and I made myself some caribou pants and socks. We were all sewing clothing for the fall and winter. Of course my aunts were also sewing complete sets of caribou clothing. My aunt was a lot older than me, she was an elder in the camp. Her name was Qairniq. She was my grandmother's younger sister. She used to be married to Angugaattiaq, and she had her first child when she was an older person. That time on the land we made all this clothing together. When the younger women didn't know what to do, she would teach us all she could about how to make the clothing.

Once we had finished sewing our caribou clothing, we started walking to the sod-houses on the shore. We made a qamutik out of the big hide of a large caribou and we loaded it up. Everybody was carrying things, even the children, but we had too many things to carry. We didn't have many dogs with us at that time. I couldn't see my husband's

head from all the things that he was carrying. He couldn't see the tops
of his feet. It was a very heavy load he was carrying, and he also had
two small children on his shoulders. Oh, how strong he was ... When
I think back on it, it was something to be envied, something that was
rare. My husband, he wasn't doing it to show off, that was just the way
he was. He was so strong.

After a little while my husband and I started falling behind the rest
of the families. The other two families were travelling ahead. I was
letting my children pee, and we were probably hungry, so we were
giving the children bits of food along the way. We were being left
behind. I was carrying Arvaluk on my back. Oopah was on a little
makeshift qamutik. I was walking and pulling the qamutik. Because
there was so much of a load on the little qamutik, it was almost round.
When we came to a slope, it started rolling. Oopah went rolling with
it. She didn't cry. She was lying flat on the qamutik. She was tied to the
qamutik. She had good thick clothing on so she wouldn't get cold. She
just rolled with the qamutik!

How silly of me! I didn't even think at the time that she would get
hurt. She was crying because she was so scared. Of course she was
scared, she had been rolling down the hill! At that time we were laughing at her, at how silly she looked rolling down the hill with the
qamutik. Of course we were laughing, we were still young. Eventually
we travelled off in a direction all by ourselves because the other families had gone ahead.

We made an igluvigaq for the night. We used caribou fat to make
candles. We would chew the fat to make sure that all the water was out
of it. We would chew for quite a while and keep it inside of our
mouths. We would place the candles next to the qulliq, and that is how
we lighted the tent. We would melt a small amount of water with the
candle so we could drink. Caribou-fat heat is much warmer than seal-
fat heat. It heats up more. It is almost like a Coleman stove – it is quite
hot. Snow melts fast with caribou candles.

Finally we fell asleep. When we were falling asleep, there was a blizzard starting up. When we woke up, the blizzard had died down. It
was really dark inside the iglugivigaq. There was no light, and my
husband was trying to light the candle, but he was having trouble lighting it. I asked him what was happening. My husband said that he wondered if we were snowed over. He wondered if there was snow on top
of our igluvigaq. I thought maybe he was right.

Arvaluk tried to cry, but every time he drew a breath he couldn't
breathe. He kept trying to cry and breathe, but he couldn't. He was
having a hard time breathing. My husband was trying to make a hole
at the top of the igluvigaq. He used the snow that he had dug out from

the top of the igluvigaq to climb on top of and he tried again to make a hole. He was digging the hole and my children were almost not breathing any more, they were not moving any more, and they were not crying. He dug and dug and dug at the roof, and after a while we began to see the tiniest bit of light. He took the children out in a hurry, and they started crying. It was still a blizzard outside. I had trouble climbing out and he pulled me. We all got out and we could breathe again. The snow was so high! There was a whole lot of snow.

When we got outside the igluvigaq, we started looking for our dogs, and we found all but one of them. We couldn't find her anywhere. We called to her and she wouldn't come. Her name was Niukittuq.[18]

My husband was trying to pull all of our bedding and skins and supplies from inside the igluvigaq. We had built our igluvigaq to try and keep away from the wind, we built it in front of a hill, and that is how we got snowed in. After this we packed and got ready to move to another place where we could find good snow for a new igluvigaq. We walked and walked in the blizzard, trying to get to a good place where we could build a good igluvigaq. Eventually we reached the beach. When we got to the beach, there was a cache of walrus meat, and there was an igluvigaq there also. My husband made another igloo beside the one that was already there. He didn't want to move into that old igluvigaq, he made us a brand new igluvigaq.

We moved into that new igluvigaq, and when we got inside, he started taking out the cached walrus meat and taking off the fat. We used that fat to light the lamp. It was so joyful not to be eating caribou meat anymore. We had been eating it all summer. He took out the thick skin of the walrus, and we spent the whole night and day there, waiting for the thick skin to thaw. When the walrus skin eventually thawed, he made a big qamutik out of it. He cut two big pieces of walrus skin, and he made runners out of them. The bottoms of the runners he covered with water and let it freeze. This was going to be our qamutik. At that time my husband could make qamutiks out of so many things. That was the first one he had ever made out of walrus skin.

After he finished that qamutik, we started travelling across the ice. The place where we were headed was still quite far. We had to overnight halfway. We started travelling with the qamutik and the dogs. Oopah was the only one on the qamutik – we were walking and I was carrying Arvaluk. We walked and walked, and it seemed to me that we were walking very fast. We walked and then after a while the sun started getting low. In front of us we saw steam! I told my husband to look over to where the steam was. I thought that it was maybe steam coming off of caribou hooves. He said that there was no caribou around there. He thought that it was a dog team.

My husband was right – it was a dog team! It was a man named
Amiimiarjuk. He was our relative, and he had been looking for us. I
don't remember who he was travelling with, but they came to find us
and we met them halfway. How they smelled! It was a grease smell. We
could really smell the grease on them because we had been inland
eating only caribou all summer. There was a big difference between
having caribou fat all the time and having seal and walrus fat all the
time. We could smell the fat on other people.

When we met them we left our walrus-skin qamutik behind, and
they put our small supplies of skins and things to travel with on their
qamutik. They seemed to have a great big qamutik. There was still
room, even with Oopah and all of us sitting on it. How joyous that
was, and how fast we were! It was just like driving a ski-doo, it was so
fast. We travelled to a camp on the shore, a camp with sod-houses, and
when we arrived we went inside. We went to Ulaajuk's place. Kalirraq
and Amarualik were already there. Amarualik couldn't hear anything.
She had been having a lot of very bad headaches, and her ears couldn't
hear at all. I don't know how but she eventually got back her hearing.
She has good hearing today.

I was really homesick then, and I was crying. I was crying and being
homesick. After staying there for a little while, we heard that my
father-in-law, Uyarak, had come in. He had left on a ship to go to a
hospital in the South, and we had heard that he had come back from
the South.[19] They were waiting for us to go with them to visit him at
the camp where he was staying, so they all started getting my husband
and me ready to go. They were getting the qamutik ready and making
sure we had enough dog ropes and qamutik ropes and stuff like that. I
was really homesick, and then eventually we left.

We went to Akkuniq. We overnighted there, then we headed to
Qupirruqtuuq. That is where my father-in-law was camped. We left
very early in the morning again and we reached Qikiiqtaarjuk. How
dreadful that was! My older stepsister was there, Iqallijuq, and her
husband Ukumaaluk. Their children were there too, Tapaattiaq and
her husband, Siqujjut, and Nuvvijak. There was lots of snow but you
could still see a little bit of the roofs of the sod-houses at the camp. We
stayed there with them for the winter, and in early spring we started
running out of meat. We didn't have much meat left, and we knew that
once we fed our dogs that would be the end of our meat. We were
worried about having enough to eat. It was getting to that point.

It was at that time that we first heard that the children got money.[20] At
that time we didn't see money very often. We didn't think about money
much at the time. Sometimes, to make money when we were getting

low on tea and flour and ammunition, my husband would make small carvings and take them to the Roman Catholic mission. We had no supplies that time and nothing to eat, so my husband brought a carving to the mission. While he was there he was told by the priest that the RCMP had told the Roman Catholic mission to give Inuit money for our children. We had two children so when he was there to sell his carving, he ended up getting lots of money! The store manager had been told to do this. He was given money for the month.

He bought a whole load of supplies that time, even wood and ropes for a qamutiq. Maybe they were cheap at that time, I don't know, but I remember he bought a lot of stuff. He bought great big bags of flour and bags of oatmeal and lots of candy. We had loose candies at the time. They weren't wrapped up. Of course there was no heat in the store, so the candies weren't placed in bags. Only things that could freeze were shipped in for supply – dry milk, great big jars of jam and peanut butter. That is how my husband came back that time, loaded down with supplies.

How joyful that was! We had been given money, and we had so much food! It felt like we would never be hungry again. We forgot that we were running out of meat. My mother-in-law would make great big pieces of bannock, really thick bannock – it was so delicious. She would start cutting up slices of the bannock. We would all watch her cut up the bannock and hope that we got the biggest piece. They were all the same size.

The people next door, they had lots of children too, so they ended up getting a lot of money from the Qallunaat. There were other people, though, who had no children of their own, so they didn't get any money. My older stepsister and her husband were like that. Whenever we came back from the trading post, my husband gave them boxes of our supplies. He didn't make them sign anything, he didn't make them pay, he just split everything up. He gave them things. The Qallunaat, they told us that they would give us more money to buy supplies the following month.

Eventually we began to run out of seal fat for our qulliit. We started to become afraid that we would end up with no heat at all. Then somebody found a drum half full of fat. It had come off the ship – maybe it was abandoned or it fell off the ship. It had floated on to the shore and that is how we found it. The oil was a very black liquid. At the time, it seemed strange to us, because we didn't know anything about oil. We used that oil for our lamps. We used it for heat. When we first set fire to it, the oil would burn out very early. We used it at night. We kept using that oil when night-time came.

We needed meat and fat, so my husband and his father went to the floe edge where there were some loose ice floes, to go whale hunting. When they were ready to come home, they realized they couldn't travel because there was too much loose ice. They were stranded on the ice floe! They couldn't come back.

It was at this time that my new uncle came from Aukkarniq with two bags of walrus meat. He started giving this meat to his in-laws, Uku-maaluk and his wife, and he gave some of that meat to us. He was not a rich man. He had only five dogs himself, he didn't have many dogs because he couldn't afford them. His clothing was wearing out, and he didn't have good skins to sleep on. He wasn't a mighty man, but he was full of love. Even though he was poor, he brought us over this meat. I really loved him back then. That is when we started eating and having meat in the camp again.

Finally my husband and his father came back from the floe edge, but they hadn't caught anything, not even a seal. Their dogs were really hungry by the time they came back. They fed the dogs when they came into the camp and my husband went out hunting again, right after he came home. We were getting cold and hungry, so he went to the other side of the island with his brother-in-law Kalirraq. Kalirraq was married to my husband's sister. They were hunting close to the floe edge again, around Igloolik. They were having trouble getting seals, but Kalirraq shot a polar bear.

At that time we were always nervous about killing polar bears. After they killed it, my husband and Kalirraq came back to camp with this polar bear. Of course there was no selling polar-bear skins then, so it was all ours. It was a very fat polar bear. We used the fat to light our qulliq. There was not much meat around the camp at that time, so my father-in-law cut the meat up and divided it equally among the people in the camp. There were some people who were very poor and very hungry, so he gave them what he could. He gave them what he had. My father-in-law had a lot of love in him. He loved everyone, especially people who were poor and couldn't feed themselves. If he went to buy some supplies from the store, even if he came back with only a package of gum, he would split it equally among all the children to make sure that everybody got their share. When Kalirraq got the polar bear, we stopped being hungry. We were happy – we were eating polar bear meat.

THE DOGS WERE BARKING REALLY LOUD

Later that summer, after we were baptized, when my husband came home from his trip with the minister, my husband and I went travelling inland. We went to look for caribou. Arnaannuk and Kupaaq, they went with us. At that time I had only two children. That couple, they had two children too. That lady, Arnaannuk, is not alive any more. She used to be Kupaaq's wife. I was really pregnant at that time when we walked inland to go caribou hunting. I was really pregnant, and I was carrying Arvaluk on my back and I had Oopah walking beside me. We used to try to hold Oopah's hand when she was walking beside us because she was so slow, but this time we couldn't. My husband was carrying the other couple's two small children, one in each arm. I had a baby on my back and I was carrying some supplies and I was carrying things in my hands. The dogs were carrying meat and bedding on their backs. We walked for a long time. We would walk a long distance, go to sleep, and then start walking again. We would not walk a whole day, but we would walk a long distance each day. I remember getting a tingling feeling in my feet. Sometimes they would leave me behind. My legs would get numb and I would get swollen when we walked. We walked inland a long ways. We were caribou hunting. We started out in late July and walked all of August.

Finally we reached the land where there were caribou, and we made a camp to live in. After that the men started walking in different directions each day with the dogs. They got caribou every time they went out. They didn't catch a whole lot of caribou at one time, but they caught caribou every day. We were all trying to collect caribou skins that time. We needed them for our bedding and clothing for the winter. I wasn't quite twenty years old yet ... It was only when Martha was born that I turned twenty years old. That is when I started acting like an adult. But at that time we were quite young. We were young but I was quite capable. I could make anything back then. When we got caribou skins, we would scrape them and cut them into patterns. I made clothes for all of my family, my husband and myself. The boots that we made were waterproof. I didn't have any store-bought patterns at that time, but I made the clothing for my family. I made Arvaluk a whole suit, a body-suit. He was just a baby. Then I made a little caribou parka for Oopah. I made a little tail on the back of her parka. I made myself a pair of caribou pants. I could make boots, I could sew all sorts of things with caribou skins and sealskins. I could make the slippers that go inside kamiks. I sewed all those things by myself, in the traditional way.

My husband used to wear out his soles a lot. He would walk and walk and walk. Every day he would go caribou hunting, and he kept on making holes in the soles of his kamiks. I was always working on new soles for him. I remember thinking that this was getting to be too much work. Do you know how walruses have rubbery palms? I took pieces of walrus palms and placed these palm skins on the heels and the front of his kamiks. He spent the whole summer on those soles! Those were really good soles. They didn't wear out at all. But when it came time to dry those soles, I wasn't able to turn the kamiks inside out. They were too stiff and thick to turn inside out. I would turn them halfway inside out, that is how I dried them.

We spent the whole summer caribou-hunting. When September came, it started snowing. We didn't have calendars at that time, but we could tell the months by the seasons. We knew that it was September because that snow was coming back. We were alone then, just us and that other couple. We had a small tent, my husband and I, a small pointed little tent. It was just big enough for a family with two small children. The older one, Oopah, didn't talk very much at that time. She took a long time to be able to talk, but Arvaluk, he learned to speak early. We would go to sleep early when we were alone on the land. At that time I used to fall asleep as early as I could. I used to read my Bible before I went to sleep. That would usually make me tired. We were told at that time to read the Bible every day. I would read it even though I didn't understand it. Even though I could say the Lord's Prayer, I didn't know how to pray back then. I remember one night the men were supposed to be away overnight, so I fell asleep with my small children sleeping beside me. I remember the baby inside me was really stiffening up. We had been sleeping for a little while and suddenly we were woken up by a voice outside the tent. It was Arnaannuk, and she was callling, "Ajakuluk!" Arnaannuk was older than I was, but she called me her ajakuluk.[21] Her mother was my older stepsister. She was calling to me, "Ajakuluk! Ajakuluk! Wake up! The dogs are barking! Stay awake for a little bit!" I had been fast asleep. When I woke up, the dogs were barking and howling really loud. It was really dark outside but it was very calm. It had been snowing and there was a little bit of snow on the ground so there was some light.

The dogs recognized me as soon as I came out of the tent. They came to me and all of the sudden they were all around me. I was scared. Suddenly all of the dogs were surrounding me, they were really scared and terrified of something ... It was only the female dogs, they were the only ones that our husbands had left behind. That woman who I was with said, "Come, move to my tent, bring your children with you!" I said, "But they are asleep!" and she said, "Well, we'll carry them then!" We took the children and their blankets and as fast as we could we moved them into her tent. I carried Arvaluk in my arms. He was quite small. I would have been able to carry him on my back, but I just took him in my arms. We moved into her tent.

This woman, she had never been very religious before. Suddenly she became really religious! She started reading from the Bible that the

Roman Catholic missionary had given her. We could still hear the dogs barking and howling, but I wasn't scared anymore. At that time I didn't know anything about being scared of ghosts or haunted things. My companion, she was really scared – she was so scared she became really religious and kept reading the Bible and saying things like, "Jesus never loved anybody who was scared and if we are scared he is never going to save us!" She was reading the Bible and talking on and on to me and my children in a loud voice to drown out the barking. Then she told me, "Why don't you go have a look?" She didn't want to go outside herself. She wanted me to go have a look outside to go see if there was a polar bear out there. I told her, "Well, I will go and see, but how am I going to see a polar bear when it is so dark outside?" We had made candles out of caribou fat, so she told me to take the little candle, take it outside with me. Since there was no wind outside, I would be able to use the candle to see what was there.

At that time both of us were really dumb. If I took the candle with me I would not have been able to see anything, because it was so dark outside. If I had not taken the candle I would have been able to see something at least, because my eyes would have adjusted to the darkness. Both of us were really dumb! I walked a little ways down to the beach with the candle in my hand, but I couldn't see anything. I came back to the tent and said, "There is nothing there, I didn't see anything." She said, "Okay." We were both in the tent. The dogs just outside the tent were still howling and running around and acting like they were scared, really scared. They were darting around, jumping around. She told me to stay awake, so I lay there listening to the dogs barking and thinking to myself, "What a nice noise that is!" I just fell asleep.

Suddenly she woke me up again and screamed, "I am going to start shooting!" She had a gun in her hands and was ready to start shooting all around the tent. I asked her, "Are you afraid of a polar bear? Is there a polar bear around?" She said, "No, I think it is Satan!" She was going to try and shoot Satan. I told her, "Don't shoot anything! I will go and see if Satan is around." I went out to go have a look but I couldn't find Satan. I came back in.

She had been sewing the door of the tent shut, sealing it from the wind. She had been trying to seal it really tight, but her stitches were too far apart. She took the barrel of the gun and poked it through the holes and started shooting outside. She was shooting like a crazy person, shooting all around! I started laughing by this time. She looked at me and she smiled. After she smiled it was much better. After she finished shooting, the dogs quieted down. Everthing quieted down. We stopped being scared and we slept for a really long time.

It had been calm earlier in the night, but by early morning it became really windy. The wind was blowing all around the tents. She had sewn the door shut so that the wind would not blow out the qulliq. It was snowing and windy, and we couldn't hear anything but the wind. The daylight was just coming back when all of the sudden I heard a noise coming from the rocks that we were using to hold the back of the tent down. Someone was removing those rocks. That is when I got scared. I screamed, "Arnaannuk, wake up! Somebody is removing those rocks!" She sat up and picked up a rock in her hand. She was going to throw a rock at whatever it was coming in the back of the tent.

It was her husband! Apparently her husband had thought that if the wind was coming in too much from the front, he was going to come in from the back so that the wind didn't come in with him. We thought he was Satan! That is how it was. I remember that incident very clearly.

We stayed in that camp for a while, and then we started moving back towards the ocean. I remember meeting one of my aunts and her husband. I don't know where they came from, but we met up with them right there in the middle of the land, and that was a very happy time. I was so happy to see them. I was good friends with my aunt, probably because she was young. The woman who was with me was young too, but she was cranky.

I remembered that this aunt who we met had been given a husband back when I was still a child, so I guess she was older than me ... But she was still young at the time. We had been headed towards the ocean when we met them. My husband and I were tending the caribou skins. He would scrape them for me sometimes. We were living in an igluvigaq at that time and we had run out of caribou fat. We met them when we had nothing to light our qulliit with.

I STARTED HAVING LABOUR PAINS, AND THIS WAS WITH MARTHA

At that time I started having labour pains, and this was with Martha. It was early March – March 3rd is when I had Martha. We had been hungry the month of February. It was still a bit dark at that time, we still weren't getting much daylight.

My older stepsister Iqallijuq came over for the birth of the baby. She said that she wanted to help me give birth and that she really wanted to pray. She wanted to be behind me, supporting my back when I was having the child. I had never had her at my back before. She was behind me and I was kind of wary of her. I was getting a little nervous. It is like that when you are giving birth – it seems that the child inside you feels what you are feeling. When you feel like you are in a strange environment, like when you give birth in a hospital, the baby feels as uncomfortable as you do. My stepsister wanted to be behind my back, and the baby didn't want to come out.

At that time we wouldn't lie down to give birth – we would sit up. We would do it kneeling down. She was behind me. I said to my mother-in-law, when Iqallijuq went out to have a pee, I told my mother-in-law that I wasn't comfortable with my stepsister behind me. My mother-in-law said that my stepsister really wanted to help me give birth and be behind my back. I told her to give me the sewing machine instead. You know how sewing machines come with the cover? Well, I put that behind my back and I was much more comfortable.

Once the sewing machine was behind my back, the baby started coming out. When the baby started crying after she came out, Arvaluk was sleeping and suddenly he woke up. He asked where the noise was coming from. Both Arvaluk's aunts had little dolls – they had been placed in the drying place high up so that the little ones couldn't take them. Arvaluk thought that the dolls were the ones who were making the crying noise. Arvaluk thought that it was the doll crying. His grandfather was laughing and said "It is your sister." Arvaluk said "But I want the doll, give me the doll!" He talked very well, even when he was so young. His grandfather was laughing at him and telling him, "This is your little sister!" That is what Arvaluk has called Martha since then, he calls her Qitungauyak.[22] When he saw Martha for the first time, he wanted me to place the baby in the drying place where we used to place the little dolls.

Martha had her birthday on March 3rd. That was a happy time for me because she was a daughter. She was almost like my first daughter because Oopah had been adopted out as a baby. Even though I had taken Oopah back, it seemed like Martha was my first daughter.

It became late spring. I am not sure what happened to us then. I don't remember what happened at that time. I remember we were having trouble with our qulliit. The sod-houses were leaking inside, and it was getting really dark inside the sod-houses. When you went outside and then came back inside, it seemed dark inside. We played outside a lot back then. We played all sorts of games! I had children at that time, but I was still playing games. After Martha was born, we were not hungry any more. We had a good supply of meat. We were playing games outside.

WE WERE STARVING, AND THAT IS HOW I GAVE BIRTH TO SIMON

Being fearful of what is going to happen takes away your courage. It keeps you from being strong and doing things that you have to do to survive. As Inuit we went through hard times. I also understand that Qallunaat go through hard times ... but being Inuit, we lived very stressful and hard lives.

There was one time when we were really hungry. We had no light and absolutely nothing to eat. We were living in a sod-house. We were in Upirngivik. Sod-houses are usually cosy and warm, but in this sod-house the ceiling was frosted over, and some of the pieces of wood that held it together were missing. We were really hungry and thirsty and cold, and we had no fat to light our qulliit with. We had no light and no heat. This lasted all of March. In April when the young seals came, that is when we finally got some food. And that time in March, before the seals, I was pregnant with Simon. We were really hungry and we had nothing to eat. We were getting ready to move from our camp at Upirngjvik, to move to where we could find food. The men were out hunting for seals to feed the dogs. We wanted to feed the dogs first so they would be stronger for the trip. This was in 1953. I was just twenty-two.

We were starving, and that is how I gave birth to Simon. It was really, really, really cold, and Simon, he was a big baby! And of course we were living in the sod-house, so there were no doctors. When he came out I thought, "What do I do? What should I do?" A woman who has been dead for many years now, David Mablick's mother, Aaluluuq, she was the person taking care of me while I gave birth. My husband and my mother-in-law were both out hunting, and Aaluluuq lived next door. It was cold, it was so cold! She took her own baby off her back and put my newborn baby, the one I had just given birth to, she put him inside her amautik. I tried to clean myself, I tried to clean up the placenta. It froze, and there was this umbilical cord hanging out of me still, and I was getting scared. I thought that it was going to be like that forever. I became scared, having that thing hanging from me, I thought I was going to be like that all the time.

When my mother-in-law came home, she told me not to worry. She said, "No, don't worry. When the cord dies, it will come out." I was supposed to keep my pelvis warm, to keep the cord from freezing. It was so cold! The next day I began to have cramps. I felt like I was giving birth again, and the placenta came out. That was March 10th, and that is how it happened.

THE TIME THAT WE WERE BAPTIZED

The time that we were baptized, I remember it was winter. That fall was the first time we were going to have our own sod-house. That was the first time we were going to be by ourselves. We had always lived with my in-laws before that, in their big sod-house, in their tent, all of us, my mother-in-law, her husband and her children, three daughters, and Peter, myself, my husband and my children – Oopah, Arvaluk, Simon, Martha, and Jakopie. My in-laws said that there were too many people in their house, and they told us that we should build our own sod-house. I remember it was a small, small sod-house. If we brought a big seal inside to skin, there would be no room on the floor for anything else, just the big seal, there would be no place for us to walk around.

That spring, in March I think, a minister came to our camp. He was a fat man. He is dead now. He came in with Nasuk and Peter Paniloo – he was a little boy then, Peter Paniloo. They came to our camp. I remember it was scary for me to get baptized. I remember they were teaching us to sing songs. When I think about that I smile and I laugh. They wanted us to sing properly, to sing nicely! I laugh when I think about that ... about trying to sing songs properly ...

They also told us that we had to be baptized. They said that baptism was like when we used water to wipe away the little bits of caribou fur stuck to us. The ministers, they told us that was how baptism worked. We were baptized on the bed of the sod-house. We knelt on the floor, and the minister and the two men sat on the edge of the bed. They had a different way of speaking, a different language, different words. When he baptized me, the minister didn't hear me properly when I told him my Christian name. He didn't hear me correctly, so he baptized me Sapphia instead of Apphia. I was scared – I thought that Sapphia would be my new name forever ... Sapphia! All of these thoughts were racing in my mind. I was being baptized without really knowing what it was. I was confused. I didn't want to become Christian, I didn't know what it was, and then on top of it all I was being baptized a different name. How scary it was! They seemed to be so holy and almighty, and it was a very scary experience.

When they finished baptizing us, they started preparing to leave. They were going to leave the next day. As they were preparing to leave, they asked my husband to go with them, to travel with them for a little while. Apparently they were going to go far away, to Qurluqtuuq.[23] It was a long, long distance. My husband went part of the way with them. They went through Pond Inlet. Yes, they came through here. Then they went to Igloolik. They left in February, and my husband didn't come back to us until late spring. Sometimes we didn't have our husbands with us for a long time back then. That is how it was at that time.

The Qallunaat, especially the priests and the ministers, they were scary. They forced people to be baptized. They pressured us to say yes.

The Anglican and the Catholic ministers, they were always fighting with each other, fighting for Inuit.

OUR FIRST OUTBOARD MOTOR

There have been happy times and there have been sad times in our lives. I remember when we got our first outboard motor, it was a nine horsepower. Before we got our motor we used to paddle or sail everywhere we went. We would paddle when the sea was calm. When we were headed to an island, it would take us a very long time to reach the island, because we would paddle the whole way, we would paddle and paddle. It was really tiring, paddling like that. We would paddle far, far away to other lands just to look for caribou.

I remember we were travelling in a boat. It was in 1953. We didn't have a motor at that time, and we were out caribou hunting. We were gone for a month, just my husband and I. We left in June and came back in September. We were gone more than a month. We paddled and paddled until the wind started. When the wind started, we put up our sails. That is the only time that we ever travelled fast, when we were sailing. My husband would steer the boat. But when we were facing the wind, we sailed really slow.

We had a sealskin tent. That time we didn't have any material to make tents like canvas tents, so we had tents made out of sealskin. We took a string and ran it across the inside of the tent to hang our clothing. I used to live the Inuit way and I never used to see any Qallunaat. We dressed in caribou clothing. I had a caribou amautik and caribou wind-pants that I wore all the time. I had kamiks. That is how we lived. Every time we went out camping or hunting, I would wear my caribou clothing. I would sew skin clothes for my husband and my children. When we were out caribou hunting, our dogs would come with us. When we got a caribou, the dogs would carry caribou on their backs and men would also carry caribou on their backs. We didn't have any four-wheelers. We had needles that we would sew with and a qulliq that would light our tent. We didn't have any tea or any biscuits. It didn't bother us, because we weren't used to them then. We didn't even think about not having tea or biscuits. It is only when we started having modern things in our life that we started caring about not having things. That is when we started leaving our culture behind.

Since there were no rubber boots at that time, we had to make caribou-skin or sealskin kamiks. We sewed them. We used caribou clothing and caribou mattresses and caribou blankets, and that is how we lived. It was all right, it didn't bother us. I would sew caribou clothing, and we would eat and drink the blood of caribou and seals. Our tent was made of sealskin. That is how we lived. My children didn't have Pampers. We would watch them closely and pull them off the bed or out of the amautik when they were about to pee. In the summers we ate lots of caribou meat and caribou fat. We would pick blueberries and blackberries, and we would mix them up with caribou fat and make Inuit ice-cream.

We would go out caribou hunting for a long time in the summer and fall. We would use different mosses to light fires to boil caribou meat. We didn't have any stoves. We would pick dried mosses and plants from the land and that is what we used to cook. We would boil our meat, fry our meat, or eat it raw. We would mix hot water with different mosses and leaves and drink it as tea. We would boil the water and put the leaves in and it would be tea. We would eat seal fat and keep it in our mouths for a long time like it was candy. We didn't have bottles at that time, so we used our breasts to feed our children. One time I had been eating lots of seal fat and caribou fat, so my youngest baby had a lot of trouble with his poops. Finally he pooed and it was just white. I remember thinking it was because of the caribou fat that I was eating. Our food gave us strength, but at times I think it gave us problems.

🔳 🔳 🔳

I remember a time when we stayed out too long, me and my husband, we ran out of matches. We didn't have any matches so my husband started looking for ways to start a fire. He took a caribou antler and he rubbed it on a rock with some moss. It started smoking, but there was no fire. He thought of something else. He took a piece of paper, he wet it and put gunpowder on it and rubbed it and rubbed it. He took a piece of flint that he picked up from the ground and he started hitting the flint with another rock. The paper and the ashes started smoking and once they started smoking, a fire started. We had fire! It was so good to see fire again! We hadn't had any heat or any fire all day long. That night we had heat and fire again. It felt like our tent was really hot.

The next morning after we made that fire, we headed back to our home camp. We folded up our tent and took our qulliq and put it in the boat. It was still lit when we put it in the boat. It was burning caribou fat. I was really careful to make sure that the fat didn't spill anywhere. We had to keep it going with caribou fat so that we could use it when we set up camp on our way home. We kept our fire going in the boat all the way home. We didn't have any matches. We were really poor that time.

The boat we had, it was one that we had to paddle. It took us a long time to get home. We didn't have any matches with us and we paddled very slowly. When we got back home, we got out of our boat and went to my in-laws' tent. We went inside, and they were very, very happy to see us. It had been a long time! My husband's mother, she boiled some caribou meat that we brought back and made tea for us on her qulliq. I remember she had two pots in their tent, one with tea and one with meat, and she was putting them on her qulliq one at a time. That is what she was doing. I looked around the tent at the pot on the floor and the teapot on the qulliq. I was so happy. My husband and I had tea. We hadn't drunk tea for a long time. It was so good. It wasn't leaves from the land like what we had been drinking, it was Qallunaat tea. We had our tea and our meat, and my husband started smoking. I think I was smoking too. I used to smoke then.

That fall when we finally went home to our camp, I was really, really happy. There were good times and bad times back then. I was really happy when we got back to our camp and had that tea. My in-laws who we had left in the camp, my in-laws, they had not had caribou for a long, long time. It is no wonder – we left them in the camp in springtime and we came back in fall. When we came home we brought them caribou. They were so happy to have caribou.

FEELING VERY LUCKY WHEN WE HAD A GOOD DOG TEAM

I always thought that dog teams were the only way to get anywhere. I never thought that anything but dogs would ever take us hunting or take us places. I remember feeling very lucky when we had a good dog team. There were always people who didn't have dog teams around. They were poorer than us, because they couldn't travel anywhere or go out hunting.

When we had dogs, we looked after them like they were babies. From when they were born until they were adults, we would take care of them. We had to look after them and feed them so they could grow up strong. We had to keep them in the house when they were small to keep them suckling, to keep them warm so they would be strong and healthy later on. When they were too young to walk or feed themselves, we would keep them in the house with their mother. Once they began walking around, we would let them go outside.

If it was winter and the puppies were walking around, the men would build them a little igluvigaq to keep them warm. The little igluvigaq would have an open roof so that we could watch the dogs from above. It was high enough so that the puppies wouldn't jump out. Some of the dogs were more aggressive and angry than others. They would see a puppy and try to kill it and eat it. Sometimes other dogs would protect the mother and the puppies. We would build an igluvigaq to protect the mother and her puppies from the angry dogs. It would keep them from getting in and killing the puppies.

When my sons were growing up, they would go out and play with the puppies and take them out running. They would do this close to the camp, close to the fox traps. My sons had little qamutiks like their father's, and they would tie the puppies to them and pretend they had their own little dog team. They would name the puppies on their team and teach them how to pull a qamutik. Since my little boys were tiny, the puppies would pull them along.

By the time the puppies became adults, after playing with my sons they were ready to pull big qamutiks. When the dogs were old enough, my husband would take them and mix them with the other dogs on the team. We looked after our dogs like they were children, like they were teenagers. We had to look after them, feed them, make sure they were warm. Some people beat their dogs and puppies, but that was never good for the dogs. We raised them to respect us. Dogs, they are like children – if you beat them all the time, they stop listening to you. They start wandering off, and they stop listening to you.

The children would name their dogs, and the dogs would know the person quite well and listen to the person. The dogs would know their names. Every time they were pulling the qamutik, if one of them was pulling back or being lazy the men would yell at them and call their name, and they would understand. They would pull harder. That is the reason why they named dogs in the past, so that they would listen when they were being scolded, so that they would listen.

Some dogs weren't as good as others. If they were hungry or cold, they would walk around like they had water in their boots. They would tiptoe, and often they wouldn't grow up to be very big dogs. My husband and I, we always raised nice big beautiful dogs. They understood my husband. If they were out on the ice, my husband and the dogs, looking for baby seals, the dogs would sniff around. My husband would hold on to the dogs and the dogs would sniff around, and when they smelled something, they would start digging on the ice. My husband would make a hole in the ice where the dogs had been digging. It was always the dogs who showed us where the seals were. It was my husband who taught them these things.

If we went out hunting for caribou, even if we didn't see caribou tracks or see caribou in the distance, the dogs would smell them. They would show us where to look for them. They knew how to protect the Inuit from the polar bears. The dogs would bark or howl every time there was a polar bear. If somebody was coming towards our camp, they would bark. The only sounds we ever used to hear in camps were the sounds of dog teams. We had no radios then. That was the only sound we heard.

That is how it was back then. That is how important dogs were to us. Dogs were like human beings. We depended on them, we needed them. We had to raise our dogs to be strong in order to pull a qamutik and in order to help us hunt. That is how we lived back then, as Inuit, before we began to live like Qallunaat.

JAKOPIE, HE WAS ADOPTED OUT

My son Jakopie, he was adopted out when he was a little baby. He was my fifth. He was adopted out to a couple. They were not my relatives, but since I was full of children at that time and that couple couldn't have any more children, my mother-in-law asked me to give him to them. He was adopted in February, and they only kept him until mid March. His mother died, so the RCMP told me to go pick him up. He was in Nirlirnaaqtuuq. When we went to pick him up to take him back with us, his backside was so skinny you could see his tail-bone. You could see his eyes were very big and he had a really long face. I felt very, very sorry for him! I started feeding him with my breast, even though I was still breast-feeding Simon at the time. He kept wanting more and more. He was quite full, but he kept wanting to eat.

His adoptive father was Ujarasuk and his adoptive mother who had died was Kuattuk. I was scared of this old person, Ujarasuk. Although the RCMP told me to pick him up, I was scared to take his child away. I told him, "I am just going to take him for a little while. I will breast-feed him and bring him back to you." The woman who had been looking after Jakopie was his older adoptive sister, Niriungniq. She was just a young child at the time, and had been carrying the baby around in her amautik since her mother's death. She told me that she had been giving Jakopie water when he cried. After I finished breast-feeding him, they asked for him back again, so I gave him back. I was scared when they said they wanted him back, so I did what they told. After a while Niriungniq brought him back again and said, "I think he is hungry again. He keeps crying." So I breast-fed him some more, and finally I fell asleep and we slept all that night until early in the morning.

The next morning when my husband and I woke up, the people next door, Ujarasuk and Niriungniq, were still sleeping. We got up and got the dogs ready to go. We were trying to be really quiet. We packed up really quietly. We left in the morning and we kept on travelling all through the day. We acted like we had stolen a person. We didn't say anything. Both of us were scared of the RCMP so we did what they told us to, we took Jakopie back. We didn't tell those people that the RCMP had wanted us to take the child. We felt sorry for the old man because his wife had just died, so we just left, we crept out of the camp. To this day we have had Jakopie with us. He was just a little baby when we gave him away. He didn't know what was going on at the time. He had no idea.

Jakopie and Oopah, those are the two children who I adopted out and then took back. When little babies are starving and skinny, it is pitiful.

THE AIRPLANE PICKED US UP

I am going to tell you about a story that amazed me very much. It was at the time that my in-laws went to go meet the ship. This was in 1955, and we were camped at Upirngivik. It was summer and the ice was gone. Kalirraq and his wife, my husband's sister Amarualik, left the camp. They went to help unload the ship. At that time we couldn't sell our sealskins, so we would do odd jobs and get paid. We wouldn't get paid much, mainly with tea, sugar, bullets, only with supplies we could use for the fall. We needed supplies, so Amarualik and Kalirraq, they took our boat and my husband's tiny outboard motor to go meet the ship. The boat they took was a big boat. It used to be a sailboat, and then we bought a small motor to put behind it. They left us behind when they went to meet the ship because we had dogs and we had to look after them. There were three dogs. There was just me and my husband and the children left in the camp, so we put my in-laws' tent on top of our tent to make it warmer and to keep their supplies away from the dogs.

We had sealskin tents back then. I would make tents myself out of sealskin. I would scrape the sealskins and dry them and sew them together. I would sew the skins together while they were still wet. It took seven sealskins in all to make a very small tent. If it was a bigger tent, it would be eight seals. Even today I know exactly how to make those tents. We would split the sealskins and separate the skin from the fur. There is a very thin layer of skin on the fur. Part of the sealskin is just plain skin. We would do this very carefully, even though we had a lot of children to look after. The children also had to have kamiks made out of sealskin back then. We didn't have store-bought boots at that time, so we would have to sew all of our boots ourselves. When the soles wore out, we would have to replace them. Soles were always having to be replaced. I chewed a lot of sealskin at that time. No wonder my teeth are worn out today – I spent so much of my life chewing sealskin!

On that day after my in-laws had gone away, we were in the seal-skin tent and it was really warm. We never thought about how we smelled. We didn't have any soap. I had a young child at that time, a baby, a small son, Jakopie. Jakopie Siqujjut Kuutiq was his full name before the Qallunaat changed my children's names. I had a small baby at that time and four other children. This was in 1955. This was just recently.

We had never ever seen an airplane close up. We had never been inside a plane to take a trip. We never used to have airplanes come up North very often because we didn't have any airstrips. I thought one of the dogs was growling slowly, quietly. I thought that he was growl-ing, but he was taking a long time – growling for such a long time.

My children were playing outside. Arvaluk had gone out to meet the ship with his grandparents, so only his brothers and sisters were with us – Oopah, Simon, Martha, and little Jakopie in my amautik. The older one, Simon, he is older than Jako, he was sitting beside me, and his father was out in the tiny boat. He paddled away to go hunting because he didn't have a motor. He had gone out seal hunting, and he was gone by then. I was tending to the udjuuk²⁴ skins. There were so many of them. My mother-in-law was supposed to have done them, but she left to go meet the ship. She left me with all the skins, so I was working hard, really, really hard. I had to clean them and dry them and scrape them and get them ready for sewing. Some of them were getting old, and I was scraping the dirt off those ones, making sure everything came off so they could be used for rope. Udjuuk skin ropes were used for dog harnesses. We used dogs to travel at that time. This was a long, long time ago, before the Qallunaat came.

I thought that one of the dogs was growling. It seemed like the dog had been growling for a long, long time. I was listening to him growl, but it seemed to be going on for such a long time, and it seemed like he was getting louder and louder. At that time I didn't recognize the sound of an airplane. Those small planes sound just like dogs growl-ing. The growling got closer and closer, and the children were still playing. The children suddenly shouted, "Anaana! Anaana!²⁵ Look! A big airplane!" They yelled like it was a large, large airplane. I was inside the tent, and I thought to myself, "I wonder if they are telling the truth? I wonder if it is a real plane?" I put Simon's little kamiks on him and we went out of the tent.

We went out, Simon and I. Oopah was carrying Jakopie. She was taking care of him. He didn't have any Pampers on, of course, at that time, and apparently he had pooed in her amautik. We had no diapers at that time and Oopah was too young to know to pull him out when she felt him about to poo.

We were amazed – there was an airplane! The dogs were amazed too. They started howling. I wondered why that plane was going over our camp. I told my children, "Oh, it is just passing us!" I remember wiping my hands. I had been working with sealskins, and I had a dirty old cloth that I was using to wipe my hands. Since we didn't wash much back then, the cloth was full of grease. The children were playing outside. The plane flew over us, and I told them all to come inside the tent. We didn't have tea or anything at that time. I didn't care about cigarettes back then, but I was disappointed for a minute or two that the plane was just passing by. I wished for a minute that it would land and give us some tea.

Just after I wished that, all of the sudden the airplane turned around and started preparing to land on the water! The water was very still. I was scared. I told the children, "Oh no, I shouldn't have wished for the plane to come, now it has come! Go look for your father. See if you can find him and tell him that there is an airplane here!" The children ran off. They were scared. Simon was really scared, so he was running faster than his sister. Oopah was carrying Jakopie on her back so she was much slower. They were running and running, and they were quite tiny children. Oopah was wearing my amautik and it was too big for her. I still remember how they looked, running away like that ...

They couldn't find their father, so they came back. By the time they got back, the airplane had landed on the water and it was trying to beach. We were wondering what was happening, so we went down to the water. We had a wooden door on the tent, and I closed the door. I was worried that the dogs would get in while we were over at the airplane. When we got to the beach, a man came out of the plane and started talking to us. He was making airplane noises with his mouth. He was making signs with his arms and talking in a language that didn't make any sense at all. Since I didn't know what he was doing, I just watched him. Simon, my son, was playing in the water. He was dipping his feet in the water, and suddenly the man picked him up and put him on the plane. I yelled at him, "That is my child! Don't take my child!" I was scared. He was trying to get us to follow Simon into the plane. I was worried about my sealskins and the dogs next to the tent. They were going to get into the tent if we left them.

Oopah kept Jakopie on her back, and they probably thought at that time, "This must be a little adult carrying this little baby." When we got inside the airplane, I saw my older sister Nattiq and her husband, Ijituuq, and her five children, Angutimmavik, Arnattaujuq, Nuqallaq, and then the last one, the one that used to have epilepsy, Renee. There were five of them. I was so scared!

My sister was saying, "Oh my God, what is happening to us?" She was frightened. Her eyes were wide open, and she was sitting down. They told us to sit down. The airplane was really full. Simon didn't have anywhere to sit. He kept standing. The pilot put him on his lap. He started talking in Qallunaatitut,[26] and Simon was learning from him. Simon must have stunk like crazy! He was probably smelling pretty bad because we hadn't washed in a while, and he was sitting on the Qallunaaq's lap. The plane took off, and the things that happened to our stomachs! When the airplane went up our stomachs dropped. The plane went down again and up again, and I started vomiting.

It was very hard to hear anything in the plane, and the trip only took a very short time. They took us to Ikpiarjuk.[27] We landed on the water, and when we landed there were a whole bunch of people there. I guess we were all being collected. Of course there were no radios or anything back then, so we had no idea that this was happening. We didn't know what was going on. We had no radios, no phones – there were just us Inuit, dogs and Inuit, our country food and our skin clothing.

When we landed, one of the Catholic priests came over to where all the people were standing and told us that they were going to take chest X-rays.[28] That is why the airplane picked us up. I asked, "What does that mean?" I had never had that done to me before. I was scared! I didn't know what they were going to do. The priest said that they wanted to look at pictures of our chests. I thought they were going to take out our lungs and snap their picture, that is how I understood it. I was really scared, and he said, "Just come on." I was scared. I wanted to keep my lungs inside of me. I had good lungs back then ... We went inside, and right away they told us to get comfortable and take our clothes off. There were some tools there, and two Qallunaat were talking. I did not understand even one word of what they were saying. The Catholic priest was the one who was interpreting for us. They told us to take everything off. We had to take our parkas and our shirts off for the chest X-ray. He explained to me exactly what was going to be done and what was going to happen to us. I asked him, "Are we going to get cut up?" I had heard of that before, about surgery and people being cut up. He said, "No, they just want to take a picture of your lungs."

All of the children took their shirts off. The third one, Simon, didn't want to take his shirt off, and he was crying. He had a small T-shirt on, a ragged old dirty little T-shirt. He didn't want to take it off, but it had to come off. The Catholic missionary gave him biscuits and candy, and while he was eating those he didn't mind so much having his shirt taken off. After we had our tea, they told us that they were going to take us back to our camp. Oh, how joyful that was! We didn't even have time to visit with all the people who were there. My in-laws had been there helping unload the boat. They found us and gave us flour and sugar and other things. They told me to put it in my hood. We didn't have bags back then. They put it inside my hood. Finally the Qallunaat told us to get back on the plane. We went with my oldest sister to her camp. We flew there first, and it was not as bad as the first flight, we were not vomiting any more. We had drunk tea and eaten Qallunaat biscuits, so we were all very cheerful. They took us back to our camp.

When we were flying above our tent, we saw our dogs, and it seemed like they were so far away! We could see the tent. I remember looking for my husband there. I didn't see him. It was really loud in the airplane, and I remember Simon touched me and yelled, "Look!" Simon yelled, "Look, my father, he is short!" I was so amazed. He had gotten shorter! He hadn't changed, but from up there at that time he seemed to have a really big head and a short, short body. He was looking up with a knife in his hand. He seemed really short. When we landed on the water and beached, he asked, "What happened to you?" And I said, "They took us to Ikpiarjuk and took pictures of our lungs. I wonder if they are going to do a chest X-ray on you too." I made sign language to the Qallunaat, asking if they were going to take my husband, and they said "No." I wondered why. That is the time I learned how to say no in Qallunaatitut. The airplane left and we had plenty of tea then.

After that plane ride my in-laws didn't come back into the camp for a long time. Apparently the ship took a long time to leave the community, and it took a while for them to help unload the ship. They made money that way, money to buy Qallunaat things. It took them a while to come back to the camp.

I remember when they came back. Oopah looked out of the tent and said to me, "Look, that ice is really close!" There was no ice at that time, but my in-laws, they weren't using a sail, just an outboard motor. It was a really small motor so it was really quite quiet. My children's father went out of the house and said, "That is a boat! It is moving!" I didn't believe him. I said, "You are lying, it is a piece of ice! There is probably a walrus on top of it." And then it got closer and closer as we were talking, and you could recognize the people. They were Amarualik and Kalirraq. When they finally came back, how joyful that was! That was the most joyful moment for us at that time. We had been alone all summer, we had been alone for so long.

WHEN RHODA WAS BORN, HER FATHER NAMED HER PALLUQ

It was my husband who was with me when I delivered Rhoda. He helped me deliver all my babies. It was just him and I when Rhoda came. Rhoda was born in the spring. We were camping with some other families, but no one assisted us delivering Rhoda. I think my husband probably waited too long before he went to ask for help. He prepared the bed and helped me give birth. After I had given birth to Rhoda, a woman, Aaluluuq, came over.

When Rhoda was born, her father named her Palluq. Palluq was my husband's adopted father when he was growing up. Palluq took care of my husband when he was a child. My husband, he grew up with his grandparents. Palluq wasn't his natural grandfather, he was my husband's grandmother's second husband. She married Palluq when her first husband died. This was just around the time that my husband was born, so he grew up in Palluq's care. To honour Palluq my husband gave Rhoda the name Palluq. He was his step-grandfather, and my husband loved him very much.

Palluq died many years before my husband and I got married. I remember him being sick and dying when I was just a small child. That was when my husband was married to his first wife, when I was very young. He was married to someone else at the time Palluq died.

So Rhoda was named after my husband's step-grandfather. I named her as well after my grandmother Kaukjak. Even though we have six girls in our family, out of all of his daughters my husband loved Rhoda the best. Because of the name Palluq, he seemed to love her much more than his other daughters. Because he loved Rhoda very much, he worked hard to provide for her. He would carve carvings or hunt foxes so that he could buy bannock and other things at the Hudson's Bay store for Rhoda to eat. He tried very hard to provide for Rhoda. Even today she is the most loved one of her father.

Because she was so loved by her father, I didn't really love Rhoda as much as the other children. I loved her, but I didn't spoil her. My husband loved her so much he would never let her be disciplined in any way. Whenever he went away, I would take the liberty to discipline her and mistreat her. I remember when we lived on the land and she would go walking with her older brothers and sisters to look for ducks or for rabbits, her older brothers and sisters would pick on her and make her cry. On the way back they would try and get her to stop crying. Once she spotted her father, she would start crying again to get his attention.

WE WEREN'T ALLOWED TO TRAVEL SUNDAYS

There was a milk can that was filled with blood from my daughter's nosebleed. Oopah was having a nosebleed. She was about twelve or thirteen years old, and we were trying to take her to Arctic Bay to get help. It was springtime, and even though we didn't have a clock or a watch, we thought it was Saturday. We were poor at that time, so we didn't have any clocks or watches. We didn't have any calendars – we knew the time and the day by the sun and the moon. While we were travelling to Arctic Bay, we thought it was Saturday. We weren't allowed to travel Sundays.

It was cold that evening, so we stopped to rest. Our daughter was really cold. She was losing blood. Oopah was the only one of our children that time who was thirsty. She kept wanting to drink. It was because she was losing blood. We slept that night, and when we woke up, we thought it was Sunday. We weren't allowed to travel on Sundays. We weren't allowed to hunt either, even though there were lots of seals around. We didn't have a choice, so we stopped and rested since it was Sunday.

My husband was restless, so he walked up a little hill beside our campsite. My daughter was having nosebleeds all the time, and we thought she might be dying. He went out and climbed the little hill, just for fun, just to see if he could find any seals with his telescope. When he was up there, he saw a dog team and a qamutik passing by. It was my husband's sister Amarualik and her husband, Kalirraq. My husband was wondering why they were travelling on a Sunday. He waved to them and when they came over they told us it was Monday. We found out that we had travelled on Sunday and rested on Monday. I was afraid.

When they stopped, Oopah's nose stopped bleeding, so we didn't have to go to Igloolik. We went back with them to their camp. She was fine afterwards.

MY BABY SOLOMON ALMOST DIED

We used to deliver in camp without nursing stations or nurses to help us. We delivered in sod-houses, and we delivered in tents, and we were fine. Even though it was fine, I used to be scared. That was when I was really young. I remember I used to be so scared back then ...

I remember it was 1959 and my mother-in-law was going to deliver a child. She asked me to come into the sod-house and help her deliver. My mother-in-law was in labour, and I went over. The baby that came out was a boy. I was really happy. I delivered the baby. I was pregnant with Solomon at the time, and my husband had heard the noises. He thought I was having my baby. I went home and said to him, "Your mother had her baby."

I remember a while later I was eating. I was eating raw meat, seal meat, and I wasn't thinking about having a baby, I was eating raw meat. All of a sudden I noticed that there was a flow of water coming through my pants. I stood up very quickly and yelled to my husband, "I am peeing!" I thought I was peeing my pants. My mother-in-law ran in and shouted, "You are in labour! You just broke your water!" My husband got up very quickly from where he was lying and started making a bed for me to lie on. He put a nice blanket down and right there I delivered. I was really frightened – I delivered in a hurry, because the baby was coming fast.

After I delivered my baby I was in really bad pain. That is when I got sick and started having pains and aches all over. We had a new sod-house. We had just moved into a new sod-house right after my baby was born. I didn't know why it started or how it started, but I was in really bad pain. I couldn't eat any more. I started wondering and thinking, "Why? Why am I in so much pain?" I found out later I was sick with an infection in my uterus. That is why my skin turned dark. Arvaluk, my son, he went out hunting. He was out hunting and while he was gone, my skin started getting dark all over. It was really dark. Then, the top of my skin started peeling off. All the dark skin started peeling off from my body, from all over my body.

Finally, when I started getting better, my skin started looking normal again. When I felt better I went to my mother-in-law's sod-house. I went to go visit my mother-in-law. I remember her telling me that her baby was sick. She said that he was having trouble with his lungs. I stayed with her for a while and then I went home. I told her that I would go back later on that night, but by the time I went back, the baby was dead. After he died, we went up the hill to dig the grave. It was dug quite easily. It wasn't too much for us. He was so small, he was only a few months old ...

A few days later my baby got sick, my little baby Solomon. I didn't even notice he was sick. I never had a sick baby before. After I got better from my infection, I began sewing skins again, and he was in my amautik. He was sleeping and my husband was out hunting. The baby was sleeping on my back in the amautik, he wasn't crying, and I never thought about pulling him out to feed him. I didn't realize he was having trouble breathing. When my husband came back, I helped him take off his kamiks. Then I took off my kamiks and went onto the bed. My husband sat down beside me on the bed and wanted to look at the baby. He pulled him out and he said, "What is wrong with the baby? He is so pale!"

I looked at the baby and he was really weak and pale. I thought the baby was dead. I had kept him in the amautik for such a long time. When I took him out, he was looking really pale and he wasn't breathing. My husband grabbed the baby and tried to help him breathe. He tried to help him to breathe, but the baby, he couldn't breathe. Simon ran out to tell my mother-in-law what was happening. When my husband's parents came in, my father-in-law grabbed the baby from my husband. They were fighting over the baby. The baby was dead. I didn't know what to do, so I just sat there. Whenever I have been scared in my life, I close up and I don't move. I went over to my husband that time and said, "Let go of the baby." He let the baby go.

My mother-in-law took the baby home, and the baby was dead. My husband and I followed her. My husband went outside and started praying out loud. He was praying really hard, and my son started breathing again. Maybe it was the strength of his prayers that brought my son back. God listened to him. My mother-in-law told us to start packing to go to Igloolik for help. We packed up our things and the next day we travelled to Igloolik. We didn't have proper winter travelling clothes with us so my husband found some wood and built a little house on the qamutik. It was January and I was only wearing my ordinary clothing and we travelled. It was so cold! I took all my children with me. I had six children and the baby at that time. Solomon was the seventh baby. There were a lot more babies to come ...

When we got to Igloolik, we went to the Catholic priest. There was no nurse at that time. There were some teachers, but they hadn't started teaching yet. That was the first year the teachers came to Igloolik. That was 1959. When we got there, the Catholic missionary gave my son a needle and told me not to breast-feed him. He gave me a can of milk for the baby to feed on. He gave him a needle and told us to go to Hall Beach.[29] That is where the nursing station was. We left Simon, Martha, and Jake in Igloolik and went to Hall Beach with the older ones and Rhoda and Solomon. My husband, he was whipping the dogs all the way from Igloolik, and it took a long time to get there. I think it would have been faster by ski-doo if we had one at that time. My husband was trying so hard to make the dogs go faster, he ran beside the sled all the way from Igloolik to Hall Beach. As soon as we got to Hall Beach, the baby was taken into the hospital. I had been breast-feeding him. That was why he was put in the hospital. I had passed my infection to him through my breast-milk. We stayed in Hall Beach for a long time, almost two months. While we were there someone brought Martha to us. My husband and I stayed in Hall Beach with the children in a little igluvigaq.

Solomon was sick for a long time but he still kept on smiling. He was sick for a long time. When he did start getting better it was the beginning of spring. He still shook a lot and I thought he was going to be like that forever, but finally he started getting back to his normal self, and we were told by the Qallunaat that we could go home. It was March by the time we were able to leave Hall Beach. It was springtime and really warm outside, so we left behind the little shed my husband had built for the back of the qamutik.

When we got back to Igloolik, my other children were really happy to see us. My children weren't well looked after while we were away. They weren't being fed well, their clothes were all worn out, and Simon, he had an infection in his eyes. His eyes were really red, and his hands were really swollen from not having proper mittens and from them getting cold. I was really upset. My little children, we picked them up and we went home again.

That is the story about how my baby Solomon almost died. I told him after all of that, I told Solomon, "Don't you ever smoke, because you almost died because of your lungs! You had a really bad infection in your lungs!" He never smoked, not until he was a lot older. Even today he never smokes in the house. He smokes when I am not around, like when he is outside working on his ski-doo. I tell him over and over again that story about how he almost died, and he tries to listen to me.

A CASE OF MEASLES GOING AROUND

When I think about the sicknesses that we have had, I really notice that there are two different kinds of bodies, the Qallunaat body and the Inuit body. Our bodies are different. Maybe it is the food. Inuit, we live on land food. Maybe that is it ... Whatever it is, Qallunaat don't get as sick as Inuit do, they seem stronger that way. Every time the ships came in, the Qallunaat brought colds and sicknesses into the camps. That is when Inuit started getting sick. Inuit, we were not used to these kinds of sicknesses in our bodies. Before the ships starting coming in, we never had measles. Measles was a new disease for the Inuit people.

My daughter Joanna, she was the first one. That was in 1962. She was born in 1961. She was the first of my children to catch the measles. There was a case of measles going around. This was in Arctic Bay. It was a pretty big community by then. We were in our home camp, Nau-jaaruluk. We were alone. We didn't know anything about measles. There was a boat travelling to the different camps. They were deliver-ing food and supplies to our camp. We heard from them that there was a case of measles going around Arctic Bay. They came to our camp with the food and sugar and tea and flour, and they brought the measles to us too. After that we started getting sick. All my children started getting sick, they broke out in spots. I had never heard about measles in the past. I saw spots on their bodies and wondered what they were.

Solomon and I were the only ones who weren't sick in the camp. Maybe because he was really sick as a child, he didn't catch the measles. He was so young he wasn't even talking yet. I remember him helping me. He would deliver water and take out the honey-bucket. Even though it was too heavy for him, he would still do it. I was really, really busy with the sick children.

I remember my husband was out caribou-hunting on the mainland that time my children got sick. It was summertime, and Oopah, Simon, and Arvaluk were with him. He got sick out on the land, so he sent Arvaluk and Simon back to the camp to tell us that he was sick. Oopah stayed to take care of her father. He got better out on the land. When Simon and Arvaluk came home, they told me about their father who was sick out on the land, then they got the measles too.

I was all alone, and all my children were sick. I would give them water to drink when they started crying with pain. They would drink water, and they would settle down. Every time they became restless in the bed, I would take them out and help them pee. Then I would give them more water to drink.

Solomon, he was so young, but he understood that I was nursing the other children. Every time one of them would get restless, he would quickly get water and hand it over to them and let them drink. I remember one time when Martha started moving, Solomon quickly went over and gave her water. She was in pain. We had a can that we used to pee in. Solomon was pretty small at that time. He grabbed the can and brought it to Martha. It was too heavy for him, but he still carried it over the other children in the bed to where Martha was lying. Martha had long hair at that time. The load was too heavy for Solomon, so he stumbled and dropped the can on Martha's head. It was about half full when it spilled all over her long hair!

We had lice at that time too. The lice stayed around until we recovered from the sickness. After a while my children got better. My husband also got better out on the land while he was hunting. After my children got better, I got sick. I was the last one to get sick, and I was really sick. Since I had never been sick in my life, I would scream out in pain. It was really painful – I was very itchy, and I was not supposed to scratch. Solomon and I were the last ones to get sick.

After a while a boat came in, a Qallunaat boat. Everybody was sick everywhere, in different camps all over the land, so a boat went around to pick up the sick people. They were worried about us, so they took us to Igloolik by boat. By that time my children were all better, and Solomon and I were sick. They picked us up, me and all my children. That was the only way I would have been able to go.

We left our dogs and brought our supplies, our hunting gear, and our tent. We were in a big boat. It had a motor on it. Arvaluk took the small family boat and followed us. I remember travelling and the wind started to blow. It got really stormy. The ice was really rough. We were travelling on the rough sea. We could see Arvaluk following behind us, but our family boat was a lot slower than the big boat. I was in the bigger boat but I was in bed. Every time we hit a wave, water would come in from the ceiling.

When we got to Igloolik, the water was so rough we had to dock at the back of the island. Arvaluk's boat was lighter, so he went straight to the front of the island where the community is. We couldn't reach that shore, the sea was too rough.

We docked at the back of the island and then people in the community came to get us. They didn't walk over, they came with a truck. It wasn't an ordinary truck, it was a big huge truck. I was lying on a qamutik and they drove us to the community. They took us to where there were some Qallunaat. That was the only way that we could travel, by truck. They brought me and Solomon. We were sick. I had Joanna on my back. Joanna wasn't sick any more, she just had a few spots. Rhoda was just a small child, so she came with us. She got sick again when we got there. There was no nursing station at that time in Igloolik, but there was a small building that they were using to treat people. Igloolik was the last place to get a nursing station. We stayed in the student hostels. They had been built for children who needed a place to stay when they went to school. That was the only place they could keep us.

We stayed in Igloolik for a long time. We stayed in a little trailer for almost two weeks. It was packed with people with measles, people were sleeping on the floor. Some of them were really, really sick. Some of them died. A lot of women who were pregnant delivered before it was their time. I think there were three people who died of measles. Another person had mental problems afterwards. That is how it was for us at that time.

I remember they treated us by giving us medication through our rectum. I was really scared of Qallunaat at that time. Solomon was quite small then, but he could understand and talk a little bit. Every time the nurse would come over to treat us, he would scream and try and protect his bum from the nurse.

They treated us, and after a while we got better. I remember them telling us we could finally go back to our families. My children and I started heading back to our camp. We were walking. Since it was my first time outside since I had fallen sick, when I started walking, my body felt sick. The land around Igloolik is full of rocks. I felt very dizzy walking along the shore. I felt like the land was moving under my feet. I think it was because of the medications that they had been giving me, the needles they had been giving me. I kept on walking and walking, even though I felt that way.

By that time my husband had recovered from his illness on the land. It was late in the fall. He was staying in the tent that Arvaluk and the rest of the children pitched just outside of Igloolik. We walked to that tent from the trailer in Igloolik, and the next day we all travelled to Naujaaruluk, we started travelling to our home camp. I still felt weak and I was scared to go home. When we finally reached the camp, all of our dogs were still alive, all except for one. There were also some other dogs that had been left behind by some other families. Those dogs were left at the camp and we had to look after them. I remember there were a whole lot of dogs that time. We had used up all our caches of meat so we had no dog food. I was still sick and I was also trying to look after my children and all those dogs. We were alone in the camp. I had no one to help me. We had to feed the dogs. If they died, we wouldn't have had any way to travel. I remember it was really hard that time. It was hard.

SHIFTING WINDS: THE FIRST TIME WE EVER LIVED WITH QUALLUNAAT AROUND US

I WENT DOWN TO IQALUIT TO DELIVER MY BABY

That time I was pregnant and I had to be sent out for delivery, it was summertime and I went down to Iqaluit to deliver my baby. I had never delivered in Iqaluit before. All of my other children, I delivered them all on the land, in our sod-house or in igluvugait or tents.

I had trouble with my pregnancy that time, and the Qallunaat said I had to be sent out. It was with Ida. She was the last baby I gave birth to and I had to be sent out with her. My daughter Joanna, she was only five years old when I left, and Phillip and Salomie were just babies, little babies. We went by boat to the plane and I remember looking out the plane window. I remember staring out the window at my children, watching Martha carrying Phillip in her amautik and Oopah carrying Salomie in her amautik. I felt so horrible leaving my little ones behind, leaving them all alone. It was August and the ice was all gone. I had tears in my eyes when I was leaving our camp and my children, my little children. I was so sad. It was the beginning of August when I left. I didn't get back to our camp with Ida until January.

❈ ❈ ❈

When I got to Iqaluit it took me four days in the hospital to deliver. The nurses put me on my back to deliver, so I couldn't deliver. I had so much trouble with that one! Before, whenever I was delivering, I did it sitting up, and usually my husband was with me. It took me four days to deliver my last one. When I delivered on the land, my husband would be with me holding my hand, helping me. I was used to that, so I couldn't deliver in the hospital. Once you have delivered by yourself or with a friend or with your husband, that is the only way that you can deliver. I was in labour in the hospital, but I couldn't deliver because my husband wasn't with me. When we were on the land, my husband was my doctor. Every time I delivered, he was the only one who would look after me. He would make my bed, put nice clean skins down, and put me in a good position. I would deliver, and he would cut the cord. He would cut the cord and wrap and wash the baby. I would clean myself. We didn't have Qallunaat doctors back then to look after us. That was our life, that was the way we lived.

WHEN MY HUSBAND BOUGHT HIS FIRST SKI-DOO

I remember when my husband bought his first ski-doo. Without me knowing, he bought a ski-doo. He bought one when he heard that ski-doos were really fast and that they travelled well on the ice. He bought one.

I remember the night he brought it home. There used to be a plane coming in once in a while. I expected my husband to come in that night, but he didn't. I was looking outside to see if he was coming in. My son Jakopie used to take out the garbage and honey-bucket. He was taking out the garbage and the honey-bucket, and when he came back in, he said that there was a light on the ice. I wondered what it was and I was scared. It was the ski-doo light. I thought that it was a star that fell out of the sky. I should have known that when lights are far away in the distance, you can see them flickering on and off. When I went inside I heard a sound, like a plane. I didn't know it was a ski-doo.

After a while a ski-doo came in. My husband was driving it, and he had a grin on his face from one ear to the other. He was so proud of himself for buying the ski-doo. He told me that he left Igloolik by ski-doo, that the dogs were following behind. My husband and I went inside, and the dogs came in a long time later. They weren't tied to the qamutik but they were tired. The next day my husband went out to get meat from our cache. He would usually stay out all day long when he went to get meat from the cache. He was back in less than two hours. He was really happy. He was so proud that he had his own ski-doo.

We went to Igloolik for Christmas, and we went on the ski-doo. My husband was driving, and I was with the children on the qamutik behind the ski-doo, and the dogs were following us. They were running behind. We had trouble on the rough ice. The ski-doo couldn't cross the rough ice, but the dogs were running along the ice without any problem. The ski-doo kept getting stuck. Every time we stopped, the dogs would have to stop and wait. I started hating the ski-doo very much because it wasn't working the way I expected it to.

We stopped on the ice to sleep that night, and we stayed there all night long. We spent Christmas Eve on the ice. The next day we woke up. Solomon said, "Listen! there are the bells, everybody is going to church." That ski-doo, that was the first time we ever got really excited about something that the Qallunaat gave to us. It was exciting to receive a ski-doo like that.

After that Christmas my husband went out with the ski-doo all the time. But he could only take certain routes because the only places he could take the ski-doo were places with flat ice. When he went ice-fishing with the ski-doo, he brought his dogs along with him just in case he got stuck out on the ice. He used the ski-doo for a long time and then, after a while, he stopped using dogs. We ran out of dogs. Dogs were all gone. It was really hard for us to stop having dogs. It was really hard ...

Ski-doos, they are good in a way, and in another way they are not. Dog teams, as long as they weren't hungry, they would take us any-where, far far away, without breaking down or running out of gas. Even if they had to climb up hills or travel on snow, hard or soft, they would still walk, no problem – they didn't get tired. If they were taught well, if they were well-treated dogs, they would respect a person and they would do lots of different things. They were slower than ski-doos, but I sometimes think that dogs were better.

ARVALUK AND SIMON WENT TO SCHOOL

The year Joanna was born, 1961, that is the year that the new school in Igloolik opened. All the children from the camps started going into town to go to school. My older sons went too. Arvaluk, he was the first. That is how he learned English. We were still in Naujaaruluk at that time and every time we took the children into the community, Arvaluk and Simon went to the school. When we left Igloolik, they would come with us back to the camp. Arvaluk, he struggled to be a good student and to learn English. He worked very hard when he went to school. He was different from other children, Arvaluk. I used to laugh at him because he was so funny.

He told me one time when he came home from the school trip, he told me that one of the teachers slapped his hand because he was speaking Inuktitut. That is what he told me when he came home. He

said that she slapped him! At that time when our children attended
school, they were not allowed to speak Inuktitut, they had to speak
English right away. Since there were no teachers in the camp, it was
hard for the children when they first went to school. They didn't know
how to speak English. Arvaluk, he really struggled when he was a child
going to school.

Whenever he came back from school, when Arvaluk and my
husband came back to the camp after picking him up, Arvaluk would
get to work teaching the other children and my husband the English he
had learned in school. My husband, he really wanted to learn English.
Arvaluk taught them the alphabet. The teachers would send papers
and pencils back with him so that he could keep on learning to write
at the camp. He and Simon were given papers to write their daily activities down on. He would write down the things that we were doing on
the papers the teachers had given him, and his father would bring them
to the teachers when he went to trade. The teachers would check them
to make sure that they were correct. I remember the papers were dirty
and greasy from children's hands. Since the children never washed their
hands, all the papers from that school were dirty and greasy. I think the
teachers could smell the dirt and the grease on the papers.

After a while we were told by the Qallunaat that our sons had to
stay in the community all year long. We left them there, but we missed
them very, very much when they were gone. We missed them so much!
They were away from us all winter, and in the springtime we would go
and pick them up. After grade six Arvaluk and his brother Simon were
sent to Churchill to go to school.[30] They left the community. Oopah
and Martha didn't want to go to school. Oopah never attended school,
because her father didn't want her to go.

Arvaluk and Simon, they went to school in Churchill, and we didn't
see them much after that. We couldn't communicate with them because
there were no phones, and since we were in the camp, we didn't get any
letters from them. We didn't hear from them for a long, long time. We
didn't know how they were down there. I remember being so worried
about them. Finally Simon wrote a letter that someone brought to us
at the camp. He wrote that he was very homesick and that he wanted
his parents to talk to the teachers and ask them to let him come home.
He wrote that he was scared of the Indians in the school. He was just
a little boy. I wrote back and told him that he had to be patient and
wait for the time to come home. I wrote to him that he had to wait
until springtime.

When Arvaluk and Simon started school, it was hard for them, and
they were confused. When they were sent back to Igloolik, they got
jobs in the settlement. Simon and Arvaluk, once they started working,

they never came back to live at the camp with us. After they went off to school, they never came home.

WITH SOLOMON IT WAS DIFFERENT – WE KEPT HIM OUT OF SCHOOL

In the 1960s it seemed as if all our children were leaving us to go to school. They had to, that was the law of the teachers, that every student had to go to school. All my children were so young when they went to school. It seemed as if they were getting younger and younger. I remember when Joanna started I went down to Iqaluit to have Ida. It was August when I left, and I came back in January. Joanna, the five-year-old who I left behind, she came to say goodbye at the plane in Igloolik. All the older children were in the community in school, and my little Joanna, five years old, she didn't want to stay in the camp all alone while I was away. She wanted to go to school with the older ones. She was only five years old when she went away to school.

When I came back from the hospital from having Ida, I stayed overnight in the community with my in-laws. I slept with Joanna in the same bed, my little Joanna ... I left for the camp the next day and I left her in the community, I left her in school with the teachers. I was on my way back to the camp and I felt hurt inside, knowing that my little Joanna was in school and I had left her behind. I left her behind and I was crying and crying as we travelled by dog team back to our camp. Later on, with Ida, she started when she was four. That was when we were living in Pond Inlet. Ida was only four years old and she started school. She stayed in school.

With Solomon it was different. We kept him out of school. This was before Ida and Joanna went away. Arvaluk and Simon were far away in Churchill, Martha was in Igloolik, Rhoda and Jakopie were in Pond Inlet. Joanna and Salomie were young, and Phillip was just a baby in my amautik, he wasn't even a year old. We asked them if we could keep one of our sons with us. We asked the teachers that if we let them take Rhoda and Jako away, would they leave Solomon to stay with us? Solomon was just seven years old, and my husband had nobody to help him when he was going out hunting and camping. When the teachers came to get him to take him away, my husband told the teachers that he didn't want his son in school. We asked for Solomon to stay with us because he was ours.

We were in a camp outside Pond Inlet that time. We were at Qaurnnak. We had moved there from Igloolik, and we stayed there through the fall. The boat came to pick up the children at the camp and take them into school. There were only a few buildings in Pond Inlet at that time, and Rhoda and Jakopie were going to live there and go to school. When the boat came, my husband started arguing with the teacher. He was telling him, "He is mine! He is my son! Since you have taken all my other sons away, I am going to keep this son! He is going to help me. He is going to learn how to hunt!" He was telling the teacher how he would rather see Solomon learn the Inuit way, not the Qallunaat way.

We were still living in a tent when the boat came. It was early fall and we had a pot of seal soup on the floor. Solomon and Rhoda were playing that day the boat came in, and Solomon accidently put his hand in the seal soup and burned his hand. I had to cut off his sweater, his only sweater, the sweater that he was wearing. When I pulled off the sweater, some of his skin came off with it. Since the boat was already there, we put Solomon on the boat so he could go have his arm bandaged in the community. We had a smaller boat and we had to pack up our camp, so we arrived in Pond Inlet a few days after our children.

It was the RCMP who looked after him when he got into town. There was no nurse around at that time. The RCMP, we called him Pang-nialuk,[31] he put a bandage on Solomon's arm. When we were ready to go back to camp, my husband was looking for Solomon around the community. He thought Solomon was visiting people. It was around 1966. Solomon was seven years old at that time. We couldn't find him. My husband went to the school to see if he was there, and he found him in the school sitting with Rhoda and Jakopie in the classroom. He was one of the students! He was the only one of all our sons that my husband didn't want in school. When my husband went into the school and found him there, he told the teacher that Solomon wasn't going to go to school, that he was going to stay with us out in camp. The teacher got very, very angry. My husband asked the teacher if he could take his son out of the classroom, and the teacher said no, so they started arguing. They got into a big argument, and then my husband just took Solomon by his hand and walked him out the door. He was very, very angry. He didn't even stop to get Solomon's parka. My husband gave Solomon his own parka to wear back to the camp. Solomon was crying that time. He wanted to be at school with the older children.

After this the teachers told my husband that if Solomon didn't go to school, they would cut off the family allowance that we were getting for him. My husband said that was okay, and that is what the government did. They cut off our family allowance. We were poor back then, not like today when we live in the community. We were out in camp. We didn't have food from the Bay or clothing from the Bay. We didn't have jobs, so we sold things like sealskins and other types of skins to make money.

After that incident we moved back to the camp that we had lived in a long time before, we moved back to Naujaaruluk, near Igloolik. We had Solomon with us. He wasn't going to school. We cried when we left Pond Inlet. We were sad knowing that we were leaving our two children Rhoda and Jakopie behind in school.

We started travelling back to Naujaaruluk. There was an Inuk, an Anglican minister and his wife living in Igloolik at that time. The minister and his wife lived in a small shack. Simon and Arvaluk were staying with them that fall, before they went back to school in Churchill. We went to see them on our way through. The minister gave us a house in the community so we could stay all together. It was a small house. It belonged to someone else at the time but they gave it to us. It was heated with a woodstove, and we stayed there for a while to be with our sons. After the school year finished the next spring, we picked up Rhoda and Jakopie from Pond Inlet and moved them to the school in Igloolik. We wanted to be near them. Igloolik was a small community at that time. There weren't very many houses. Our children stayed there and we stayed at Naujaaruluk, not far from town.

When we settled back in Igloolik, Solomon was asked to go to school again. At that time, ITC had just been formed.[32] We talked to ITC. Since Solomon was taken off the Family Allowance, we talked to ITC about him. They told us that when he got to be fourteen, he would have to go to school. They told us that when he was fourteen he would be a student and learn how to write in English and Inuktitut. He would learn about the animals in school – that is what we were told. We were told that he would be an interpreter. We were told that in the future, Solomon was going to take Qallunaat out hunting and out to see all different kinds of animals. He was going to learn the names of animals in English and Inuktitut. When Solomon turned fourteen, we agreed to let him go to school. He stayed in school for one year, until he was fifteen.

There was a company called Panarctic at that time that used to take Inuit on tour to drill oil. Panarctic was looking for Inuit, so Qiluqqisaaq[33] asked him if he wanted to go. Qiluqqisaaq asked Solomon how old he was, and he said he was fifteen years old. The job would only hire men who were sixteen and over. They have to be old enough to know how to look after themselves. He was only fifteen, but Qiluqqisaaq put his age down as sixteen and put him on the board to go to work. That is how he learned his English, not from school but from working with the Qallunaat. Jakopie also started working at the Panarctic site.[34]

We sent our children to school at such early ages. We sent them to Igloolik and to Pond Inlet and to Churchill. They only went because we were very poor at that time, and we couldn't support all of them. It hurt us very much that we couldn't get jobs and keep our children with us. I think that is the only reason why we left them in the schools. We couldn't support them by ourselves.

PHILLIP, HE NEVER ATE MEAT

One of my younger children, Phillip, he never ate meat. He only drank from a bottle, and he only drank milk. He would drink a lot of milk from the bottle. I tried giving him meat and other land food, but he wouldn't take any. He had two sisters and a younger brother that I had to look after at that time. He wouldn't eat any of the seal or caribou meat that I fed him, he only took milk from a bottle. We were out at Naujaaruluk and we didn't have any money at the time to buy Bay food. We didn't have any candy back then. Even though we didn't have chips or pop or candy in the camp, he still would not eat any meat.

Every time we sat down to eat meat, he would start running around. He would run until he was close enough to us that Oopah could grab him and try and feed him seal meat. She would put the seal meat in his mouth and ask him to swallow, but he wouldn't swallow. After a while he wouldn't even take the seal meat in his mouth. It was like his stomach couldn't take any of the seal meat that we gave to him. Since Phillip wouldn't eat meat, his father had to buy lots of milk, and he had to buy oatmeal as well, even when he never had any money. We had no money so it was hard to look after Phillip.

MOVING BACK TO THE SETTLEMENT

We were happy living on the land. We never really thought about moving to the settlement since we were barely ever hungry. My husband was a really good hunter. In later years Qallunaat started living in the community. There was a nurse, some teachers, and the Hudson's Bay Company. The teachers had our children, and they were trying to get families to live together in the settlement. Many of the Inuit were moving in. They were moving in, leaving behind their camps and their sod-houses or the cabins they grew up in.

In the camps of my childhood, in Kapuivik – that's near Igloolik – there were only a few people left. All of my relatives were leaving the land. When people started meeting Qallunaat, they started moving into Hall Beach and Igloolik. It was hard for me at first when I saw Inuit living in a different way, not hunting any more, using fuel stoves to heat the houses. I remember when they started building houses in Hall

Beach. Some people didn't move right into the settlements. They set up their camps near the settlements. That was around 1955. That is the first time we saw Qallunaat in Hall Beach. People from the camps began to move to Hall Beach.

My husband and I, we stayed in our camp for a long time. We stayed for as long as we could. I remember going to Igloolik to visit during the years that everybody was moving in. This one time when we got there, there was a committee meeting happening. It was the first committee meeting I had ever seen, and it was all about houses. People were meeting to discuss whether elders and people who weren't married should get free houses or not. They asked the people how they felt about it, and they said they should have houses of their own. The government said that once they gave them a house, it would only cost them two dollars a month. After the meeting they gave two of the new houses to these two old women. Those two women were widowed women, so people gathered in those two houses, just to see what the houses were like. Compared to now, I think it was pretty cold inside those houses. We didn't have heaters at that time, but I remember thinking about how hot it was when we were inside. We thought they were so hot!

We would come in from our camps at times to visit the community, not very often, though, just once in a while. We would come in, maybe during Easter or Christmas, to visit our children or sometimes in the summer to watch the ship come in.[35] We never really thought about moving into the community during those years. At times we worried about our children getting hungry, but most of our children were in school so we knew they had food. Yes, most of our children were gone. They were in school. I didn't have many children left at that time.

In 1966 or 1967 we moved in off the land for the first time. The first time we moved into Pond Inlet, my oldest daughter, Oopah, was there with her new husband and we wanted to be close to her. When we moved into the community, the Qallunaat gave us a house. It was a really, really big house that we moved into. We had been living in small houses out on the land, sod-houses, tents, then a shack for a while. That house seemed so huge to us. There was so much space and it was very, very hot. That is how it was.

We had been in Pond Inlet for a while in that hot, hot house when all of our dogs were shot. It was our dog team that we used to travel with, the one we used for hunting. They were the only travelling dogs that we had! The RCMP came around and shot them all. We were about to move back to our camp near Igloolik, Naujaaruluk, and they shot our dogs. We were very upset – our dogs were beautiful dogs. We had taken care of them from the time they were puppies. They were trained very well. They were healthy and young, just a few years old. They were beautiful, beautiful dogs.

After the RCMP shot our dogs, we still had to get back to Igloolik by dog team. We didn't have a ski-doo at that time. Only one person had a ski-doo back then. We weren't sure what to do. After a while people in Pond Inlet started feeling sorry for us. They started giving us dogs to put on a team, but they were only small, silly dogs. They were small, small dogs. Even my brother Maktaaq's dog that was tied up beside his house was given to us to use on our team! After we got these dogs together, we started travelling again back to Igloolik. It took us a long time to get there with those little dogs, over a month.³⁶ We were eating mostly seal meat.

We moved back to our camp for a while, Naujaaruluk. There were barely any Inuit left there and there were no Qallunaat. Then we moved to Igloolik for a while. In 1972 we moved back to Pond Inlet and stayed. It was my mother's idea and also my mother-in-law's idea that we stay in Pond Inlet. My mother, Suula, was getting old, and she wanted us to be close to her. That was the first time we ever lived with Qallunaat around us. We have been here ever since.

MARRIAGES BY THE MISSIONARY

Marriages back then, there were two different kinds. When we lived on the land, we had our own kinds of marriages. Then when we moved in off the land, there were marriages by the missionary. Me, I married my husband in 1967. We were married by the minister because the government told us we should. The government told us that men were supposed to work and support their wives. My husband was working, he was working for the government and even though we had lots of children, he was getting paid only enough money for himself. He couldn't get money for the children. We were told that if we were married, he could write down who he was supporting. That way he could write down all of our children's names and myself. That is why we got married, to support all of our children on his salary.

It was 1967 when we got married, and we got rings, beautiful rings. They told us to wear them on our hands. I still have mine. It was when I was pregnant with my eleventh child, my daughter Ida, that we got married. We got married because he was working and we needed money. If he hadn't been working at the time, I wouldn't have married him. It was the government's idea that we get married. They told us to get married, so we did.

THE OLD CULTURE: STORIES SINCE A LONG TIME AGO

I HAVE HEARD OF SHAMANS

I don't really know about shamans. I grew up when God and Jesus and Christianity were around. I never hear people talking about shamans any more. Today they talk about God, about Jesus. I have heard of shamans, but I don't believe in them.

My husband's father, when we lived with him, he never talked about shamans, even though his father was a shaman. His father, he was the shaman Awa, my husband's atiq, the one with the picture in the Qallunaat books.[37] The people in the camp treated his father like an ordinary person even though he was a shaman. He had the power to visit other settlements with his spirit. He was a strong man, a good hunter, a powerful man. He would catch many animals and would feed the different camps. He would share with people. Maybe it was because of his powers, because he was a shaman, that he fed all the people in the camps. He was a rich person back then. He had lots and lots of children, and none of his children ever starved. He used to provide a lot of food to his family and his friends when he was younger. He had a big family, he had lots of brothers and sisters.

※ ※ ※

There were many different kinds of shamans back then. Some shamans had powers to kill people, some had powers to find out where the animals were. Others could heal sicknesses and disease. There were bad shamans who hated people and tried to kill them, and there were good shamans who could find people when they went missing on the land. If someone was lost out in a boat, or if someone was stuck on a piece of ice that had broken away, shamans would turn into spirits and go out looking for that person. The shaman who found that person would say, "He is wherever," and the dog teams and the men would go find the lost person. Shamans would tell Inuit in camps where to look for people. Those were the shamans' powers.

There were shamans who knew how to find out the cause of something. Like, if people were starving and they were wondering why the animals weren't coming to them, they might ask a shaman and the shaman would try and find out why. Shamans had the power to find out why animals stayed away. Sometimes the shaman would find out that a woman was eating raw meat while she was menstruating. Maybe a woman was eating raw meat. In the old days there were many rules for women, many things that they were not supposed to do. If a woman ate raw meat while she was menstruating, starvation might come to the camp. Starvation was like that. After finding out from the shaman why the animals weren't coming, the Inuit might ask that woman, "Did you do that? Did you eat raw meat?" She would admit it and she would explain why. It was like being in court. The woman would be brought to court. She would not be sentenced, not like now. She would just confess what she had been doing. She would apologize to the camp for what she did wrong. After that everything would be fine, and they would go out hunting again and they would catch animals.

When shamans were around, pregnant women had a hard time. If they were about to deliver, they would have to stay away from the camp for a whole month. They would have their own little igluvigaq in the winter or their own little tent in the summer, and they would be kept away from their husbands and children. They would set up their igluvigaq or tent a little ways away from the camp, not too far but a little ways out. The husband could look through the door but he was not allowed to go into the igluvigaq. The woman, she was not allowed to eat raw meat. Other women would bring in meat and she would boil the meat before she ate it, because she wasn't allowed to eat raw meat. The other women would have to stay there and watch her to make sure that she wasn't eating raw meat. Those women helping her cook the meat weren't allowed to be menstruating. Right after she ate, the women helping her would leave the igluvigaq and go home. This would go on for over a month. She would stay until she had her baby and had finished bleeding. That is how long women had to stay away from their families. Those were the rules they made back then. A woman would do this because she believed that the camp would starve if she was with her family eating raw meat. It was an important thing. She would stay alone in the igluvigaq, and when she was ready to come out of the igluvigaq, she would be given new clothing. This clothing would be made for her, or maybe she would make it before she gave birth.

❀ ❀ ❀

We Inuit, we went through hard times. We struggled through hard times in order to obey the rules in the camp. At that time, the people before my time, they were full of superstition. Life before my time was even more difficult than it is today, than it is right now. They were bound by superstition and by all these beliefs based on superstition. The shamans, they were very strict people. People lived in fear, fear of the shamans, fear of breaking their rules.

When the minister came to our camp – this is what I remember – when our minister came, he preached to us about life and God. He said that God would give us everything we wanted, he said that God's power was stronger than the shamans' power. When the missionaries came, they talked about being freed from the laws of the shamans. They talked about Jesus Christ being the breaker of those laws and creating a new set of laws. They told us that we did not have to abide by the shamans' rules to be righteous before God.

I remember a story from back then about a minister using a seal heart as communion. We weren't supposed to eat seal hearts back then, we weren't allowed. This minister cut up the seal heart into little pieces and gave it as communion to show that it was okay to eat the heart. The ministers prayed for the shamans, and the shamans agreed to give up their power. They thought they would be able to live easier and not have to struggle. The ministers, they would cut up seal hearts and hand them out. Every time they did this they would say, "This is the body of Jesus that you are eating and your sins are forgiven." Sometimes Inuit would start confessing their sins. They would be so happy that they were forgiven they would cry out and scream, they would cry out in joy. They would cry out in joy because their sins were forgiven. It is like they were freed from their superstitions. The ministers would say, "Your shaman power is removed from your body by the blood of Jesus. I am giving you this heart so that every time you have your period you can eat raw meat. After this you can eat raw meat when you have your period."

The ministers who first came to our camps made new rules for us. We could eat raw meat whenever we wanted. If we were pregnant we could eat meat and live with our husbands and our families. We were only allowed to have one husband. Some of the people back then had many husbands. For example, a woman could have two husbands, or a man could have two wives. Now we are not supposed to have many husbands, we are only supposed to have one husband. We were told about Sundays by the ministers because they had rules about Sundays, we were told not to hunt on Sundays. Even if we were very hungry, if the calendar said it was Sunday, we weren't supposed to hunt. My children weren't supposed to play outside on Sundays or throw rocks on Sundays. Even if we were out on the land all alone, it was a sin. The rules were given to us when I was a little child, so we followed them.

❀ ❀ ❀

We used to believe that animals all have spirits. Birds, lemmings, seals, caribou, all kinds of animals have spirits. Even weasels and foxes have spirits. Sometimes shamans would turn into animals. Their spirits would move into animals' bodies. They would go in quickly and come out very quickly. Shamans were able to do that. There were shaman gatherings once in a while. When shamans got together, they would laugh and have a good time together, they would try out powers for each other. They would play together and practise things, like turning into animals. They would turn into polar bears, walruses, and weasels for each other. They would use their powers on each other, just for fun. They had fun together. They would laugh ...

✼ ✼ ✼

Some shamans relied on evil spirits. Some of these evil shamans had so much power they could make themselves appear just as eyes or in the form of an animal. They could take possession of an animal. That is how they did evil.

I remember my grandmother, Kaukjak, telling us a story one night. I was just a child, a little girl, and we were all together in the sod-house. We didn't have much seal oil left that time for the lamp, and we were trying to save our oil so we didn't have the flame going. We were all together in bed and it was very, very dark. She was telling us stories, stories about spirits and shamans. Just before I was about to fall asleep, I heard a noise in the entrance-way of the sod-house. I turned in the dark and saw a pair of eyes. I was so scared, I thought they were the eyes of demons!

My grandmother, she told us about a time when she saw a polar bear possessed by a spirit. It was a time when there were many polar bears around. The polar bear came to their camp. The dogs started attacking him, but the bear did not turn on the dogs. He didn't even look at them. He headed straight for the people in the camp. The people began shooting at the polar bear, and eventually they killed it.

The polar bear had really yellow fur and when they killed it they did not use the polar-bear skin because it was possessed by the spirit of an evil shaman. They learned that the shaman was angry at one of the people in the camp, so he tried to get revenge by turning himself into a polar bear.

✼ ✼ ✼

Some shamans were really friendly and really kind people. I knew one like that. It didn't bother us being around him. We believed in Jesus and the Devil at that time, but it didn't bother us having him around. He was just around to help out if people became sick or having a hard time.

This shaman, he had the power of healing. He really liked having this power. He didn't want to give up this power. He was told by the missionaries that if he gave up his power and became a Christian, he would live forever. He wanted to go to heaven, he wanted the eternal life that the missionaries were telling us about, so he gave up his power. He gave it up and started to worship Jesus.

This shaman, he told us how it was for him. He said he cried a lot during his conversion. He thought that once he gave up his power to Jesus Christ, he would not be able to heal loved ones who were sick. He cried a lot when he gave up his power, but he was happy in the end. His shaman power did not guarantee eternal life, but Jesus Christ's power did.

When the ministers asked them to give up their power like that, some of them did and some of them didn't. Some of them became Christian people. But they would still follow their old ways. Sometimes they would do things, shaman things, that they weren't supposed to do. Sometimes they wouldn't do Christian things that they were supposed to do. I wasn't around when they started doing these things.

I am tired of talking about shamans. This is very long.

WHALERS FROM BEFORE

I only heard about the whalers from before, from stories since a long, long time ago. I never actually lived with them or saw them. In the old days, before I was even conceived, there were whalers who would visit Inuit in their camps. I heard about them from the elders when I was growing up. Between Igloolik and Pond Inlet, that is where the whalers were.

There is a story that was told to me. I was with my husband and we were visiting his mother, his real mother. My husband and his mother, they had been separated when my husband was a child. He was just a baby when she moved away. They lived apart and didn't meet each other until many years later when they were both quite old. My husband had been raised by another woman, his father's wife. My husband and I, we went to see his real mother not too long ago. We went to see her, and he started asking her questions about his ancestors. He could never accept the fact that he had Qallunaat blood in him, so when we met her after all those years he confronted her. He asked her why she was half Qallunaat, why she had a Qallunaat father. My husband, he wanted to ask her that. He never liked the Qallunaat blood that was in him, so he confronted his mother and asked her why he had a Qallunaat grandfather.

My husband's mother, when he asked her that, she told us about a whaler called Sakkuartirungniq who was up here for awhile. He was a Qallunaaq, and he had lots of children up North. My husband's mother was one of his children. That is the reason why my husband has Qallunaat blood in him. We were asking my husband's mother some questions because he wanted to find out, he wanted to know. Before she answered she started laughing. She said, "Those whalers that came up here, they were just men!" She told us how there were no women whalers. Lots of the whalers were married and had children already in the South. They left their families in the South for many, many months to come up here to work catching whales. They stayed up here for a long, long time.

She told us how the whalers back then travelled with sails, they didn't have motors. I have seen pictures of whaling boats, and the ends of the boats are pointed and they have sails on them. Sometimes when the ships were frozen in, they would stay all through the winter. When the ice melted, they would go back to their towns.

My husband's grandfather's name was Sakkuartirungniq.[38] The Netsilingmiut were the ones who named him. His English name was George Washington Cleveland, that was his English name. When my husband asked his mother why her father was Sakkuartirungniq, she answered, "Before the whalers, there were no Qallunaat men up here. Then the whalers came." She explained how Inuit had never seen Qallunaat before the whalers. They brought pots and beads and rifles from the South, and the Inuit started trading with them. The whalers would put their things out and ask the Inuit men to trade the women they were living with for a rifle or a pot or some beads. They would trade. They didn't think about having Qallunaat-blooded children – they traded their wives for things like rifles and pots. My husband's grandmother was happily married. It was her husband's idea that she should go to the Qallunaaq and then she got pregnant. That is why my husband is Qallunaat-blooded. He has Sakkuartirungniq's blood. I guess my children do too.

Lots of Inuit had the Qallunaat whalers' children. It was their husbands' idea to trade their wives for stuff. My husband's mother, she remembered meeting somebody from Igloolik. That person's father was also Sakkuartirungniq, so he was her half-brother. Sakkuartirungniq, he was a famous whaler, and he moved around a lot, so there were lots of women who had his babies. He had children all over the place, not in Pond Inlet but in South Baffin, Pangirtung, and the Hudson Bay and Keewatin areas. He had lots of children in the Keewatin area. Myself, I know of four other Inuit besides my husband's mother who are also Sakkuartirungniq's children. Only two of them are still alive.

They all have separate mothers. One time I was in Iqaluit and I found out there was someone living there who was named after Sakkuar-tirungniq. He was one of his grandchildren, just like my husband. I have seen this man lots of times when I go to Iqaluit.

※ ※ ※

My father, Arvaarluk, told me a story once when I was a child. He told me about how when he was young and he lived in a sod-house, they were given tea, tobacco, and biscuits from the whalers. He said that he only used the rifles and the bullets that the whalers gave him. At that time the Inuit didn't drink tea and eat biscuits, they ate Inuit foods from the land. The tea, biscuits, and tobacco, he didn't know what to do with them. He put them on the shelf above the sleeping mat and left them there. Every time the sod-house began dripping from the roof, they would get wet. The Qallunaat food started to rot, so he threw it away.

A lot of times when Inuit would receive things from whalers, they would get confused and not know what to do with the stuff. My grandmother, she told me about how back then they didn't have any knives. Ulus were made of stone at that time. Every time they had to sharpen an ulu, they would use rocks. To find out if they were sharp enough, they would hold them up high and see if the sun shone through them – that is what they used to do. When the ulu was clear and thin at the end, then they would know that ulu was sharp. My grandmother said that when the whalers brought knives in, they didn't know what they were. They didn't know that steel could be very sharp, even if it was not clear or thin. There weren't any Qallunaat around back then to tell them about steel. That is what my grandmother told me. That is what she knew from before.

※ ※ ※

Yes, my grandmother, Kaukjak, used to tell me jokes and stories about whalers. I can remember being a child in my grandmother's sod-house. After my grandfather Nutarariaq died, and my father went out hunting, Kaukjak used to take care of us. I remember all of us children, we would all be lying in bed together before we fell asleep, and my grandmother would lie beside us and tell us stories about the whalers. She didn't remember all that much about the whalers either, but she told us a story about how one day she was given beads. A whaler brought them to her house. She said she was very afraid of Qallunaat. She was very afraid at that time, and she thought that the whaler was giving her the beads because he wanted to have sex with her. She was with her children in a tent not far from the ship, and he arrived at the tent with the beads. He walked in the door with the beads. She said she remembered staring at the beads and being terrified of this Qallunaaq. My grandmother, she said she remembered how he stood in the doorway, and she was looking up at him, she just stared at him and didn't move. She was scared! She said that the whaler was nervous and red and that after a while he sensed that she was afraid so he left her with the pot of beads. He left in a hurry. She had never seen beads before, my grandmother, so she put them in a bag and took the pot. When she was telling the story she used to motion with her hands how big the bag was.

There were a lot of beads in that pot and my grandmother said she was so happy to have received them. They were different colours. She said that at first she thought they were food, so she started chewing them. She put them in her mouth and then spit them out. After a while she took out a beautiful sealskin she had been saving and sewed the beads onto it. That is what she told us ...

She told us this story because the pot that the beads were in was still around when I was a child. She was so old then, my grandmother. She used to tell us the story about the pot because it was unusual to have a pot at that time. There were no Bay stores, no trading posts when she got it. She got the pot from the whaler that day, and many years later when she was my grandmother telling me stories, that pot was still her prized possession. She kept that pot the whaler gave her until the day she died.

❋ ❋ ❋

When my grandmother told me another story, I was shocked! She said that sometimes the whalers ran out of food from the South and then they would eat whale meat and maktarq.[39] Since they couldn't get the Bay foods or Qallunaat food, they would eat Inuit meat. They used to help each other a lot back then, the Qallunaat and the Inuit. Inuit people would make caribou clothing for the Qallunaat, and the Qallunaat would have their own dog teams. They lived and talked just like us after they had been here for a long time.

At that time there were no interpreters. Some of the whalers would learn Inuktitut, and the Inuit who were working with them, they would start speaking English. They would start speaking English even though they didn't go to school. After working with Qallunaat, they would learn English. We used to call people who could speak two languages "tusaaji."[40] Inuit, they lived a miracle life in the old days. They knew what Qallunaat food to eat and what not to eat. If they thought that the food was bad for them, they wouldn't eat it. They wouldn't touch it. Not like the Bay food now ...

My grandmother said that the whalers used to have small boats, tiny boats that they used to go hunting. They would row the boat and they would sing songs. It was the Qallunaat who would sing. The Inuit learned those songs. I think Inuit had an easy time learning whalers' songs and music. The whalers would give them candies or sweets. Even if they were frozen, they were still good. There was no pop at that time. Sometimes when the whalers would come, they would bring big barrels of molasses. They would make wine out of it and they would drink wine – just once in a while, not all the time, they would make a big barrel of wine. The whalers who were up here, at times they acted just like the Inuit. They used to have great dances back then, the whalers and the Inuit, not drunk dances but with an accordion, they would dance. They were all very happy. In the igluvigait, on the decks of the ships, or in the qaggiq, they would dance. After a hard day of work they would dance. In the summertime they would dance outside. The whalers would bring record players up, and they would wind up the record player and put the needle on and play the record player. They would dance away until it had to be wound up again. That is how they danced. Towards the end it would slow down. The records they had, every time they would drop them they would break into small pieces. I guess they were not made like today's record players. The songs and music that the whalers had, we knew the songs quite well, even after the whalers had left, when I was a child ... We used to sing whaler songs. We still sing them today.

That is what it was like back then, when the whalers were up here. That is what my grandmother used to tell me. That is what I have heard.

WOMEN WOULD GET TATTOOS

I am talking about trying to look good. I am talking about that time long ago when women tried to look beautiful. Women back then, they were always trying to look beautiful. They put marks on their faces and they dressed like women. If a woman didn't try to look good, there would be talk about the woman's face looking like a swollen gland. She would look like a swollen gland if she had nothing on her face.

When a girl became a young woman, she would start putting make-up on. Nowadays when girls become adults, they colour themselves. They colour their eyes the Qallunaat way, putting eyeliner on their eyes and lipstick on. At that time when women tried to make themselves beautiful, they would fix up their faces too, but the stuff they did didn't get removed at all until they were old women. Women would get tattoos, colouring right underneath their skin.

Tattoos would be designed the way a woman wanted. If she didn't want such a dark shade, the thread that was placed under the skin would be more wet. Soot would be taken from the lamp, and they would run the needle through the skin. As they were pulling the thread, the thread would leave the soot behind. They would make little designs, little lines on the chin, here and there, two at a time. They would put two on the forehead, also on the eyes, from the end of the eye, across and out. Around the cheek they would put three across. They would thread the needle with a thread soaked in soot and pull the thread through the skin. They would leave the soot underneath the skin. There would be short lines in between the long ones. They made designs on womens' faces.

Right after tattooing was done the woman's eyes wouldn't open because they would be swollen and sore and hardened. There would be little stitches on the eye, on the wrist, and on the shoulders. The designs on the shoulders they looked like fringes. The woman would be really sore, she would be sore all night. Her eyes would be swollen shut in the morning. This was done to make a woman beautiful. She looked good when it was all healed. A woman would look very beautiful. It was like she always had make-up on. She wouldn't have to put on make-up everyday and then remove it – tattoos were permanent. They would be added to and changed sometimes, but that was all. That is how make-up was applied for women.

This tattooing, it wasn't just for young women. Women would keep on getting them all through their lives, from puberty right to old age. When I was growing up, we didn't tattoo anymore. It was just the old women who had tattoos. It was from their young-woman days that they got them. They would grow old with them. Some women had fewer tattoos than others. They had just a few tattoos on their faces, just barely enough for people to notice, maybe a little, maybe only three on each cheek. Maybe they wouldn't have any on their eyes.

Some men had tattoos too but not on their faces, just on their shoulders. They would have a picture of something, maybe an animal ...

THE HUDSON'S BAY COMPANY

Yes, the traders, I remember them very well. I was born when the traders were around. The Hudson's Bay Company, they would buy furs from us and sell us food. People used to trap foxes to trade for food.

The Hudson's Bay, they were the people who bought foxes and sold food and ammunition. They didn't care much about polar-bear skins, narwhal tusks, walrus tusks, and carvings back then. Sealskins weren't being sold. They just wanted white foxes, and they only wanted them in the winter. We were living in camps back then, so I didn't go to the trading post much, my husband did all the trading. I didn't have much contact with the traders. My husband would bring the foxes back from the traps and I would prepare the furs to trade. In the winter he would go to the trading post and sell them. He would buy enough supplies to last all spring and summer. There were a lot of things we could buy with those furs. The most important things to buy, in order, were ammunition, tobacco, flour, sugar, and tea. We could get a lot of things for one skin. If the price of the fox skin was five dollars, that is not much today, but back then sugar and flour and everything didn't even cost a dollar. At that time flour came in great big hundred-pound bags. They didn't give you a whole bag, they would just measure you a portion of the bag. A gallon of sugar was not even a dollar, it was a lot less than a dollar. They never told us how much all the foxes were worth. They just counted them and pressed some buttons and they never told us how much they were worth. Maybe they thought it was useless to let us know how much they cost because we wouldn't under-stand anyways, they thought we didn't know the value of money. The trader would just measure out supplies and give them to us.

The value of the fox depended on what the skin looked like. If a fox skin was really yellow or if we didn't take the time to dry the skin prop-erly, it went down in value. Some people when they were desperate for money – like if they needed something in an emergency, like ammuni-tion or oil or something – sometimes people used to hand in raw skins, unprepared skins. They didn't get much for them. They weren't worth as much as dried and cleaned skins.

The springtime, that was when we would travel with our furs. People from different communities would travel together in groups. We were travelling everywhere back then. Nowadays lots of ski-doos come and go to different communities in the springtime. It was the same back then. We would travel with our families. We would go by dog team. We would gather our skins together and go to the trading post and buy things we would need for the whole summer, like bullets, flour, tobacco, and stuff. Then we would take a big load back home. We would be very careful about our supplies over the spring and summer, take a little bit of sugar at a time, take a little bit of tea. Even children had certain times to eat certain foods. Like bannock – they would have bannock first thing in the morning for breakfast and that is all, they wouldn't have bannock for the rest of the day. They wouldn't even ask for it. They wouldn't be hanging onto biscuits or carrying bannock around all the time. Maybe a few days later mothers would make some more bannock, but we would be very careful about eating it. We needed to save the supplies because we wouldn't be getting any more until the next time we went trading. We would try to make sure that our supplies lasted a long time.

THE LAND AS TOOLS

We knew lots of things back then. We had names for many different things, different winds, types of snow, mountains, clouds. The stars also had names, lots of stars and constellations had names. Because they were always just above the horizon, we would use the contellations for clocks. We had no clocks back then, so we would make a hole in the igluvigaq when it was dark and look out. If we saw that the stars were far enough away from the horizon, we would go back to sleep. If they were close to the horizon when we woke up, we would know that daylight was going to come soon, so we got up. That is how we told time.

When it was dark, in the dark months, we used stars for navigation. Nowadays we have a navigation tool for boats, it looks like a little watch. Now we use this little watch with its hands moving different ways, that is how we navigate now. Back then it was different. When there was a clear sky and there were no trails, we used the stars to find our way home. The stars were great for navigation.

It was the same with wind – we could tell if a wind was coming by looking at the clouds. Even if it was a beautiful day outside, even if all day there was no wind at all, we could tell from the clouds that a wind was coming. We were always looking at the sky back then. Even if it was a beautiful day, the clouds would tell us that there was going to be a blizzard. We wouldn't leave or go hunting, the men wouldn't leave. The whole day would be beautiful and then a blizzard would come.

We used the land as tools back then. If snow was drifting on the land in a certain direction, we would know where the wind was coming from. We were always using the land like that. If it was really foggy and we didn't know where we were going with our boats, if we saw a little bit of the sun, then we would know where the land was. If there was a little bit of rough water, then we would guess that the land must be over there. That is how we figured it out.

We were told to make note of the weather very carefully back then. We were taught these things when we were very young. We were taught to look at the sky and the land. Today we don't even think about the weather. There are lots of things that we used to think about that we don't today.

Back when I was young, the ice used to tell us things. We would watch it all the time. If it was springtime and we could already see big cracks across on the ice, we would know that the ice wasn't going to go away for a long time. It might look like the ice was going to go away soon because the cracks were wide, but if the ice was cracking easily it meant that the ice was really thick. If it was thick like that, it wouldn't go away in the summer. It wouldn't melt.

In the springtime if there were hardly any big cracks in the ice, it was scary because we knew that the ice would move a lot more and it would melt faster. If there were only a few cracks on the ice, the ice would leave early. That is what we were told. We were told that it was going to be a nice summer if warm weather didn't come too early in the spring. If it was cold enough in the spring, even if there were little puddles in the snow, but it was cold, then when summertime came it would be really warm and it would stay warm right up until September. It would be a long, warm summer.

This past summer was not a good summer. The plants hardly grew. It wasn't very warm, but in the springtime it was hot. It was a hot spring, and then the heat went away. Back then we would have known in the spring how the summer was going to be. We were weather observers, that is what we were.

ANIMALS, BIRDS, WILDLIFE

I will talk about a different subject now. Animals, birds, wildlife, you were not supposed to treat them badly. Even little snow buntings, if you injured a little snow bunting on the wing by throwing a rock at it or something like that, and you broke the wing, if it was still alive but not able to fly, you were not supposed to remove the feathers. You would be abusing it if it was still alive.

I remember one time there was a person from around here, he removed the feathers from a duck that was still alive. He left just the wing feathers and let the bird fly away without any feathers on its body. After awhile that same person got a big sore that went all over his skin. He still had bones and meat left on him, but he had lost his skin. He was still alive. That happened to him because he had abused wildlife. We had to kill animals right away when we caught them and not let them suffer. If you were abusive to wildlife, that is what happened to you.

When it comes to wildlife, we were told that we should never be proud. We should never think we are more powerful than polar bears and walruses. We should never act like we are not scared of them. We should never think that we are big powerful people, that we are so fast that an animal cannot get us. We are not supposed to be proud or act proud when it comes to wildlife. That is what we were taught.

There were different kinds of polar bears. An angutjuak was a big male polar bear. The younger ones, the young big polar bears, were called nukauq. The second older from the youngest were called tiqituar. The young ones are really fast. I knew a man who went out hunting, he was a very proud man, he thought he was really fast. A young polar bear showed up for that man. The polar bear was heading towards him. Because the man was proud, he thought he could beat off the polar bear and harpoon him, so he started walking towards the polar bear. The polar bear and the man met and when the polar bear rushed, the man got out of the way without the polar bear getting at him. He was a fast man. He went to remove his clothes to make himself lighter and while he was taking off his parka, the polar bear hit him and killed him. That man was too proud. That is why you are not supposed to think you can beat animals. You should never think that you are stronger than animals. The animals know that. They can hear you ...

People who talk like that, people who say that they aren't scared of polar bears, they can't catch them. It is the same with walruses, with their big tusks, they can stab a person. They can even put a hole in the boat and make people drown. That happened once when a Qallunaaq came up here. A walrus put a hole in the boat and the Qallunaaq drowned. The Inuk who he was with lived. It is because human beings are not supposed to feel more powerful than wildlife. Walruses, when they are not scared, they give themselves up. They go to you. They die easily.

The way we should act is that we should say things like, "I can't catch any animals. I don't know where the polar bears are. Even if I did see one, I could not catch it." We should be humble. If we respect them, then the animals will come to us. That is all I want to say about that.

FROSTBITE

When I was living in the Igloolik area back a long time ago, there was a floe edge near us. The men would go to the floe edge to catch whales. They would have to travel really fast since the ice was thin. Once they caught their whales, they would travel back to Igloolik. At times when the ice was too thin to travel on, men would have accidents and fall into the water. At times they would come back with frostbite on their feet or hands, and sometimes they would lose one of their toes or fingers.

I knew one man who was out hunting and he fell in the water. He took off his kamiks and socks, and the only reason he survived was that he killed one of his dogs and used the fur to make a new pair of kamiks. He made kamiks with the fur even though it wasn't dried up. That is how he got home.

Sometimes when the men froze their feet, they couldn't take off their kamiks. Their kamiks would freeze to their feet and they would lose some of their toes. That was before nurses or planes were in Igloolik. I knew a man once who froze his feet. His feet were dead and he couldn't feel anything any more. His feet blistered and the skin started coming off. He could see the muscles. The man, he got his knife and he cut off his toes. He cut them off himself! That was before there was a doctor. That is how he survived. He didn't walk for a long time, all summer, all year long. There were lots of people who lost toes and fingers back then.

In those days we had to struggle to live. It is the same thing with Qallunaat. They struggle to live when they don't have a house or food to eat. They struggle through hard times too. It was like that for us. We had to struggle to live, especially in the winter and fall time.

We went through hard times but our life was okay when we lived it. I am telling you about things that I experienced myself. That is how it was. Now we are not that way at all.

THINGS THAT WE USED FOR MEDICATION

The medications that we get from the nurses today, we didn't have those in the old days. We had lots of different ways to treat ourselves. I will tell you some of them so you will know.

If a person had a really bad stomachache, or really bad diarrhoea with a stomachache, and if the diarrhoea went on for a long time, and if every few minutes the person had to go to the bathroom, we would use cotton that we use for lighting the qulliq and mix it with dirt. There was a special dirt that we would use. We would mix it with the cotton and baby-seal fat and eat it. It would get stuck in the intestines, and the diarrhoea and then the stomach cramps would stop. We would block the intestines with that stuff. That is how stomachaches were treated in the old days.

We used to catch colds once in a while, not like we do now, not that many ... maybe once a year. If a person had a cold for a long time and if there were dogs around, we would use their urine. Dog urine has medicine in it. It tastes like Vicks' and it clears up the cold. It has a really strong taste. You could vomit from the taste, but it gets rid of the cold.

There were lots of things that we used to use for medication. A lot of them I have never used, but I heard of them from before. I used the cotton and dirt mixed with the baby-seal fat, but I never used the dog urine. My father-in-law, one time when he had a cold he asked me to go out and get some ice with dog urine in it. I went outside and brought it back in. Since he was my father-in-law, I loved him very much. I didn't want to see him eat the dog urine, but since he asked, I went out and got some for him. They were both sick in the house, my father-in-law and mother-in-law. Since I was not sick at the time, I did not eat the urine. He was coughing and at the same time gagging on the ice when he was eating it. The next day his cold disappeared.

If we cut ourselves back then, if we were out hunting and we were cutting meat, and it started bleeding, we would pee on our cut. The acid of the urine stops the bleeding, and it stops the pain. If we didn't pee on it, then the cut would bleed more and it wouldn't heal properly. If I cut myself on the hand and if the cut was really big, I would be told to keep my hands up. I would be told to keep them up so that the blood would drain down in my veins. That is if I was alone. If I had someone around to help me, this person might have bandages, like the mushroom-type plants from the ground. You know those mushroom-type plants that every time you break them, they are like powder? We would remove the powder and use the skin to put it on the cuts.

The seal's gall bladder is really bitter. We used to use them to bandage a cut. Gall bladders would heal the wound. It is good to use gall bladders, they kill the germs. If someone burned themselves, we would use fish fat, cooked or fried fish fat, for ointment. We would use that fish oil on the burn.

I think I forget most of the medications that we used a long time ago.

INUIT WERE GIVEN NUMBERS

There was one thing that I was really amazed at. I remember this really well. A miracle happened – numbers, numbers were given to us! I was about six or seven, and I was living with my adopted parents. This was before my mother died. My parents and other Inuit were given numbers.[41] I could remember my parents receiving their numbers. They were little circular things made of steel or wood. I remember the sound of them clicking. They were beautiful! They were red and they were round. Some of them were dark red, and some of them were bright red, with names on them, plus a number.

My adopted parents were given numbers, but I didn't get one at the time. I was just a child. The Catholic missionaries didn't have translators back then, so they could speak Inuktitut. They were living among Inuit all the time and they learned our language. My adopted parents were told by the Catholic missionaries exactly what the numbers were. They told us that the numbers began with E-5 and then each person's number. Different settlements had different numbers. It was all organized around numbers. In Igloolik, Pond Inlet, and Arctic Bay the number was E-5, and in other settlements the number was E-7 or something else, something like that. I can remember when I started playing with the numbers, my mother told me that we weren't supposed to lose them or get them dirty. The Qallunaat told us that we were to carry them with us at all times and never get them dirty. They told us that if we went to a hospital down South, we had to take our numbers with us. That was the only way the government could recognize us, was by our numbers. We didn't have second names at that time, we only had our own names. My mother made little pouches out of cotton so they wouldn't get dirty and she put them around her neck. They held on to them for a long, long time.

Finally I got one! When I was older and married, they gave me a number too. My husband and I both got one, and all my older children got numbers as well. I wondered why my children got numbers when they were young and I never did until later. I can't remember my children's numbers, but I can remember mine and my husband's. Mine was E5-345, and my husband's is E5-344.

Today we get first names and last names from the Qallunaat. They give us names. In the old days, though, before we had two names, we were given numbers. If a person died in the hospital down South, before they buried that person, the government would put the E-5 number on the coffin. They would bury the person with the number stamped on the coffin. The government never took back a number after a person died. Today when people go out down South to look for their relatives' graves, they use the E-5 number to locate the grave.

Those numbers, those disks, we always carried them. Some of the people carried them around their neck. I kept ours in the bag. We had these numbers for a long, long time. We kept them for a long, long time.

BORN WITH THE NAME OF SOMEONE WHO DIED

The government has been giving out names to the Inuit ever since we stopped having numbers. Before we started using Qallunaat names, we would use only Inuit names. We named our children after people who had died. Usually they were relatives.

In the old days it was difficult for us. People used to travel a lot. If we found out somebody had died far away, it was really painful for us. Since we didn't have any telephones or radios, it was really hard for us. We would really miss that person. We would mourn for them. If it was a relative or a close friend who died, we would name our newborns after that person. When a baby was first born, if the baby was crying all the time, the elders would say that the baby hadn't found its right name yet. The baby would stop crying when we named it its proper name. It didn't matter if the baby was male and the person who had died was female, that didn't matter, we named it the name anyways. We named it whatever its name was. Names were carried through the generations. We were born with the name of someone who died, someone who was close to our family, someone we cared for, and that is the name we would use. That is what we did. We have been doing this for a long, long, time ago.

My grandmother and grandfather are named in my children. My adoptive mother and father are named in our children too. My son Arvaluk, he was named after my adoptive father, Arvaarluk. Oopah was named Ilupaalik after my mother who died. They all have Inuit names, all of my children. Martha is named after one of my sister-in-laws, Umik. Simon is Mala, after Uyarak's older brother, my husband's uncle. Solomon's name is Qajaaq after my father Arvaarluk's daughter. Jakopie is named Kuuttiq, after my brother. Everyone is like that. Thinking back, I didn't even have a name from the Bible until I had many children, that is, when I was baptized and I finally got the name Apphia. We never had Qallunaat names before that.

When I was younger and my parents were still alive, I was called Siqpaapik. I was named after my mother's sister-in-law. I knew myself as Siqpaapik, that is what people called me. Then, when I was still a child, my adoptive mother died and I became orphaned. My father was still alive, but he was old and people treated me like an orphan. People poked fun at me, they wanted to make me feel bad. They did this because I was an orphan and I had killed my brother when we were children. After my mother died, in the years after she died, I was neglected and kind of abused. People used to say mean things to me. I didn't have a mother, and my father, he was hard of hearing, so he used to miss a lot of this.

I was given a lot of names as a baby. That was because I was adopted and I was my parents' first child. One of my names was Agalakti, I was named after Agalakti. He was a man, a crippled man. He had strength in his arms, but his legs were paralysed. People knew that my name was his so they poked fun at me. They tried to make me feel bad. I remember asking my father, Arvaarluk, one time why they had named me that name when I was a baby. I didn't like the name Agalakti. He said that Agalakti was his relative. He looked at me very hard and told me not to reject the name Agalakti. He said that even though Agalakti couldn't walk, he could drag his legs and still go walrus hunting. Even though he couldn't walk, he was a very brave and capable man. That is what he told me about this man, Agalakti.

I have been Agalakti and Siqpaapik, both those names, for a long, long time. Then I got a Christian name, Apphia. When the missionaries came around, I took that name. They came to the camps to baptize people. I remember when the missionary came to our camp, he baptized us and told us to pick out names from the Bible that we liked. I told my husband that maybe the name Mathias could be his name. I said that my name would be Apphia. I like that name, it is short and easy to say. We never thought of the meaning of the biblical names, who they were or what they did in the past. We just used the names.

Some people didn't pick the new names for themselves. They used their Inuktitut names for their baptisms, like Mablik and his wife. The missionaries, they told us to use our baptism names to talk to each other but we didn't listen to them all the time. Me and my husband, we still use our Inuktitut names when we talk to each other. He is Awa and I am Agalakti. We had used these names for a long time. But in public, in front of the Qallunaat, we would use our baptism names. We would laugh and smile and use our names Mathias and Apphia. Oh, we laughed! Then after that we would use our Inuktitut names, Awa and Agalakti.

As soon as my children were born, I gave them Christian names even before they were baptized. The ministers told us that we should name our children after Christians so we gave them both Christian and Inuit names. We took names from the Bible to name our children. My children, I used to try to address them by their Christian names because the minister at the time, he didn't like Inuktitut names. Once that minister died – he shot himself by mistake – once he died, I started calling my children their Inuktitut names again.[42] James Arvaluk I called Arvaluk, and Martha, our daughter, I called her Umik. We called Rhoda by one of her names, Kaukjak. She was named after my grandmother.

When my children started going to school, they went by their Qallunaat names. When my son Arvaluk went to Churchill, the Qallunaat used his baptism name, James. When Arvaluk came back, he told us that his name was James Arvaluk. We didn't call him James, though, we only called him Arvaluk. When we all took on two names, Arvaluk took Arvaluk as his last name instead of Awa.[43] That name was very precious to him, so he wanted to keep it. Rhoda, when she went to school, her name was changed to Rhoda and we started using that.

✹ ✹ ✹

I think it was around 1969 when we started using two names instead of one, it was around that time. We weren't living in the settlement at the time, but I remember the federal agent going around registering people. Everyone was giving him their husband's name as a last name. My husband, he was named after his grandfather Awa, so that is the name we took. We were out on the land when all this happened, so we weren't around when the administrator gave us a second name. When I started going to the hospitals, the name that was written down in the hospitals was Apphia Awa. It was my husband who was Awa – I was Siqpaapik and Agalakti – but that was the name given to me in the hospitals, Apphia Awa. Ever since then my name has been Apphia Awa. We changed to surnames so that the Qallunaat wouldn't get confused.

Today, the younger generation, they name their children Qallunaat names at birth, they don't wait for the baptism. In the old days, when we were named Inuktitut names, they were easier to remember, easier to say. Today, there are names that we can not say. Today there are names that we have never heard before, names from the television, like Hazel.

ALWAYS ASKING TO BORROW THINGS

We do not live in igloos any more. We don't do a lot of things we did back then. Back then, with our relatives, we were always asking to borrow things.

If my husband's younger brother's wife didn't have anything to use for soap, if she didn't ask me, I wouldn't know. I was told never to talk about my husband or his relatives. If things happened, like if my brother-in-law wouldn't let me have tea or flour, I wouldn't say anything to my husband because my husband would be protective of me and not like his brother any more. This would create problems and the family would be distant. We had to act a certain way if we wanted to have good relations.

If I had a mother-in-law and she had needles and thread and I needed them, even if I was scared of her, I would still have to ask her. I would still have to go to her and say things like, "I really need thread." I would say, "I wonder if you could give me a sharp needle?" If she knew that I didn't have a needle, she would give me one. This was the way daughters-in-law were loved. We would try not to be strangers to our in-laws. If daughters-in-law did not ask their in-laws when they ran out of things, rumours would start. If daughters-in-law said little things to their husbands like, "I don't have a thread any more. I am not sewing," her in-laws would hear her and her mother-in-law would not have much love for her any more. If the daughters-in-law acted like strangers, after a while that is how the mothers-in-law would treat them, like distant strangers.

When they came back from the trading post, people would share their supplies. If one person had certain things and the other person had other things, they would share. If you had a teapot and I didn't have one, I wouldn't think about going out and buying one. Even though I wanted a teapot, I would borrow yours for a while instead. This was part of being related and being a proper person. It was our way of being close to our relatives. This shouldn't be forgotten. The reason why we used to ask for things from our relatives is that we used to be so close, we used to really be close back then. If we borrowed and shared, then men would not hear bad things said about their wives. Saying bad things and not wanting to borrow and share would cause bad relations in a family. That is how the Inuit life was.

As Inuit, we would trade things. We didn't pay each other. Paying makes you distant from your relatives. We would trade things. If my husband needed kamiks and I didn't have any bearded seal for the soles, I would ask someone, "My husband is out of soles, can you give me soles?" And of course that person would say, "Yes, come take what you want." There wouldn't be any talk of payment. That is how families were kept together. Asking for things, it is not part of our life any more. I never thought that we would end up thinking so much about asking for things. Now we are trying to be like the Qallunaat. Qallunaat want things to be paid for right away.

I do not like this business of paying for something that you get from your relatives. It makes me sad, it makes me very sad. When Rhoda couldn't make warm clothing for her husband, I used to help her. I used to make clothing for my son-in-law all the time. She never paid me, and I didn't ask for a payment. I never mentioned anything about payment. My son-in-law knows that I am his mother-in-law, and he knows that I will make things for him without wanting money. When he gets animals, he is very generous. I can have anything that I want from what he hunts. I never thought about them having more money than me. They always bring things to me because we are not distant. They give me everything that is available ...

This business of paying for things makes you distant. I want this to be known. Just thinking of my grandchildren, if one of them says,

"Grandmother, I want you to make me something," I will say to her, "If you chew this particular caribou skin, I will do that for you." If she says that when her money comes she will pay me, I get lazy. I get lazy because I am sad that my own grandchild wants to pay me. It makes me very, very sad. I don't know where they learn this from, that they have to use money to get things. I don't know where they learn that there is a cost to everything. I try to instruct my children and my grandchildren, I try to tell them that we are relatives and that there is no need to pay for things. That is the way it used to be ...

HOW THE JUDGING WAS DONE

I remember an incident in a tent one summertime. There was this one woman who was not bonding to her husband at all. Her parents had married her to a man in the camp, but she was always going off with another man. She wouldn't agree to be with the man her parents married her to. Her parents didn't know what to do.

We were all in a tent having a prayer meeting. We used to have prayer meetings in tents or sod-houses. At these prayer meetings women would take off their kamiks and sit on the bed. The men would sit on the floor. That woman who had been causing trouble, she was with us on the bed. She didn't know what was going on. After the praying was done there was an announcement that something had to be said. The elders wanted to say something. We were told not to leave. No one left. Even though I was a child at the time, this really scared me. I didn't want to be like that person at all.

They were talking to her. This elder – she was a really important elder – she talked to that girl and then another person who wasn't as scary also talked to that girl. There were three of them, three elders who talked. They told her that she was not supposed to do what she was doing anymore. How scary it was! That same man who she had been going to bed with was with us in the tent. She never did that again. She stayed with her husband after that ...

It was like that. If there was a person who was gossiping in the camp, if there was a person who was visiting different houses and gossiping and spreading rumours, then the people would gather together and the elders would tell that person that they were not supposed to do what they were doing. They would tell that person that they were not supposed to gossip anymore. The elders, they would fix up a person's life that way.

That is how the judging was done. People would meet together and deal with things that came up. We had only small communities back then. There weren't that many people, so we would all get together to deal with things. It was a scary time on those occasions. You did not want that to happen to you at all.

HOW ELDERS WERE TAKEN CARE OF

I am going to talk now about being an elder, an old woman. Even though I am quite capable and I can do a lot of things, I get tired easily. When I tire easily, I can't get any ice from outside of the house and I cannot carry garbage bags to the box outside. I can't look after my whole house. I get tired easily.

When our elders were like the way I am now, a long time ago, when I was a child, we children were told to look after them. If we looked after them properly, the elders wouldn't get so tired and they would live longer. Being exhausted makes elders' lives shorter. That is what we were instructed. That is what we were told.

When I was growing up, the elders were treated with respect. The elders would sit around and we would serve them. We would prepare their tea for them, we would prepare the oil for the qulliq, prepare the seal fat. We would bring them ice for tea or water. We would take out the honey-buckets and clean their sod-houses. We did what they told us to do. Back then we were told to visit elders, not just our grand-mothers, but all the elders who could not take care of themselves. We were always visiting them. Of course, elders at that time didn't have telephones, so young people wouldn't phone them. We would visit all the time to make sure the elders were not alone. If there was meat and delicacies around, like fish or maktaq, we used to make sure to save pieces for the elders. Even if it was a small little piece that we gave to them, the elders wouldn't say that it was too small, they would be really thankful. They would be thankful for the little bit of meat they were given. At that time our job was to serve the elders. People didn't have jobs back then like they do today. The only job we had was to serve the elders. If we did things for them, they would live longer. That is what we were told and instructed.

A long time ago there were a lot of good elders in the camps with us. They were our teachers. They used to instruct us all the time on what we were doing. They were always telling us how to act, and they organized all the important work. They organized the hunts, and they organized the skin preparations. They distributed the meat and told us how to prepare it. Young people listened to the elders and did what the elders said. If a son wanted to go to the floe edge and his elder told him, "No, don't go to the floe edge. I want you to go check my fox traps before a blizzard starts," the son was sup-posed to do what he was told. He would listen and do what the elder told him. If the elder wanted him to go hunting, he would go hunting. If the elder wanted him to stay home because it was too windy, he would stay home.

Every so often I realize that in the past few years I have become an elder. Some of my grandchildren are young mothers and young fathers. When it occurs to me all of a sudden that I am an elder, I feel that I should be able to be like the elders when I was young, boss people around. Sometimes I ask younger people to do things for me or to lend me their ski-doo. I am like that nowadays, I don't walk far because I tire easily, I need a ski-doo. Sometimes I feel that I should be able to sit down for long periods of time. I say to myself, "Since I am an elder, I should be able to sit down and get somebody younger to do the work." I feel that I should be able to act like an elder, so I call up my grand-daughter Mona and say, "Come and do the dishes. I am just going to sit here." Mona will say, "Yes, but later ..." She won't come, so I end up doing them myself.

❈ ❈ ❈

I now have a life that is not the exact same as it was a long time ago. I don't feel old, but I know that I have become an elder. I am an elder now, but I'm not treated the way that we treated elders when we were growing up. Inuit today have to go to jobs all the time. The children, they are always in school. Elders today, we know that the younger generation have full-time jobs. We know that when they get home they have even more work to do, taking care of their children, their houses. The elders today realize this, and that is why we don't ask to be waited on. That is why we try to do things ourselves.

Also, things are different because of the alcohol. The elders today are just as knowledgable as before, but we don't talk or instruct the young people as much anymore. If an elder disciplines someone, when that person gets drunk he might get mad at the elder for having said those things. He might go over to the elder's house and start yelling. He might scream at the elder when he is drunk, and say things like, "I won't take it anymore!" The alcohol, that is why the elders don't want to talk anymore. It is because when young people get drunk, they get abusive towards the elders.

Even though the elders are still capable of instructing people, they don't want to do it anymore. They are scared. Alcohol leads to divorces and violence in marriages. People fight and get divorced because of alcohol. Alcohol is causing the problems.

❈ ❈ ❈

Now that we consider ourselves elders, my husband and I work very hard to act the way elders are supposed to act. We work very hard at being elders. I am proud of the fact that we work so hard governing the family. Our parents, they taught us that we should look after our children. If my husband and I have things that could help members of our family, we give them or lend them out without requesting money in return. We even lend things to our sons-in-law. If one of our sons or our sons-in-law wants to go out polar-bear hunting and his ski-doo doesn't work very well, we lend our ski-doo to him. We don't charge him money. We do it because it is less of a worry to us to see him with a good ski-doo than to see him go out with a bad one. We would rather lend it to him than see him get into trouble out hunting with a bad ski-doo. We make sure our children are well prepared when they go out hunting. If they are going long distances, we make sure they have gas and proper caribou clothing. It is not that we are bossy. We try not to request anything of the children or the grandchildren without reason. We would never tell our son to go over there, to buy this, or to do that without a good reason. We just make sure that we do what we can to help out, make sure they are okay.

Our children and grandchildren, when they go somewhere, they let us know what their plans are or what they want to do. We try to keep good communication with all of the children in our family. Sometimes it surprises me. People will tell me now about how I have children living all over. I have children in Pond Inlet, Igloolik, Iqaluit, Resolute, Yellowknife, Winnipeg, all those places. Sometimes I forget how far away they are, because we talk on the phone so much. I believe that families have to talk to each other, they have to help each other out. When our sons and sons-in-law in town go out hunting, they bring back meat for us. They give us whatever they catch, and we decide who we want to give it to. We distribute it to whoever we want. We might have a feast, have a group of people over, or we might just give it to people in our family, it depends how much there is. All of this has nothing to do with money. We don't even think about money when we are sharing like this.

AN ELDER IN THE SETTLEMENT:
THERE IS NO ENDING TO THE STORIES OF MY LIFE

SOME REALLY HARD TIMES

When I think about the stories I have told on these tapes, those times, the 1950s and 1960s, those were really hard times in my life. I went through some really hard times. Those things before, the tough life I had, after a while it started making me ill. By the time the 1970s hit, I was ill, I was very sick by that time. We moved in off the land for a while in 1970. We moved to Igloolik in 1970. Because of my illness, the Qallunaat sent me away. They sent me off to Iqaluit. They found out that I had something wrong with my uterus so they sent me away. I got better down there, and then I came back home to the camp.

At that time there was just a few of us left in the camp outside the community. My in-laws had moved to Igloolik. My mother, Suula, was living in Pond Inlet. Most of my children had been in school for several years. Oopah was married, Martha was married and was living in Pond Inlet, Simon also had a wife and they were living here. By that time I had my first grandchild and my younger children, Phillip and Salomie, were both in school. Only Ida, the youngest, was still with us. She was just four at the time. We had nobody left except my husband and me and Ida. I had diseases and sicknesses in my body. I was barely forty and I felt like I was getting old very quickly. I was sick all the time. I felt old. After a few visits to the nursing station, travelling from our camp, we were told by the doctors that I had to live near a nursing station. They told us I had to be close to Qallunaat facilities if I was going to live.

When I was forty-three years old, that is when it hurt me the most. We had moved in off the land and we were living in a house in Pond Inlet. Rhoda got married, and the other three, Solomon, Joanna, and Salomie, left town to go to school in Iqaluit. Four of my children were married and having children. I was left with the three little ones, but my illness was so bad I could hardly stay home with my family. I was going to Iqaluit all the time for hospital visits. In 1972 when we first moved here, I was really sick. I was sick to the point where I had a bottle full of pills that I was supposed to take for the rest of my life to help me with my lungs. The doctors, they told me that I was going to be taking those pills for the rest of my life. The doctors, they saw what was happening to me. Maybe a lot of people did. They started talking to me, telling me that if I kept all the tension in my life, it wouldn't be long before I died. They told me that I was still young and that I could have a long life. They said that I should try to live longer because I have so many children. It took me a long time to decide what to do about all of that. Finally I decided that I was tired of all of my problems and that I didn't want to die. I decided at that point that yes, I wanted to live longer.

From that point on I started turning my life around. I started talking about all the problems that were inside of me. I started talking about the things that were bothering me in my life, the things that upset me, the things that were causing my illness. I guess I decided that if I was going to live for many more years, I was going to have to stop trying to keep eveything inside of me. When I turned my life around, I decided that I was going to stop taking all those pills they were giving me.

I turned my life around in 1985. That is when I was saved. That is when I became a Christian. In the past, when we lived on the land, we lived in deepest, darkest sin. We lived the very worse sins. Now all those dark sins no longer affect us. I don't move as fast as I did at that age, but I feel a lot younger today than I did back then. Jesus has helped me. Our family is reunited. My husband and I love each other. Even though we were oppressed in the past, we are better now. The whole family is reunited and we are a lot closer. We are living a much healthier and happier life now. I am fine now. I am happy.

KNOWING TODAY THAT MY CHILDREN HAVE ALL GROWN

When I think about my children and my grandchildren and what the future holds for them, I think about a lot of things. I think about how happy I am that I am now an elder. I am at a point in my life where I am teaching my children and grandchildren things that will prepare them for a happier future. I teach them the things that they must learn, I teach them now so that I don't have to worry about them in the future.

The elders today are used a lot for teaching. Sometimes I feel that is all I do, teach. In my life I have learned a lot. For me, I feel the most useful and knowledgeable when I am teaching young people about sewing skins, about making traditional clothing, mostly caribou-skin clothing. I worked for the hamlet as a janitor a long time ago, but I was sick at the time, I was getting old. The doctors told me that I had too much stress in my life and that I should quit. So now I teach young people how to sew skins. That is what I do now. I make skin clothing for people and teach people about skin clothing. I have even set up a tent outside my house so I can teach sewing to young people who aren't in school. I think it is important that young people learn this. I make clothing for my family. It takes up almost all of my time.

Looking back on my life, the stories that I have told, a lot of them are from difficult times that I went through when I was younger. Looking back, I realize that the life I have had has been a difficult one. I needed to be strong to survive. Back then I was always working, I was always struggling to make sure there was proper clothing for the children, a warm place for them to sleep, water and food for them. Today my children have all grown, and I know that my life is a lot easier. I am happier now. This is the last tape, the last session, but I want to mention that there is no ending. I would say now that there is no ending to the stories from my life. That is all I have to say.

Suula Atagutsiak Kublu (Apphia's mother) and some of her children, approximately 1964. *From left to right*: Lucy Kublu (Quasa), who worked with us on the life history project and translated a third of Apphia's stories for this book, Joannie Maktar, Bernadette Kublu, Suula Atagutsiak Kublu, and Leno Kublu

Apphia Awa, 1972; photo taken at the
Adult Education Centre in Pond Inlet

Mathias Awa, 1972

Rhoda Awa (right) and her friend
Oopah Arreak, June 1972

Salomie and Martha Awa (stirring the bowl).
Taken in the Awa family's first house
in Pond Inlet, 1972

Phillip and Oopah Awa, spring 1973.
Taken on the beach beside Pond Inlet

Rhoda Katsak with Sandra in her amautik, August 1973

Sandra and Rhoda Katsak, 1974

Apphia's in-laws, Uyarak and Panikpakuttuk (Hannah Uyarak).
Photo taken in their home in Igloolik, 1976

Rhoda Katsak and Mona, on the sea ice with Pond Inlet in the background, spring 1977

Joshua Katsak, 1978

Apphia Agalakti Awa and her family, Christmas 1980.
From left to right: Joshua Quanaq (sitting),
Martha and Solomon Awa, Salomie Awa (behind
Apphia), Phillip Awa (at the back), Sipporah Awa
holding Minne, Ida Awa, and Jake Awa;
Front row: Mona Katsak and Apphia

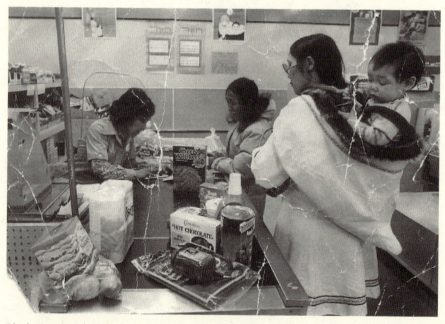

Rhoda Katsak with Sheila in her amautik, at the Hudson's Bay Company store in Pond Inlet, 1982.
Apak Kippomee is ahead of her in line, and Hanah Quaraq is calculating prices

Mona Katsak, Sheila Katsak, and Sandra Katsak, 1982

Spring festival on the ice in Pond Inlet, April 1992. *From left to right*: the two adults at the back are Mary Arnetsiak and Elisapee Ootoowak. Rhoda and Sandra were not able to identify the two small children in front of them. On the left in the front row, Christine Awa, two unidentifiable kids beside Christine, Martha Awa behind her, beside Martha: Rhoda and Josh Katsak with Ruby between them, Inootiaq Mucpa, then Apphia Awa. In front of Apphia is her grandson John Awa. In front of John is Paingut Peterloosie sitting with her grandchild. Beside Apphia are Solomon Awa, his son Jimmy Awa, and Joanassie Mucpa

Rhoda Katsak and Ruby, spring 1992

Sandra, her uncle Shem Katsak on her left, and Apinasi Mucpa, summer 1994

PART TWO

Rhoda Kaukjak Katsak, 1993.
(Photograph, Nancy Wachowich)

Rhoda Kaukjak Katsak

✤ ✤ ✤

When I was young I used to have dreams about my future,
about what I wanted to be when I grow up. I always thought of people
from the South, movie stars and musicians like the Supremes.
They were my idols! I would have given anything to be able to sing
like them, or look like them, or be as popular as them at that time.
People loved Elvis Presley.

INTRODUCTION

Rhoda Katsak is Apphia's sixth child and third daughter. She was born on 18 April 1957, when Apphia was twenty-six years old. At the time that we recorded her life history Rhoda was thirty-six. Born in a spring camp outside Igloolik, she was named Kaukjak after her mother's maternal grandmother and Palluq after her father's step-grandfather who was his guardian as a child. Rhoda spent the first part of her life living on the land, hunting and travelling with her family. At the age of eight and not speaking any English, she was forced to leave her parents and her family to attend federal day school. The effects of this separation from her family and her life on the land figure prominently in her narratives.

Rhoda attended Grade One in Igloolik's federal day school. Skipping Grade Two, she completed Grade Three in Pond Inlet, then moved back to Igloolik to live in a student hostel and attend school there until the age of fourteen. When she was fifteen she moved back to Pond Inlet with her family, where she met her husband, Josh, and began working at a job and raising a family. She and Josh lived with her in-laws for the first years of married life, and then moved to a series of houses before building and settling down in the one they own today. Rhoda has six children: Sandra, Mona, Sheila, Dawn, Lucas, and Ruby, and (at the time these stories were recorded) one grandson, Terry. She has worked at a number of jobs in the settlement, from local newspaper reporter to legal interpreter, from finance clerk to her longstanding job as hamlet accountant.

While Rhoda's testimonies are somewhat less elaborate than those of her mother, the recollections converge on early childhood experiences travelling on the land, motherhood, and challenges of adapting to settlement life. Rhoda is forthright and candid in telling her stories. Her narratives are direct and to the point, and yet they evoke powerful images: a hungry young child anxiously awaiting her father's return from the trading post; an eight-year-old girl waking up in their tent on the DEW-line site to the delicious smell of fried wieners; a young mother overwhelmed with child care and laundry. Rhoda experienced first-hand the politics of assimilation that shaped 1960s Canadian Arctic policies. Her stories often return to the watershed event in her life when she was taken from her parents and placed in Qallunaat school culture. Deliberately leaving the more objective descriptions of Inuit culture to her mother, Rhoda speaks to her own displaced generation of Inuit, describing her encounters with teachers, ministers, nurses, researchers and other outsiders. She relates her feelings about being born into one cultural milieu and compelled to train for another.

At the time of our life history interviews together, Rhoda lived in a house on the beach in Pond Inlet with her husband and five of her six children. Described by neighbours and family as a woman constantly on the go, she was working full-time at the hamlet office, tending to her children, and studying by correspondence to become a certified general accountant. She was also spending her scarce free time learning from her mother and mother-in-law how to sew caribou, seal, and polar-bear skin outdoor clothing for her husband and her family. When we discussed this project, she expressed her desire to see Inuit texts, including her own family's stories, replace the Euro-Canadian school texts which she was taught with as a child. As she declared one afternoon as we were chatting over coffee at her kitchen table, "I want to make up for lost time."

The opening story was recorded late at night in Rhoda's living room. Her three youngest children, Dawn, Lucas, and Ruby, were sprawled out asleep on the couch and on the floor, and her husband was out seal-hunting. She had just finished doing the dinner dishes after a long day of work; accounting books were stacked on the table beside her and the television was on the CBC news with the volume turned down. She lit a cigarette and filled our coffee cups. I turned on the tape-recorder and asked, "Where were you born?" She began to talk.

GROWING UP ON THE LAND: MY BEAUTIFUL LAKES!

I WAS BORN ON APRIL 18, 1957

I was born on April 18, 1957. That was just before Eastertime, Easter weekend ... My parents were supposed to go to Igloolik for the Easter holidays, and my mother gave birth to me on the 18th. They went off to Igloolik the very next day by qamutik.

It was possibly my grandmother who helped my mother give birth, my father's stepmother, but I am not sure. My grandparents were the ones who were living with my parents at the time. I don't know ... I suspect it was my grandmother who helped my mother deliver me. They had been living with a few other families at the time I was born, Mablik's family and some other family. I think they moved down into the Igloolik area before I was born. I think they hit some hard times ... Yeah ... my mother loves that story! She always used to tell me, "I gave birth to you one day, and the next day we went off on the qamutik." I am number six of eleven kids, right smack in the middle.

It was springtime, so I have no idea how we travelled at that time – by dog team, I would imagine. By summertime we would start to use boats. My family usually went to Igloolik at certain times of the year to trade. We would go in the fall to get set up for the winter, either September or October, and this would be by boat because the ice hadn't frozen up yet. We would go again around Christmas, during the Christmas holidays, and do some shopping. We always went shopping every time we went into the community. Then another time would be during Easter break, because that is when everybody would play games and activities and stuff, and another time would be early summer ... or late summer, depending on the ice. We would trap white foxes to trade for things.

My parents stayed in that outpost camp outside of Igloolik until 1970 or 1971. I think it was 1970, because it was a very short while until they moved here to Pond Inlet. They stayed in the same camp from my birth, but way before that they moved around the area.

After I was born, and I am not sure where I was born, but after I was born, possibly a year or two later, we moved into a shack, a little matchbox shack at Naujaaruluk. That is where we had our winter camp. We would stay there all winter, and in the springtime we would go to another camp, Upirngivik, which was about six or ten miles from this winter camp. We would do our fishing there. Our summer home was a tent, a cloth tent. The land was kind of flat, but not too flat. It was part of Baffin Island. It was on the mainland. Igloolik was on an island facing it, about fifty miles away from the camp we were in ... not that far, unless you have to travel by dog team or a nine horsepower motor. By dog team it took one day, a little bit more than a day. Yes ... that is where I lived until I went off to school.

THREE SMALL LAKES

My beautiful lakes! This is a story about my lakes. Growing up, we had both a winter and a summer camp. They were about ten miles apart. The summer camp, Upirngivik, it was a little bit further from Igloolik than the winter camp. We camped at that same spot every year. We used to camp there all alone. By the time I started remembering things, we were all alone on the land. My grandparents had moved to Igloolik. We were by ourselves.

In this summer camp there were three small lakes. One lake was really close to where we put our tents. That is where we used to get our water. On the left side facing the water there were two other lakes. Both of these other lakes were set on solid rock. The one closest to the water was quite small. We only used it to wash our clothes. There would always be a soap film on the edge of the lake. We would just go there and wash our clothes. The third lake was a little bit farther away. This lake was solid rock all around, like a swimming pool, and it had this rock canopy overhanging. We had a great time there. That is where we would bathe ourselves. The sun used to hit it mid-day and warm the water. It would get quite warm in the summer. The swimming lake had little fleas or lice in it – some of them looked like tiny turtles. They die very easily with heat up here. You might see them swimming around in the water tank, but when you heat up the water tank, they die.

For some reason in this area there is also a place where I thought there was a buried treasure. Maybe I had read about buried treasures at school. There was this one spot, and I used to stomp on top of the gravel because it sounded hollow underneath. I thought that buried treasure was hidden there. My husband tells me that is where there is frost or pieces of ice between the layers of gravel. That is why it sounded hollow.

Just next to this summer camp, not very far away, there was an old camp. It had maybe four old sod-houses. It was a very old camp. Even at that time, in the 1960s, the sod-houses were there, but there was maybe about six inches left of the original buildings. There was a big lake up there too. Apparently this old camp – this kind of surprised me because it was inland, not on the shore, just a little bit inland from the summer camp – apparently my grandparents and Mablik's family had lived there for quite a number of years. I think that is where I was born. It was an old, old camp. It had been used for years and years, maybe by some other people who lived before my family's time.

WE HAD MEASLES, MY WHOLE FAMILY

I had a fair amount of contact with white people before I was shipped off to school. One time we had measles, my whole family, every one of us. We spent maybe a month in Igloolik before I went to school. I remember we stayed in one of the transient centres, where they boarded the students. They used these transient centres as extra hospitals when people came in sick off the land. My family stayed in different rooms, but we were close together. There were four beds in one room, two bunk beds, and there were three rooms in the centre we were in. I don't know how many people were in the other houses.

My mother got sick, and my older sister. I don't know who else got sick at this time. I was okay. We went to Igloolik by boat. I remember it was a very cold trip. I remember being very cold. Igloolik is on kind of a U-shaped island with the community inside of the inlet. Our camp was behind the island, so we went to the back of the island because the waters around the bay were too rough. It had been storming. I think the people in Igloolik knew we were coming. They came to pick us up on a Bombardier, a great big vehicle with skis. As usual I was crying and crying. I didn't want my mom to leave me, so I went with her to the hostel. I was about three or four years old, just a small kid, a baby. I didn't want to leave my mom. I was fine, healthy at that time, but I didn't want to leave my mom, so I went along to the transient centre. My mom had Joanna on her back and me and Solomon at her side. The transient centre, that was where I got sick.

I WAS CRYING, "I AM HUNGRY"

The incident that I am thinking about was maybe when I was five or six years old. I was a very picky eater. My mother always used to complain that I was a picky eater. I wouldn't eat any aged meat or old meat, like day-old meat or anything like that, I just wanted delicacies. I don't know what my disposition was at that time, but I don't think it was linked to me being a picky eater. I ate meat all the time then, so I don't think it was because I was fussy that I didn't like old meat. I felt nauseated or vomited after I ate it ... I only liked delicacies, like caribou fat, caribou bone marrow, eyeballs, tongues – things that the elders would get and the children weren't supposed to have. So my mom didn't really like me for that reason ... I was hard to please.

At the time that I am thinking of we were quite hungry. I remember now the incidents when we were hungry. I don't remember starving, no, we never starved, but we would go a couple of days without food. We would go hungry for a while ...

The incident I remember happening was when we could get good daylight. It was springtime, so the sun had come back. We had been hungry and I was feeling really nauseated, I was hungry. I hadn't had anything to eat. I was about five or six. When I woke up that day, I hadn't had anything to eat the day before, no tea, no biscuits, no bread, no meat. Whatever meat we had was about a week old. It was an old seal. I remember feeling like eating, but not wanting any of it.

That day my father took off early in the morning. When I was a kid I never thought my father slept. He was up early in the morning before I got up, and I was always asleep before he came home. When I woke up that day, he wasn't there, I thought he had gone. He had made some plans to go to Igloolik by dog team. He wanted to buy some supplies because we were hungry, so he took off that morning. I had no idea where he had gone. By late afternoon I was crying and crying. I was crying, "I am hungry! There is nothing to eat. I wish my daddy would get here!" – stuff like that. And my mom kind of screamed at me, she screamed, "Your father is never going to get here if you keep on crying!" Something like that. I remember I cried and whined all day long.

By late evening it was just starting to get dark, but we could still see out on the land. My older sister went out and climbed to the top of the little hill just behind the matchbox house. She was looking around to see if any dog teams were coming back. We didn't think they would be coming back. My mother had said that they'd be back the next day. They couldn't make it in one day. She knew that when she scolded me, that they couldn't be back in one day. It was a one-day ride to Igloolik each way. My older sister went out, and I went out of the house with her for a little bit. I remember not having a parka on. You know how kids are – they'll run out for a minute just dressed in a sweater. I saw her up on the hill and she was yelling, "I think there are dogs coming!" She came down from the hill and we went into the house and we were all kind of getting excited. There were dog teams coming! We thought maybe they were from another camp or something, stuff like that. About half an hour to an hour after she sighted the dog teams, my dad came in with his supplies, everything. He wanted to make it in one day so he came back in one day. He had bought all of his supplies and come home, and it was not the end of the day yet. It had only been dark for about an hour.

We went into the house and my dad came in and we were all excited, getting all these supplies out of the boxes, all these treats like chewing gum and oranges and candy. I still had tears on my cheeks from crying. I was telling my mom, "I thought you said that if I cried my dad wouldn't come! I cried and he came! You liar!" She accused me of being spoiled – all I had to do was cry and my dad comes home.

THE NEXT DAY WAS SUNDAY, SO WE WEREN'T ALLOWED TO TRAVEL

One time I remember being hungry. I was maybe six years old. I remember the incident very clearly. It was late fall, and we hadn't eaten for days. All we had in the camp was a great big seal carcass. I think that most of the meat on it had been eaten already so all it had was skin and a bit of fat. Most of the ribs had been cleaned away, but there were still slivers of meat on a few of the bones. That was the only food we had in the camp, this old seal carcass. Everyone else in the family had been taking bits and pieces off this old seal, but I wouldn't touch it. It wasn't good, aged, meat, it was just old. It wasn't fresh, fresh. I was a picky eater.

I remember we left the carcass in the shack we lived in and tried to go to Igloolik because we were so hungry. We thought we would go to our relatives who lived in Igloolik and get food from them. We travelled, I don't know how far, maybe fifteen miles, but the water was really rough. That was normal weather for the late fall, windy and rough on the water. The water was so rough we had to stop at an island just past our camp, Mitilik. It was the island where all the eider ducks usually nest ...

We stopped at that island and I remember being really, really hungry. The food we would have been hunting at this time of year were seals, but because it was so rough, we couldn't catch anything, no seals. The next day was Sunday, so we weren't allowed to travel. We spent the day on that little island with absolutely nothing. I remember my sister was braiding my hair, my brothers were playing outside. By some lucky streak so late in the fall my older brother caught a snow bunting, a small little bird. In this season most of the geese are gone, ducks are gone, and the buntings are on their way. In windy weather, anyways, they would have been hiding. Anyways, he ignored the rule that we weren't supposed to hunt on Sundays. We were starving, and still we weren't supposed to hunt on Sundays ... Snow buntings are tiny and they have skinny little legs. He took the bunting and he cut it up really nicely, he cooked it, and he gave it to me. Nobody else had anything that day. I had the snow bunting. He gave it all to me so that I could eat.

WE WOULD PUT THESE SUPPLIES IN A LITTLE CAN

We had bannock and tea and other store-bought things a lot as children, but we didn't have them all the time. Quite often we would run out of things and have to do without for a while. My mother, she was a cigarette addict. I mean, she was worse than I am today. We all knew this, so when my father brought supplies, the first thing we would do as soon as we got the supplies is put away a little bit of tobacco, a little bit of sugar, a little bit of tea, sometimes if we were feeling good maybe something else, but those three basic things, just a little bit of each. This was Oopah and myself, usually. We would put these supplies in a little can, maybe something that wouldn't get wet, usually the can that the tobacco comes in. We would hide these cans in small cracks between rocks or caves, we would cache them. We would hide them like that and not let my mom know. Then when we ran out, and if my mom was going haywire thinking about cigarettes, we would get the cache out and bring over a little bit. That is what we would do, surprise her with our caches.

One time my mother was going into hysterics about not having any cigarettes. Our caches were all gone, and I think she spent the whole morning screaming. That particular time she was screaming at Joanna. Joanna was standing there by the doorway, just a tiny kid, just standing really still listening to my mom, and here we were behind my mother on the bed all cringing, wondering what was going to happen next. Poor Joanna, she was getting the worse end of it. My mom was screaming. She was standing in front of her and then finally my mom stopped screaming and turned away. Joanna looked at us and said, "Oh good, she stopped talking." She didn't really care!

I remember one of my mother's tantrums. She didn't have any cigarettes and she was screaming at us because she lost her sealskin scraper. My older sister Oopah used to be scared of my mom a lot when she was like that. Oopah was like a mother to us because we had such a big family. When my mother started having her screaming fits, Oopah would try to listen to everything she wanted us to do and get us organized. My mother wanted to clean some skins that day. She couldn't find her scraper in the house, and so we were all ordered to look for it. She had been spending that morning screaming or being generally grouchy at the rest of us. Oopah was telling us where each of us should look for it, saying things like, "You check the outside. You check the floor," stuff like that. She was telling my little brother Solomon to look for it in the bed.

Solomon was just a little kid at the time. He went to the bed and he put his head on the bed, like, he was crouching on the bed hiding his face in the covers. Oopah kind of bumped into Solomon, he was scratching like that in the bed. She was pulling off bedsheets and looking under the mattress. She kind of pushed him off and asked him, "Solomon, what are you doing? You are supposed to be helping me look for the scraper! Solomon, what are you doing?" Solomon answered, "I am looking for the scraper." Apparently he had heard one of my father's stories about how if the shamans lost anything, or if they were looking for things they had lost, that is what they would do, crouch over and maybe pray or something. That is what he was doing. He was pretty funny.

MY BABY SISTER GOT SICK

I remember one story from earlier on, early in my childhood. I had just
got a little sister, Joanna. She was just born when we were out a long
ways from home, a long ways from the outpost camp. At that time
there were hardly any caribou around Igloolik. We had to travel a long
ways to get food. My father spent so much time looking for caribou!
This time he took us with him. We travelled all over the place. I don't
know whether my sister was born before we left the outpost camp or
whether she was born while we were out there. Solomon, my brother,
he was younger than I am, and Joanna was younger than him. I
remember being out on the land. We were at Tasiujaq. We had been out
there for a long time, and my baby sister got sick. She looked awful. It
was something I had never seen before. Her head was swollen, really
swollen. It wouldn't have been meningitis because now she would be
dead, but she was sick for the longest time. Her head stayed swollen.
It was winter, and it was dark outside all day long. We were at least a
week's travel away from Igloolik. That was pretty far back then, especially if you were moving a family. We stayed at that campsite when
she got sick – we stopped moving for a while. She got well afterwards,
and we moved on. I was just a child at that time but I remember it quite
well. It was a very bad sickness, very scary.

WE USED TO KEEP DIFFERENT KINDS OF BIRDS, SORT
OF AS PETS

We used to go egg hunting a lot when I was a kid. We would look for
eider ducks' eggs and – what are those called, those birds, they are
smaller than eider ducks, tiny ones? Arctic terns, that is what they are.
They are tiny, tiny birds. Anyways, we had these little islands not far
from our winter and summer camps, and we would go there to look
for eggs. The birds, they have their nests up on these cliffs, under the
big rocks. They built their nests right under the rocks high on the cliffs
of the islands, so we would have to climb up and find the nests. The
eider ducks, they have great big fluffy nests and great big eggs. They
taste good, those eggs. The Arctic terns are really scary birds. They are
small and fierce. When we were gathering eggs we would have to put
on little metal hats. We put pails on our heads when we were egg
hunting to protect ourselves when the terns got too fierce. They would
come rushing down and hit the metal. It was kind of scary.

We used to keep different kinds of birds, sort of as pets. We would find
them as little birds and feed them throughout the summer. They would
get used to us and hang around. The pets that we had came from this

area, they would follow us sometimes, but they wouldn't travel outside their nesting area if we were going far away. One time, one spring that we were here, I had a snowy owl, a baby snowy owl. I can never tell the difference between a falcon and a hawk, but we had one of those too. They are kind of fierce, though. They are very demanding as pets, they eat a lot. So do owls, owls eat a lot. We used to feed them fish. Seagulls also love fish, fish and seal fat. In the fall they would migrate.

Every summer we had pet seagulls. Just next to our summer camp there was a seagull nesting area, and my dad would get tiny little seagulls from there for us to keep. They would get so used to us they would be like pets by the time summer was over. Once they got used to us feeding them, they would just hang around the camp until they went south, they wouldn't go anywhere else. There was one seagull we had once, he was my brother Arvaluk's pet. He was hardly ever in the camp. He would come in maybe just to have a meal. He knew our family, he was used to us, and he could recognize our boat from all the other boats when we went out on the water. Arvaluk's seagull would fly around, and when he recognized us, he'd come flying down alongside the canoe and stay with us the rest of the trip. I remember it was late fall and Arvaluk's seagull had been gone for days and days. We thought that he had headed south for the winter. It was late fall. Most of the gulls had migrated already. When we got in the canoe and went out on the water, there he was, hanging around again. He wanted to stay with us, so he held off migrating. My brother started throwing meat on to the water for him to catch. I don't remember seeing him after that day. He must have gone south after that.

MY BROTHER JAKOPIE HAD A DOG

One incident I remember, I think my mother would remember this better than I would ... I just get flashes, eh? My brother Jakopie, he had a dog. He wasn't a St Bernard, but he looked just like one, a really big, brown, dark disgusting dog. My brother really liked this dog, though. This dog was the love of his life or something like that. I felt so sorry for the dog. One summer we were out caribou hunting, we had gone by boat, and we had brought the dog with us. We were going back home to the outpost camp from somewhere, I don't remember where we were. I remember we were ready to go, and the dog was nowhere in sight. We all got into the boat. My brother was getting pretty upset – his dog was being left behind! Then, after we had left the shore and were on our way home, we saw the dog on the beach. He jumped into the ocean. He was splashing in the water, swimming, trying to catch up with the canoe. I remember watching him swim. The dog caught up and we pulled him into the boat. He got the boat all wet. I remember that incident really well, because I knew Jakopie really loved his dog. He was heartbroken that we were going to leave it behind, but that was what you had to do back then. You couldn't wait around for dogs to show up.

JIGGING ON THE ICE

The incident that I am thinking about happened when I was a kid. This happened when I was just a young girl. Growing up, we had a winter camp and a summer camp. The winter camp was the one where most of my stories come from, because it had a shack, a matchbox shack, and it was more of a permanent home. We also had a summer camp which was about five to ten miles away, and we would go there in the early springtime when the ice was still good. We would go by dog team. We would pitch our tents there for the spring and summer. That is where a lot of the good fishing spots were. We had fish for most of the spring and summer, hardly anything else, maybe an odd seal. If the men went out caribou hunting from there, it would have taken them a long time to travel to where the caribou were and then come home. I don't remember having caribou in that place.

That summer my older brother Arvaluk was home from school in Churchill. He was maybe fifteen at the time, and he was home for the first time in a long time. Usually when he came home for the summers, he spent his time working at jobs in Igloolik instead of coming to the outpost camp. He hadn't been in the outpost camp, our home, for a long time, so this was kind of a rejoicing.

My uncle was with us too at the time, my dad's brother. He was there just for a little while, maybe to spend a week or a couple of weeks with us. We went there that spring before the fish started running. When it is springtime, the fish start coming down from the lakes on the land and into the ocean. They always go down from the lakes in the springtime to the ocean. Usually we would have to wait maybe a week, maybe a couple of weeks before they came by on their way to the ocean. There are a couple of weeks where you couldn't find any fish, even if you did some jigging on the ice. When someone caught the first fish from the ocean, we would know that the fish were on their way. We would start our jigging on the ice right next to the land where we would set our tents. We would just go down onto the ice. The ice on the beach had cracks that go right into the water, and you can jig from there. You don't have to drill a hole or anything, because the cracks are already there to fish from, so that is what we usually did in the springtime in the camp.

Anyways, my brother Jakopie, he and I had ongoing childhood contests. He is almost two years older than me, but ever since we were children we acted like we were the same age because we were born so close together. We would do things like compete to see who could learn syllabics first, see who could be the first one to be fluent reading syllabics – or running, who could be the fastest runner. We were always competing, and I was always trying my hardest to beat him, because in his opinion I was just a woman. He thought that because I was a woman and two years younger than him I didn't ever know what I was doing, that kind of thing. So we had this ongoing competition, and he was challenging me that spring, saying that he would catch more fish than I could. That spring we were jigging, counting all the fish that we caught, both of us. I got up to about two hundred fish the whole spring, from mid June to July, before the ice went away.

When the ice went away that summer, Jake quit jigging and started helping my older brother and my father. He was helping them pull in the fish nets and take the fish from the nets. They were using the nets to catch fish at that time because the ice had left. At that time we had a canoe with an outboard motor and a little tiny boat. The tiny little boat was just for the net, it didn't go very far. We used it mostly to get easy access to the nets from the shore. Me being a girl, I wasn't allowed to get on the boat or help out with the nets. Jakopie and I, we were still having this contest, and he told me he was at about three hundred fish. He had counted the fish that he took off from the nets! He said he was winning and I got furious, eh? I thought we had finished our contests when the jigging was over, and here he was continuing to count his catch from the nets.

Everybody was in the tent, my uncle, my older brother, Jake, my dad – everybody was in the tent, playing cards, I think. I remember they were not outside. Everybody was inside. I think they were playing cards, hanging around, waiting for the next fish to hit the net. They would wait for a little while before they would pull in the net again. They would pull it in maybe two or three times a day. My father was painting the canoe. He painted it over and over again in the summertime to seal everything up so that it wouldn't leak. He would re-do the whole canoe with paint. It is because canoes were made from canvas cloth at that time. When the paint peels off, the canvas shows and water gets in.

He had just painted the canoe that day and had it upside down on the land, drying. All we had besides the canoe was this small little boat. Everybody was inside, and I decided it would be a great time to go pull some fish off the net so that I could catch up to Jakopie in our contest. I took the little boat and pushed it off the shore. I was hanging on to the net. The net had these bobbles I could hang on to. I was moving along the net like that, pulling it up, looking at the net to see if there were any fish, I was going along like that. I don't remember whether I found any fish in the net, but when I got to the very end, I was supposed to turn around go back the same way, hanging on to the net and heading for the shore. By some freak accident I let go. As soon as I let go, the small boat started drifting away. There were no paddles in the boat. All there was was the little dipper to get rid of the water that leaked in.

I started drifting away, so I started screaming, "Hey, somebody help me! Come get me!" The water was a little bit rough. It was a little bit windy outside, just enough to push the boat off the nets. I was drifting away, drifting ... Finally I started screaming and crying, because I was getting so far away. I was trying to paddle with the dipper and the boat was getting more and more water in it because I wasn't bailing it out. Finally they started coming out of the tent. I guess they heard my shouts. They started coming out of the tent, and my dad came roaring out to get me with his outboard motor and the newly painted canoe. He wrecked the paint job. I thought he was coming to get me. He came with Arvaluk, and I thought he would put the small boat next to him and put me in the canoe and we would be right home. He screamed to me "Paddle!" He wanted me to paddle with my hands. The water was so cold, the ice had just left, and I was paddling like this with my hands. I paddled all the way back into shore. He was running the motor slowly right behind me. I had to explain to everybody why I was on the net. Oh, I was mad at my brother, I was furious with him!

WE PITCHED OUR CANVAS TENT ON THE DEW-LINE SITE

This warm feeling, this good feeling, I have it when I remember this incident. My mother was away, I think she was in the hospital having Ida, my younger sister. I don't know how long she was gone, most of the summer, I think. I remember her going off to the nursing station, and I didn't see her again for a while. By that time my mother was a little bit older. She had given birth to a lot of children. Because of her age and her condition, she ended up being hospitalized for her last two kids, Ida and Phillip. Ida was the first one that she went away with for the last part of her pregnancy. She went to Hall Beach. It had a nursing station that she stayed in and had close access to a hospital. We went there from Igloolik by boat to be near her, my father, my oldest sister, and all the kids. My older sister was looking after all of us. We went to Hall Beach to see my mother.

When we got to Hall Beach we pitched our canvas tent on the DEW-line site, probably three miles away from the community.[1] My father at that time was a bit of a loner. He didn't mingle well with other people, especially Qallunaat. Thinking about it, maybe that is why we took so long to move off the land, he didn't mingle well with people ... Anyways, we pitched our tent. There was Joanna, Solomon, myself, Salomie, Oopah, Jake, six of us. Martha was with my grandparents in Igloolik. Both Simon and Arvaluk were out at school. I remember it was probably early summer, because it was really, really warm.

I don't remember much about the DEW-line site itself. I remember there was a great big airstrip. There must have been a construction crew working there. Also, there was a garbage dump there for the community as well as for the DEW-line workers. People would come to visit us at our tent. It was very nice. Some workers and people from the community of Hall Beach would walk over and stick around for the afternoon. There were some Qallunaat men from the DEW line hanging around, maybe buying carvings from Dad sometimes. I remember we didn't have much to eat because we had moved off the land to the edge of a community. We were far away from everyone in the settlement. We weren't sharing any of their meat, and Dad wasn't hunting. In the Hall Beach area the water was shallow. I think the only hunting there was walrus, which was maybe twenty or thirty miles away. It was hard for us.

When we were back at home on the land, we always had meat around. Dad would go out hunting every day and come back with meat. We usually had a cache of seal meat five miles away, a cache of caribou forty miles away. It was like that. We would have a supply of frozen meat next to the house, or dried meat, like fish drying on the tent. We always had meat around. This time we were away from home, and Dad, he was just hanging around. We didn't have much to eat.

Maybe it was kind of hard for me, maybe I was acting up, maybe I was hungry, or maybe I was just cranky, but for some reason I think maybe my father felt sorry for me. I remember falling asleep one night not having eaten anything, except maybe tea or something like that. I was whining and making a fuss. The next morning I woke up to these wonderful smells! It was a nice sunny day, a beautiful day. I woke up and my father had fried up hot dogs in a pan. I don't know what else he had, some type of luncheon meat or something. When I woke up, some beautiful smells were coming from the stove, and he was frying them up and putting them on the plate. I hadn't even gotten up yet, and he gave me tea and gave me some delicious sausages, wieners to eat. I remember that morning so clearly because it was sunny and I was late getting up. I had a good night's sleep, and it was kind of a lazy summer morning and my father gave me this beautiful stuff to eat, Qallunaat food, hot dogs.

I found out later that he had gotten those sausages from the DEW-line dump, where all the DEW-line guys tossed out their garbage. They were unused meat, packages of unused meat – they had never been opened. I don't know why the people at the DEW-line site didn't just give the meat to us directly, they just dumped it out. And it wasn't ... you see, I know what sausage smells like when it is old, I know what meat tastes like when it is dirty. It wasn't like that. They were fresh wieners. That sort of stuff happened all the time – teachers or workers would leave perfectly good food out because it was frozen or old, things like packages of meat, oranges, and apples. We would just take the top off and they would be fine.

I mean ... getting meat from a garbage dump, thinking about it today, it is kind of disgusting ... but for me it was a treat, to get that kind of food on a nice morning, summertime, and the smell was just delicious! Even today when I fry wieners – my mom boils them, but I always fry them – when I fry them, the smell always reminds me of that morning, the first time I ate wieners. I never thought of it as my father feeding me from a garbage dump. He was doing me a favour. He brought me food.

FROM INUIT TO QALLUNAAT CULTURE: I REMEMBER MY FIRST DAY OF SCHOOL

THAT FIRST WINTER I WAS IN SCHOOL

It was really rough that first year, going into Igloolik to go to school ... My grandparents were in Igloolik at the time, and I was staying with them. I was only about eight years old. I remember my father taking us into school. I remember my first day of school. We had this Qallunaat teacher, I can't remember her name. My aunt had already been in school there for a couple of years before me, so she was helping me out the first day, trying to take care of me. When I first went to school I didn't speak any English at all, absolutely nothing. I was eight years old. My aunt was showing me where things were, telling me that I had to ask to go to the bathroom, that I had to raise my hand if I wanted to ask a question, stuff like that. She was telling me all this in Inukti-tut. I remember all morning that first day of school she made me prac-tise the words, "Can I go to the bathroom?" Those were the first English words I learned – "Can I go to the bathroom?" It was hard to learn English.

That first winter I was in school was really difficult. I had a terrible winter those first three months. Just thinking about it, that first year, I think, "Gee, I feel sorry for that kid, she was only eight years old and she was all alone!" That was the first year I had ever been away from my family. I had never been in a day-care centre, never been away from my parents, I had never even stayed alone visiting my grandparents. I had always been right next to my mom. That was the first time I had ever been out of my family's sight, and I was in a totally different community. I couldn't just go out and walk home. Maybe for a child it is worse. I knew that my parents were going to be coming at Christmas time or at Easter time, but it seemed like a million years away. Kid mentalities are like that – one day is one day too late, that type of thing. I think that was why it was really difficult.

There was so much I was not used to, different schedules, set schedules. We had to get up even if we were sleepy and go to school at nine o'clock. In the outpost camp we used to get up when we wanted to. It is not as if we slept all day. We got up early in the camps. My dad was always out hunting before we got up. But we got up when we were finished sleeping. In town we had to get to know the teachers, the Qallunaat environment. We had to learn a new language and all that. All that time I stayed with my grandparents and my other grandmother, my father's stepmother. I didn't know them very well at that time. I hadn't spent much time with them when we were in camps, and I was the only kid in my family living with them. Jake and Martha were being put up in other places. That year I felt really alienated, maybe because I was away from home.

I remember that first Christmas that my parents came for the holidays, I remember having a really difficult time. I was enjoying myself because my parents were there, being with them and staying with them, but when they were ready to go back to the camp, that was heartbreaking for me. I was crying and crying. I remember my father was sitting upright on a chair and I was kneeling at his knees, crying and crying into his lap. I stayed like that for hours and hours. I was crying and begging him to let me go with him, but he couldn't do anything. Even if he had wanted to he couldn't do anything. At that time I was really mad at him for not taking me home with him. Later I realized that we had to be in school. He had no choice. The Qallunaat authorities in the settlement said so, and there was nothing he could do. Yes, the first time I saw them come and go away, it was really hard ...

When school ended, going back out on the land in the summertime was fun. Arvaluk and Simon had been in Churchill. Martha, Jake, and I had been in Igloolik. The whole family was back together again! We came back from Igloolik around June, and my older brothers didn't get back until late July. Then, after a little while, they had to head back out again. They had the long trip to get to Churchill.

That first year was really, really hard.

MY FIRST HAIRCUT

It was my first year at school. I was in Igloolik. It was winter, maybe
the first month of school, and my parents had just brought me and Jake
into the community to go to school. I was away from my parents for
the first time. I was living with my grandparents, and I think I was in
shock a little bit. I think we had some lice or something like that,
because I remember we were told that we had to go to the nursing
station. I can't quite remember who was with me at that time. I remember there were other children besides myself. I was eight years old and
I had long hair at that time. It was at my waist and I always used to
wear it combed and hanging straight down or braided. I had never had
it cut. It had been long since I was born, that was the Inuit way. It was
shameful for us to have short hair as a girl.

I remember it was my first month of school and the teachers, they
noticed I had lice. I went to the nursing station with some other kids,
and they washed our hair with some sort of shampoo, a special
shampoo, I can't remember the name ... The nurses washed my hair,
got it all clean, dried it up. Then for some reason that I don't understand, they cut it. They hacked it off just below my ears, just at the
neck. I don't know what the idea was because the other girls that were
with me at the time, they didn't get their hair cut. I was the only one.
Mine was cut.

My hair was really thick and they didn't try to taper it off or anything, they just kind of chopped it off, hacked it off. I remember it was
crooked. I had never had short hair before, and I was kind of embarrassed walking around the settlement with short hair. In those times,
when you went to church you either had to wear braids or have your
hair fixed up, pulled back. If you had a haircut, then you had to wear
a kerchief. You couldn't go to church with a haircut and show it off,
you had to hide it. I had short hair when my parents came to visit us
that Christmas and then all that year. I grew it out again as fast as I
could. That was my first haircut.

THE BOAT CAME TO PICK US UP

The first year that our father took us to school I was eight years old.
This was in Igloolik in 1966. The next year we moved here to Pond
Inlet. I was nine by then. I remember we were out at Qaurnnak, we
spent the summer at this outpost camp outside of Pond Inlet. It was
early fall, early September, and one of those big Peterhead boats that
we have here came to Qaurnnak. My father was probably intending to
take us into school, but the boat came to pick us up instead.

I was nine. I know that my father had taken us in to school in Igloolik the previous year. The previous year had actually been my first year of school. I don't know what it was with that particular year in Pond, whether he had decided to keep us out of school for the whole year or whether he was going to wait until the ice came in to travel. I don't know what he was planning at the time. All I knew was that he wasn't planning to take us to school, at least not that particular week when the boat came. I think he was planning to take us back to Igloolik. He hadn't planned to take us to Pond.

We were still in tents, it was early fall, and people in the camp were starting to work, building sod-houses. Well, actually, the only sod-house that was being built was my father's, because everyone else already had a sod-house that they could just fix up for the winter. We had just moved to the Pond Inlet area, so we didn't have one yet. That was our first winter there at that camp so we were building a new sod-house. Everyone was working, taking out the peat, that hard stuff. Most of us kids were just playing outside, running around. It was still summer outside.

Just a couple of days before, my brother Solomon had burned himself quite badly. My brother and I had been playing around in a tent, and there was this great big cauldron of soup beside us that we had been eating. I can't remember what kind of soup it was, but it was quite hot. There must have been some oil in it because it was very, very hot. It was on the floor cooling and my brother and I were play-fighting. I think we were playing ball with socks, rolled-up socks or something crazy like that. I remember he was falling down and he stuck his hand out to support himself. He stuck his hand in the pot by accident. That is how he burned himself. This was about a couple of days before the boat came. Solomon had this burn on his arm and it was sore and infected by the time the boat came in. It would have healed eventually, his arm ... When the boat came, most of the men were in the camp. I think they were all working building my parents a sod-house. I remember there wasn't anybody out hunting.

I don't think anyone in the camp knew the boat was going to come, I am not sure. All I know is that I had no idea that a boat was coming to pick me up. Anyways, the boat came. It was the local administrator. They were called "administrators" at the time, the government people. He was not a teacher or a principal – principals and teachers were not involved in this kind of thing. It was the administrator who ran the community. He was the one who came to pick us up. I think the boat was probably driven by somebody else, probably a local person employed by the government, someone who knew where the camps were. I think they had planned to leave the next day, the day after they got there, but the weather changed so they stayed a few days. It was kind of stormy, not very rough, but it was cloudy. It wasn't like the nice summer days that had been around when we were building our sod-house. I remember getting ready to get on the boat, and I remember that the weather was not that great. It was cloudy and the water was a bit rough, a little bit rough, not too much. I remember there was some discussion about my brother Solomon. I know it wasn't a smooth process. I think there were some heated words about my brother getting on the boat.

From what I know, what my father understood from all this discussion was that Solomon was going to go to the nursing station because of his arm, the one he had burned, but that after that he would be coming home. My father was bound and determined that Solomon was going to stay out of school. If his girls went, okay, fine – and Jake had already had a couple of years – but Solomon, he was going to stay on the land. We had the afternoon to pack, get our things together to go off to school. Jake and I got on the boat. Solomon got on the boat. I don't know who else was on the boat, maybe the driver and the administrator. My parents were certainly not there.

I think my parents had been making plans to come to Pond sometime in the fall in their own boat. I think there were some plans to go get some shopping done before the early fall, because in early fall the water begins to freeze and you have to wait until the ice is thick enough to travel. There is nothing you can do when the ice is just starting to freeze. You can't travel by boat and you can't travel by dog team because the ice is still too thin. There are about three to four weeks in the fall when it is really impossible to travel. My parents, they had their own boat, much smaller than the administrator's. So I thought fine, okay, we're going to see them in a couple of days maybe. I wasn't hysterical like I was that first winter in Igloolik. When we got to Pond Inlet, we had nice foster parents, Rhoda and Joe Koonoo, so I was quite comfortable with them. Solomon's burn was treated at the nursing station the day we came in, and the next day Solomon and I went to school. He had his arm in a bandage when we went to school the next day. They didn't bring him back to my parents' camp like they said they would, they put him in school instead. He was in the same class as I was. I had gone to school the previous year, but this was his first year.

I remember the incident so clearly. It was the first day of school, we were sitting there getting ready at our desks, and then, in the middle of the afternoon, my father came into the school and grabbed Solomon by the arm. He walked in, took his arm, and dragged him out the door. I didn't even know my father had come in from the camp. I remember that so well – at the time my father was a great big man, muscles and all, quite a bit bigger than he is now. He stalked into the room, grabbed Solomon's arm, and walked out. Never mind the procedures or the teachers' ways. He did this because he told the people on the boat that they could take his kid to the nursing station, not to the school. Solomon got to stay at home with my parents that year. I was so jealous of him! That much I remember from the incident.

I think the reason my father pulled Solomon out of school was that he had seen Simon and Arvaluk and Martha leave for Churchill, they had been there for two or three years, and he decided that he was going to teach Solomon the traditional hunting. He was determined to teach Solomon that. Maybe it was because of Solomon's personality. Looking at my other brothers, Simon and Arvaluk, I think they're more the administrative types, intellectual types. I think my father recognized that, so he left them there and decided that Solomon would be the one to learn to hunt. He was the youngest at that time.

My father came and pulled him out of the classroom. I think it was 1968, I don't know. He didn't go to school that year. I think he missed a few years after that as well. It might have been in 1970 when my parents moved into Igloolik that he started going to school. He is younger than me, but even today he doesn't have the same grasp of the English language that I have. He could only speak Inuktitut before he went to school. Even when he was brought to school, he didn't always complete the school year because he had been brought up to go hunting. That was what he liked most.

Jake and Martha and I, we spent the rest of the year there. That winter I learned how to smoke and how to find cigarettes or butts. I learned what a cigarette was. I did this with a friend of mine. There used to be a wooden bridge that crossed the creek near the hamlet office, and there would be all sorts of butts lying around there, and this friend of mine and I would go down there looking for butts. I didn't smoke very much at the time, but I found lots of butts for her. Yeah, I learned what cigarettes were that winter. I learned how to smoke.

I WAS LIVING WITH FOSTER PARENTS

Once my dad took Solomon away, when he took him out of the classroom, there was just Martha and Jake and me in school in Pond Inlet. I was living with foster parents at that time. I remember my foster parents clearly. They were Rhoda Koonoo and Joe Koonoo and their family. They were in their twenties then. There were maybe ten of us there at the hostel, and they had three children of their own, little ones.

We spent the winter in Pond Inlet. There must have been some Christmas holidays, because I remember my parents being here. I remember there was a lady in town that made a big impression on me. She had a great hairdo – you know that style where they kink up their hair and make it really puffy? That was the style then. She was a local lady in town. She had gotten this new style from either Churchill or some place like that. I remember those few days at Christmas time. I remember not being in the hostel, like I was free. It must have been around Christmas time, because it was dark. In the hostel we had a curfew, but at that time I remember being free.

That spring we moved back to Igloolik. It was after school had ended, just before the ice broke. I was ten years old when we moved back to Igloolik. We were there until 1972, spring of 1972. I was ten in 1967, so how many years is that, five? I had Grade One in Igloolik, skipped Grade Two, had Grade Three here in Pond Inlet and then Grades Four, Five, Six, Seven, and Eight back in Igloolik.

When we went back to Igloolik from Pond Inlet after Grade Three, we didn't move in with our relatives again, we stayed in the transient centre. It was called a hostel. I think we stayed there quite a number of years, me and my sister Martha. Solomon wasn't around. Jake must have been somewhere else. Me and my sister Martha were there. Joanna was still too young to be in school.

I remember my sister Martha got her first boyfriend at around that time. She was having a romance with the guy she married later on, the RCMP's son – I mean, the "Special Constable's" son.[2] It was difficult for me at that time, because I had to take the love-letters back and forth. She used to get me to take love-letters to her boyfriend in the middle of the night, 10:30 at night. We had a curfew in the hostel, and we weren't allowed to visit around very much. We could visit, but we weren't allowed to hang out for too long. Understandably so – we weren't allowed to burden someone's family because they were supposed to be taking care of us in the hostel. My sister would wait until the foster parents would go to their room. The foster parents had a room at the very back. There was a long corridor. She would wait until they had gone to bed, and then she would ask me if I wanted to sleep with her in her bed. Then a few minutes later she would ask me, "Want to deliver this letter?" So I would have to get all dressed and sneak out. They lived in the RCMP staff house a few houses away. Of course, at that time they had a house of their own, so everybody was wide awake at that time of night and kids would be playing around. Nobody was curious about this little kid coming in the door.

I would sneak the letter to my future brother-in-law, and then I would stick around and wait for him to answer, take his letter, and sneak it back to my sister. If it wasn't good news I had a rough night because my sister cried or kept waking me up telling me she didn't want to be awake all alone. I was Cupid. I am just thinking how silly that was ... A few years ago they got a divorce, and that really boiled me. All that trouble that I went to for them, and they went and got divorced!

FLOUR USED TO EXTINGUISH FIRE

The first time I saw flour used to extinguish a fire was when my brother Arvaluk came back from Churchill. He had been to school there and he had learned some stuff. I remember he always had lot of fun teaching my dad and the rest of us all of the things and the English he learned in the school. There was this one time he taught us all about cakes. He had learned about cakes in school, he had eaten them there. When he came home, I guess he missed them so he started imagining making a layer cake for us out of walrus meat and walrus fat. He was explaining it to all of us. I guess the walrus meat and fat reminded him of cakes. I guess the fat was the icing. We were always really amazed at all the neat information Arvaluk brought back with him. That was the first time I had ever heard of cakes, layer cakes.

There was this one particular incident that happened one spring when Arvaluk came home for a while. We were home from school for summer, and there were two other men with us at Naujaaruluk that time, one was from Igloolik, the other guy was from Pond Inlet. They came from town with my uncle. They came into our camp. I think that was the same spring that my sister Oopah's husband came with them. I'm not sure.

Anyways, we had a small stove in the shack in our camp, a wood-stove, and it had a chimney. It was just one of your standard steel chimneys attached to the wood-stove that we used. We put wood in it to keep the stove going. It had an iron top to it. A lot of people were in the shack at the time because there was a big blizzard outside, and for some reason the stove had been overloaded with firewood. It was getting so hot that it was melting the pipe – the chimney was very thin steel, it didn't have any insulation, just the steel. I was asleep at the time and I remember being woken up and told to get out of the house. I remember I had no clothes on. I was maybe eleven years old. It was quite cold outside. It was still spring. They put a blanket on me and my mom. It was kind of a surprise to be woken up to this fire in the stove and have to get out of the shack. We went out and the men were trying to put out the fire with water and cloths. Arvaluk helped put it out by grabbing my mother's flour and throwing it all over the fire.

When we got back into the house, the fire was out and the shack was getting kind of cold. There was all of this flour on top of the stove, flour and baking powder. My mom was yelling, "My precious flour, what did you do to my flour!" She knew she wouldn't get another supply for three months or so. Apparently Arvaluk had learned that you could use powder to extinguish gas flames and stuff like that, and so that is what he used. That was the first time I ever heard of powders being used to put out flames.

A STORY ABOUT PIERRE TRUDEAU

I wanted to tell you a story about Pierre Trudeau. It was 1970 – I was about fourteen, and Pierre Trudeau had just recently become prime minister of Canada. We had learned all about him that year at school, and he was due to come to Igloolik in the springtime. Before he came we were told to make a poster about him. We had to depict some sort of thing that we knew about Trudeau, opinions or whatever. This was the year that freedom of speech came to school. We were "free to do whatever we wanted," that is what the principal told us. Maybe it was 1971 ... [3] Anyways, I cut out a newspaper clipping with a picture of Trudeau in Toronto. He had sandals on, thongs, and his arms were up and out to his sides. He was talking to a great big crowd in Toronto. I cut him out, just him in his sandals, and pasted him on white paper. I drew a line. At that time I was really dumb about animals. I didn't know much because I was always in school. I drew a walrus coming out of a seal hole. He was in the seal hole. Then I drew a question mark above the walrus's head. I pasted Trudeau beside him. He was talking to the walrus, and the walrus had a question mark above his head, sort of like, "What the heck is he saying?" That was my political viewpoint, like, "Who the heck are you?" – that kind of thing.

Trudeau came into town maybe a day after the posters were all put up. He came in on the weekend, so we weren't in school. Apparently he viewed the school and looked around at all the things the kids had done to celebrate his visit. He saw my picture and he really, really liked it. He apparently told my teacher that he wanted to meet me and give me a medal. My teacher relayed this message to my mom. Early on a Saturday morning, my mother woke me up and said, "You have to go to this teacher's house to meet Trudeau! Wake up, hurry up, he is waiting!" I got up, got all dressed, and I didn't look very good, eh? I had just woke up! I went over to the principal's house. He had stairs. When you went in, you had to go past a crawl-space on the main floor and go up the stairs. I went in, and someone told Mr Trudeau that I had arrived. He started coming down the stairs. I remember he was wearing a very fancy sweater, a very nice sweater. He shook my hand, said, "Hello, how are you? Oh, you are Rhoda!" You know, that sort of thing. Then he gave me a medal. I said, "I am fine. Hello. Goodbye. Thank you," and then I took off. I mean ... I didn't even stay around to chat. I was outa there. If I had thought about it a little at that time, about who I was meeting, I might have tried to talk to him more and be more courteous. It didn't sink into my head back then that this was the prime minister of Canada!

That statement that I made with the question mark and the Inuit not knowing what the Qallunaat or the politicians are saying to Inuit has been a big part of my attitude towards politics up until just a few years ago. Right now, today, I think I can make politicians understand if I have something to say, but at the time when Trudeau came to visit, most of the Inuit didn't speak English. They didn't express many political opinions. There were so few of us younger people who could speak English that even if we voiced a few political opinions, they didn't count much anyways. I mean, we were seen as savages who didn't know what we were doing. So at that time – I was fourteen – that was my big political statement.

THIS GROUP OF SCIENTISTS

I was telling Josh last night about how my scars were itching. They were itching and itching, and it reminded me of the story about how I got them. It was in 1971 or 1972. We were in Igloolik and I was probably about thirteen or fourteen, and this group of scientists, or whoever they were, they came into town. They called themselves anthropologists. I remember it was a big deal for these guys to come in. We heard about it before they came. It was like major news in the community, a big study going on in our small town.[4]

The day after they came in, my family was told to go to this little building next to the nursing station. That is where they were working, this little building. We went over there, my mother, my brother Jakopie, my older sister Oopah, and myself. I think my mother had somebody on her back, Ida, maybe, I don't know. I don't know if it was just my family that was tested. I don't think it was everybody in the community, just certain families. They had some sort of a list, and I think they were picking names from that list or something. I remember us walking over there.

We didn't know what was going on. First they had us climb up and down these three wooden steps, three steps up and three steps down. We climbed up and down. They wanted to see how much we could do without getting tired. They watched us while we did it for a long time, then when our hearts sped up they got us on this little bicycle, and they put respirators on us. I had never been on a bicycle before. I didn't really know what to do, but they put me on the cycle and told me to breathe into the respirator. They made us take turns on that for the rest of the afternoon. They did some other tests too. I don't remember all of them. I remember they tested our blood pressure and took blood samples from us.

The big thing I remember, though, was that they took bits of skin off our forearms. First they made the whole skin area numb, then they took this very long, thin cylinder, like a stick, sharp on one end, and they kind of drilled it into my arm to cut the skin. They took the skin off, it was at the end of this little cylinder thing. It was all inside. They did that twice. Once they took the two pieces of skin off my arm, they put in skin from my sister Oopah and my brother Jake's arm. I got their skin, Jake got my skin and Oopah's, Oopah got Jake's and mine. I think my mom was there. Of course we were her children, so she had to be there, maybe to consent or something like that. But I don't think it was a matter of her consenting, I don't think she thought of it that way. Then, after they did that, they put bandages on. It didn't hurt that much at the time. It hurt later, like a regular cut would, but it didn't hurt at all at the time because of the anaesthetic.

My grandfather Uyarak had been on his way hunting that same day the researchers were in. He was probably in his sixties at the time. I heard they were quite amazed that he was out on the land hunting every day at that age, so they chose him to have this heart monitor thing attached to him. They wanted to know how much stamina he had, how much his heart could take. The heart monitor thing was attached to his body with a set of straps but it was attached outside his caribou parka. To me it seemed kind of silly, because the monitor itself was quite heavy, so I am sure his heart would have beat much differently if he hadn't been carrying anything for the scientists. He spent the whole day with this thing strapped to him while he was hunting. We heard about this story afterwards from my grandfather.

There was this other time, kind of like that one with the anthropologists, when I got my teeth checked. All of my life I had never thought that my teeth were any different than anybody else's. That time, though, we were told that we were going to have our teeth checked for some sort of study by some Qallunaat who were coming into the community. I don't remember them doing any fillings or dental hygiene or taking any teeth out. I think they were doing some sort of study on Inuit teeth.

At that time when they looked at my teeth I didn't have any cavities. I didn't have cavities until I was twenty or twenty-five. I was eleven or twelve then. They looked at my mom's teeth and my teeth and maybe my sister's teeth too. They were really amazed at my teeth. I had white spots, white chips on the front of my teeth. The dentist thought that was really strange. He kept looking at them and looking at them, opening my mouth up and looking at them, looking at the bottom. He kept looking at my teeth. Finally he told me to smile, and he took a picture. He asked me certain things, like what sorts of food I ate. He thought that maybe the spots were from a big concentration of calcium. That is what he said. He thought they were there because of big concentrations of calcium. I guess I had strange teeth compared to everyone else. I don't know. They don't bother me.

Those situations for us, like the ones I just described with the anthropologists and the dentists, there were lots things like that going on when I was growing up. In Igloolik there was lots of research going on about the "Eskimo." There was study after study after study about us. I don't even remember all of them. It was like they couldn't get enough! There were always researchers in the community and questionnaires going around asking all sorts of questions, what we did, what we wanted, that sort of thing.

The researchers, most of the time they just did whatever they wanted when they were up here. A lot of the time they didn't bother to explain themselves very well. A lot of times we didn't really understand what was going on. We just did whatever they told us to do. People in the community, Inuit, would complain to each other during those years. They would say stuff like, "Oh, here they come again to study us." I think that maybe even today there are some of the same attitudes in town when a researcher goes into a house and starts asking questions. We might think, "You again," that kind of thing, but we would still be, what is the word ... "polite" – I guess that's the word. We would still say yes to being interviewed. Even though we might talk about it between ourselves, talk about all the researchers coming to study us, even though we might say those things to each other, a lot of times we would still be polite and agree.

Sometimes I wonder why people agreed all the time even when they didn't want to. I guess what it comes down to is that the Qallunaat have always been the people with the authority. I learned that in school. Even my parents always treated them that way. It was normal for Qallunaat to ask us to come over and do things for them, even things like giving them our skin ... We just did whatever they told us to do. They were the ones who ran the town. They were the ones who said what is appropriate and proper and told us what needed to be done. If the Qallunaat say so, then it must be so. We always agreed.

I mean, people wouldn't follow what the Qallunaat say about hunting and stuff like that, but I guess we figured that the Qallunaat must know about beef, salads, scientific research, books. With those sorts of things we figured they were the authority. So, if a study was being done in a particular way, I guess we didn't question it. We figured that we didn't have any sort of scientific knowledge, so there was no way we could disagree. We have lots of knowledge about being on the land and hunting wildlife and stuff, but if the Qallunaat told us that a study was going to be done a particular way, Inuit agreed to it. Even with my skin grafts, even then I don't remember my mother being upset about what was going on. It never would have even occurred to her that she could say no to the Qallunaat.

I remember with my skin grafts they told us that they were trying to find out if a person got burned if they could get a graft from sibling's skin. Maybe they thought Inuk skin was different from Qallunaat skin, I don't know. It sure would have been nice to know what they were doing at the time! Anyways, the grafts didn't heal into my skin. Jake's and Oopah's skin fell off, and the holes healed over. Those anthropologists are very lucky the cuts weren't on my face ... We were told to go back to that place a couple of times because they wanted to check to see if the grafts were staying. We went back, but it was nice to see them go and not stay. I remember being happy when Jake and Oopah's skin fell off my arm. I was happy that I disproved their theory. I have had the scars ever since. They don't go away.

I RAN STRAIGHT HOME FROM CHURCH AND GRABBED MY MOTHER

I think it was the eighth grade, my last grade in Igloolik. I had the same teacher for a couple of years, for the seventh and eighth grade. The first year he was here, it was just him and his wife and his child who were here. The second year, that summer, his sister Cheryl came to town. She was about my age, maybe a little bit younger. Since I was friends with the teacher, I hung around with her. I became friends with her. We were friends for a long time. She was kind of like, what are they called ... dumb blondes? She was kind of like that, not really, but kind of ... We weren't used to that kind of behaviour, Qallunaat behaviour, at that time. Even though she was a Qallunaaq she treated us as equals. She was no stranger to us at all. She played with us. She hung out with us. She had a boyfriend, one of the boys in town, that sort of thing. It was the first time I had made friends with a Qallunaaq my age. There had only been adults in the settlement, the teachers, the nurses, you know.

So we were quite good friends, really good friends. I hung out with her a lot. She would come over to our house. My dad would give her a hard time. He teased her about her hair, told her he wanted to cut her hair, dye her hair black. I don't think she learned much Inuktitut, maybe a little bit, but she didn't try very hard. After all, we were all supposed to learn English at that time.

Around that time there was a thing that went on at the church. During Sunday school the preacher or a lay person used to stand up and announce who had done something wrong during the week. It wasn't always the same lay person – different adults, different lay people did it at different times. They thought that the teenagers should be taught lessons in public. It was a way of embarrassing people, shaming people into being good. That is how they dealt with bad incidents in the traditional culture, so that is how they did it in church when I was growing up.

I think there was a pressure from the church at that particular time to be a, how would you say, a "goody-two-shoes." We weren't allowed to visit the Roman Catholic people, not unless we wanted to get a reputation as a sinner. My mother's family was Catholic, my grandmother and my cousins were too, so it was a pretty big restriction for me. Usually I ignored it and visited them anyways, so I was considered a sinner.[5] Also we weren't supposed to have boyfriends at that time. We were like whores or prostitutes if we did that. There were stories always going around about bad boys. People had seen me hanging around with those boys, so I had a reputation as a bad girl. It was like "you outpost-camp tramp" kind of thing. I think that all those judgments from the adults started getting to me.

Anyways, this incident that I am thinking of happened one particular Sunday. I was about fourteen. The Sunday-school teacher stood up in front of everybody and told the whole church that I was smoking drugs. It was the early 1970s and there had been drugs around the settlement, but I didn't know anything about drugs at that time. I had only heard about drugs and their existence from Cheryl. I remember hearing my name and jumping a little on my seat. I couldn't believe it. I was so embarrassed to have my name mentioned in the church – I wasn't expecting it at all! There was no way at that moment that I could defend myself and say I didn't. I was just sitting there. I couldn't believe it was happening to me.

I was furious. I mean ... if I had done drugs that would have been one thing, but I hadn't. I remember it was spring, early spring, March or April. I remember it was light outside. I learned from the people at the church that it was the teacher's daughter who had told them that I was smoking drugs. I ran straight home from the church and grabbed my mother. I said, "Come with me." I didn't explain to her why. She followed me over to the Sunday-school teacher's house. The guy was sitting at his kitchen table. I don't know what he was doing, he was reading his Bible or having tea. He had just finished his service. I told

him that what he had said was a lie. I told him that I didn't know anything about drugs or what they looked like, or what to do with them.
My mom was just standing there behind me. She didn't say anything.
I don't remember his reaction. I don't think he said anything either. I
was crying by that point, I was so angry.

Cheryl's brother's house was just behind the Sunday-school
teacher's, just right across the street behind it. We went across to his
house after that. I remember that house had an upstairs. There was a
living room, a kitchen and bedrooms upstairs, and a basement or rec-
room downstairs. My teacher came down, probably to find out what I
wanted. I told him I wanted to speak to Cheryl. He went up again.
Cheryl came down the stairs. As soon as she got close enough, I
screamed at her, "You liar!" and punched her in the face. I was so
upset! She ran up the stairs crying. My teacher was probably wondering what the heck was going on. My mom was really shocked. She was
standing behind me and her mouth was hanging wide open. Her eyes
were really wide. She didn't know what was happening. She wasn't
used to seeing Qallunaat being treated that way. In her day they were
always treated like gods. We left. We went home.

I might have told my parents about the incident, explained what had
happened, because my parents didn't punish me at all for all the stu-
pidity that I caused. I spent the rest of the afternoon crying and being
very upset. That was not like me to scream at my Sunday-school
teacher and punch somebody. I was really upset.

After church in the evening, about eight, eight-thirty, the minister's wife
came over. Evening church service was between seven and eight. She
wanted to know what the heck was happening with me, because I was
supposed to have done choir service that evening and I wasn't there. I
didn't go to church that night. Later on the teacher came around and
wanted to know what was happening. I explained it to him and apologized. I cried on his shoulder and he held me. I never saw Cheryl again. A
few days later or a week later he sent his sister home. I guess she had been
causing all sorts of trouble besides the thing with me, something to do with
one of the boyfriends. I think that is why he decided to send her home.

I was good friends with her except for that one incident. I think I
probably still have her picture somewhere. I think that was the first
and only time I ever punched anybody.

WE MOVED HERE THE SPRING MY FATHER GOT HIS FIRST SKI-DOO

Our first trip into Pond Inlet was in 1967. Our second trip was when
we moved here. We moved here in 1972, the spring my father got his

first ski-doo. It was a Bombardier, a small one. It was yellow. I don't know what horsepower it was, fifteen horsepower or maybe something like that. The spring that we were getting ready to move to Pond Inlet, that is when he purchased it. He was working at the time, carving, I believe. I am not sure exactly what he did to get the money for it, but just before we left he purchased the machine. I remember right after he bought it I was enjoying myself terribly, ski-dooing around, having a great time within the community. I was about fifteen at the time. I remember my sister Martha and her husband came to Igloolik before we took off, and they were with us for a few days. They were getting ready to go with us to Pond. Oopah and her husband were coming as well as Simon and his wife.

Both Simon and my father had bought ski-doos, but Martha's husband didn't have one. He was going with us by dog team. My older sister Oopah had gone to Hall Beach to adopt a little child, so she was going to meet us in Pond Inlet by airplane, a Twin Otter. At that time there were only Twin Otters.

So we took off from Igloolik with our ski-doos and the dog team. The dog team fell behind, it fell quite a ways behind. We would wait for my brother-in-law at the end of the day to catch up with us. I started getting envious of my brother Solomon. They were letting him drive my brother-in-law's ski-doo with the qamutik behind it. I kept bugging my dad to let me drive the ski-doo. I had been driving it in town and I knew a little bit about how to drive one, so my father finally consented. By this time the machine had heated up quite a bit. The ski-doo used to get very hot while we were travelling. The hood was off so it would not get too warm running for so long. The muffler was not very good so it was a very loud machine. After one stop for tea, I was going to start driving.

We had our tea and I got on the ski-doo. I was going to pull the qamutik which had my father and mother and sister on it. I don't know who else was on it, maybe my mother was carrying Ida in her amautik … My brother Solomon took off, he started travelling. He didn't rush off, but he started going, and I thought I had better start the ski-doo myself. I got on the ski-doo, put on the throttle, and started going forward. I hadn't thought about the slack on the rope that led to the qamutik. I started going forward quite fast, and all of a sudden the sled I was pulling stopped the ski-doo in its tracks! I didn't think to go slow at first, I hadn't realized it was such a heavy load. It stopped suddenly, I flew forward, and my whole body went upside-down on the ski-doo. My legs were up in the air and I was bent over the steering rod on the ski-doo and my head was right next to the motor on the ski-doo. The hood was off and it was really, really loud because of the muffler. I was upside-down with my legs hanging in the air. I was stuck like that for a few minutes until my father came over and put me right-side up. That was my first experience with ski-doos and qamutiks. Looking back, it was quite funny! I was scared and shocked to be upside-down right next to the muffler with the noise of the motor in my ear.

We travelled quite a ways towards Pond Inlet, and one incident I remember quite clearly from that trip had to do with my sister Joanna's cat. It was a tiny little kitten. We had just gotten it in Igloolik. We stopped for tea, and I noticed that the kitten was on top of the qamutik when we stopped. Everyone started preparing for meal-time, getting all the grub out and lighting up the stove and everything. We were having a rest. The kids were all playing ball, and the older guys like Simon and his wife were teasing each other and stuff like that. We were all playing around in the snow beside the qamutik, and my parents were trying to make the tea and get the food out. My father thought it was a good time to ice up his sled, because it had been dragging a little. He turned the sled over, upside-down, and he added some soil and watered it like they did in the old days. He was driving with a ski-doo, but he thought that icing the sled would help it slide. It would wear less on the metal runners and make it move faster, so he did that. He put water on it while we were having our tea. This was early spring, so it took quite some time for it to freeze. By the time we finished our meal and we were ready to go, the soil and the water that he had mixed and placed on the sled was frozen. He got it all smoothed out, turned the sled right-side up, and there was the poor kitten, dead. It had been squashed under the sled. Poor Joanna, we felt so sorry for her! Her little pet kitten had just been squashed. This thing about cats having nine lives, it seemed kind of false at the time. I don't know whether Joanna felt bad back then. I never asked her. I reminded her about the story once, but I never talked to her about it again.

IN 1972 WE MOVED HERE PERMANENTLY

We visited Pond Inlet in 1967. I remember 1967 quite well, Expo year. We learned all about Expo at school. We learned with southern curriculum at that time, *Fun with Dick and Jane* books, things like that. I went to school like that until 1970. In 1970 the principal announced to us that it wasn't a federal day school any more. We were all free to do just as we pleased ... That is how the principal put it – "free to do what we wanted." We had more freedom in class after that. We started taking Inuktitut classes, but our Inuktitut classes consisted of readings from the Bible because that was the only syllabic work around. A lay person came in once or twice a week to teach us syllabics and reading from the Inuktitut Bible. Then we started taking sewing, sewing duffle socks and stuff like that in school. My mom had never taught me those things because I had always been in school. I remember when I was fifteen, just before we moved here, I was just like Sandra, lying around in my room, reading a book, sometimes for a whole day, listening to records. My mom didn't teach me much.

That year, 1967, we came to Pond Inlet to visit. My mother was in the hospital. She was in Hall Beach or Iqaluit, having Phillip, maybe. My father was all alone, and he took us all here, me, Martha, Jake, and the smaller ones, Ida and Joanna, with him. I was about ten or eleven, and my older sister Oopah was getting married. We moved to Pond Inlet to be near her. We were only here for a visit, then we went back to our shack in Igloolik.

In 1972 we moved here permanently. My mother wanted to be near her mother, my grandma Suula, before she died. My parents, I think they were the last family from around this area to come off the land. I remember travelling towards Pond Inlet from Igloolik. It was spring-time, and we had all finished our year in school in Igloolik. I think it took us about six days to get here. We had sewing machines with us, washing machines, and whatever else we could afford to bring with us. We arrived in Pond Inlet in the very early morning because we had been travelling all night, and by the time we reached Pond Inlet the weather was quite a lot warmer than when we had left. I was quite enthusiastic about moving here and thinking about what beautiful scenery there was around this area. We had visited Pond Inlet before, but I guess I had been too young to notice the scenery.

I had a friend, Oopah, who was travelling with us. She was my brother-in-law's sister, and she and I were teenagers together. I had just turned fifteen, and we came into Pond Inlet at the end of May. Both of us were wearing heavy fur clothing, and I think at the time we were kind of pretentious teenagers. We were kind of showy, and we decided that we weren't going to let anybody see us with all these caribou kamiks and heavy furs. We were embarrassed to be seen in skin cloth-ing! I remember we started walking on the far side of the road so we could get into her parents' house without anyone seeing us. It was spring and there was no snow in the middle of the roads. There was still snow all around the roads, and that is where we walked. We walked towards her father's house, and it was quite a long walk. It took us even longer walking on the snow. I remember going over to Arreak's right after we came in. We got there and everybody welcomed us to Pond Inlet.

When I got here, during the summer my parents started discussing whether I should go down to Iqaluit because that was the next grade up, Grade Nine. I couldn't go to Grade Nine here – school stopped at Grade Eight. I told them I really didn't want to go to Iqaluit. I was thinking about my boyfriend at the time, and I really didn't want to go. They gave in and let me stay here. I lived with my grandmother, my mother's mother, Suula. My grandmother's house was almost next door to my friend Oopah's house. My parents had a little house of their own. It was quite small. They didn't have any space for me. My grand- mother had room for me, so that is where I stayed. That same summer I met Josh. He was at Qaurnnak the same year I was there, 1966, but I didn't know him then. He was older than me. I only remember his brother and sister.

MARRIAGE AND FAMILY:
ALL THIS STUFF IN MY HANDS AND CARRYING LUCAS ON MY BACK

WE WENT OFF TO GRISE FIORD

In the winter of 1972 when Josh and I had been together for a few months, we went off to Grise Fiord through Resolute Bay to go to a home-economics course that we were supposed to attend. It was called a home-economics course, but it was more of a money-management course for young families. We were supposed to take the course and then come back and teach it to people here. There were only a few people that were doing it. His grandparents were living in Grise Fiord at the time, in 1972. They were some of the "Arctic exiles" – that is what they are called now. That is why they were living in Grise Fiord, because they had been moved up there from Pond in the '50s.[6] Josh's grandparents were the only relatives that we had in Grise Fiord, so that is where we stayed.

I remember my first impression of Josh's grandmother – I was quite scared of this old lady who was in the house. They had one grandchild, Samson, I can't remember exactly his age, he was maybe four or five years old. Samson had a whole bunch of gum in his room, and we stayed in Samson's room. He had a whole lot of gum and a whole lot of cereal. I don't know where he got them from, but back then it seemed to me that this family was really rich. They were rich enough so that Samson could have this huge supply of southern treats. In our family we ran out of things like that overnight. He was the only child there, the others were all adults. We stayed in Samson's room, and he had a whole bunch of these treats, and it was quite enjoyable.

One day Josh's grandmother asked me to braid something, I think it was rope for a pair of kamiks. I had braided three strands of wool

before, but I had no idea how to braid four strands. When she asked
me to do this braiding, I was scared to ask her how it was done. I was
embarrassed. I was almost sixteen, I should have known how to braid
four strands. I was old enough, but they had never taught us that in
school. I was scared to death of asking her and I was very embarrassed.

When she gave me this wool to braid, I went in the bedroom. I had
no idea what I was going to do, and Josh was with me. Josh taught me
how to braid four strands that winter in Grise Fiord. If I had known
then what I know now, I would not have been scared, because Josh's
grandmother is such a nice woman. She is very quiet. She is not talkative, she's a very nice lady. From Grise Fiord we went back to Resolute
Bay. As we were going back to Pond Inlet – this was all by airplane, a
Twin Otter – in Resolute, I got quite sick. I went to the nursing station
in Resolute Bay, but they didn't do much. When we came home to
Pond Inlet I went to the nursing station again to get a test, and I found
out I was pregnant. I had problems a few months before that, before
we went to Grise Fiord. I suspect I had a miscarriage. The nurses at
that particular time gave me birth-control pills. By the time I left for
Grise Fiord, I was on those pills. I guess I must have gotten pregnant
before I started the pills.

I REMEMBER WHEN SANDRA WAS BORN

I remember when Sandra was born. At that time when we had babies,
we were supposed to go down and have them in the hospital in Iqaluit.
She was due the end of July, and I think I left the last week in June or
the first week in July. Josh had gone to a fishing camp to do some
work, so I left before he came back. I stayed at this residence, this
home where they take in people going to the hospital. I stayed there for
a little bit and then I found out that I had an uncle there. I don't know
how I found that out – we had telephones by that time, and we had a
local operator, so I guess I had called my parents. I moved over to my
aunt and uncle's house. They were a family, so I was a lot more comfortable there than I had been in the hostel. It didn't feel so strange for
me in Iqaluit after that. My uncle looked just like my dad. It was the
first time I had seen him, and he looked just like my dad, so I was com-
pletely at home in their house. My aunt was very nice. They had all six
of their children living with them at that time except the youngest one
that they have now.

They had eggs every day, fried eggs every day for lunch. My other
aunt, my mother's sister's, her daughter Blandina, she was a very
good friend of mine. This sister of my mother's, she wasn't from
Suula, maybe from Kublu? ... Blandina and I, we were hanging

around together a lot during the month I stayed there. I didn't have anybody else to spend time with. It was her first year working for the government. She had her own apartment, so we hung around a lot together.

One afternoon – this was in July, so it was quite warm – we went out for a walk. We were picking some plants to eat. There were hardly any buildings past the high-rise in Iqaluit back then. Up in the neighbourhood they call Happy Valley now, there wasn't anything there, that's where we were. We were wandering around, just picking plants and eating. The afternoon that I had Sandra, we had been out for a long walk. I was squatting down to pick a plant. I was quite big, nine months pregnant. All of the sudden my cousin screamed behind me. I got up and ran like crazy. I hadn't run in about two months and then all of a sudden I got up and just ran like crazy, because she was screaming from fright. I thought there was a polar bear or something, and she was running beside me. She said, "There's a bee in one of those tires!" I was running just because of a stupid bee! If she had told me that it was just a bee that she was afraid of instead of screaming her head off, I wouldn't have run.

We came home. We went to her apartment, and I stayed there for quite a long time, the rest of the day. By midnight I thought it was about time I went home. It gets dark in a hurry in Iqaluit in July, and this was almost the end of July. We were looking out the window. My cousin was telling me that there were people drinking downstairs. The bar was on the main floor of her building. I didn't know that there was a bar there until then.

Anyways, I went downstairs and tried going out the front door of the building. All of a sudden I saw a person right in front of the door – there was this guy coming out from the bar, and he was trying to take a pee on the side of the building. He was hiding himself, he didn't realize that there was somebody there who saw what was going on. I thought, "Oh heck, he's going to be embarrassed!" so I closed the door again. I waited there for a few minutes and he started walking away, so I opened the door and started walking home. I started walking down the hill towards where my uncle was staying. The high-rise is on a hill, there is a little bit of a hill that you have to go down to get to where the houses are.

As I was walking down, the guy who had just been peeing, he started coming towards me! I didn't realize he had been following me because my back was turned. He started shouting my name – not my name but "Hey, you!" that type of thing. I looked back and he was quite close. He caught up to me and he said, "Hi, honey, wanna go to my house?" I was nine months pregnant! He must have been quite drunk. Anyway, he was kind of flirting with me, and he said he wanted to have sex with me and stuff like that. And I didn't know him at all! To this day I don't even know who he is. I was kind of scared, and I could smell the alcohol on him, so I walked away.

I was trying to pretend that I was not scared, so I didn't run away, I just slowly walked away. He grabbed my arm and he tried to kiss me all over, so I finally decided that I'd had enough and I pushed him away. I started running down the hill. There I was, I hadn't run for quite a few months and I sprinted twice that day! I ran all the way to my uncle's house. It was a ways away. I got home and fell asleep. I didn't have any contractions when I first got home. I fell asleep.

Then in the middle of the night, maybe two or three in the morning, I got up. I was in pain. Both my aunt and uncle were sleeping, so I went to their room and told them I was having labour pains. Since this was my first baby, I didn't know how bad the pains were going to be, so I told them as soon as I knew that I was having pains. They probably weren't all that bad. They got up and my aunt got all excited. She was pacing the room, her room. She just got up out of bed and started pacing. She didn't know what to do. She was a nervous wreck! I think she kind of realized at that point that I was very young and she was baby-sitting me. Somebody called the hospital, and a van came to pick me up.

I had just turned sixteen in April of that same year. I went up to the hospital, and I was there for the longest time, eighteen hours labour. There were people coming into the room, and I wanted to scream, "Go away, I don't know you, I don't want you in my room!"

When I first got there, there was this lady in the bed next to me. She was in the room just about to have her baby when I went in. It was the middle of the night, and she was screaming her head off and swearing at the nurses. I had just come in, I wasn't in too bad shape yet, and here was this lady next to my bed, screaming and swearing, saying terrible things to the nurses! She had an elder with her, and sometimes she'd swear at the elder. I think she was having a difficult time. It was her first baby too.

Finally I was in bad enough shape that I had to go into the delivery room. They put me on this stretcher. I was so bad off that I was screaming and I was crying, I didn't know what was happening. There was nobody to talk to. I didn't have any elders or anyone to talk to. I didn't know what was happening, whether I was dying or whether it was the real thing. I was yelling, "Josh, Josh," even though he was a thousand miles away. We went into the delivery room, and I don't remember much of what happened in there, probably because I was in a lot of pain. I screamed my head off. Sandra was a big baby.

After I gave birth to her I went into the room and I was really, really hungry. They had taken her to the nurses' station, they had this little room next to the nurses' station where they took all the babies. They put me back in my room and I was really hungry. I told them I wanted to eat something, and they had already served supper by the time they were finished with me, so they gave me a great big steak. It was really big – it covered the whole plate! It was even bigger than the ones we buy here nowadays. I ate the whole thing. I was surprised by how much I could eat. Then, after that I had a pretty full stomach, and I felt better.

I remember I could recognize Sandra when she cried. They had me take a bath every day, and every time I was in the bathtub, I could hear Sandra crying. I could recognize her from all the other babies. She was quite noisy, you could hear her all the way from the bathroom to the nursery. They made me stay in the hospital maybe three, three or four days. Nowadays they don't keep women in the hospital for very long. Back then they made you stay in the hospital for longer periods. Then I went back to my aunt's place to stay for another week, because they wanted to watch to see if Sandra developed jaundice. That's what they did at that time, they held the baby for seven days.

When I came back to Pond Inlet, I remember everyone was at the airport to meet me. It was so embarrassing to come off the plane with a baby – at sixteen, it was so embarrassing! Everyone crowded around me when I got off the plane. Everyone wanted to see what the baby looked like.

When I got home I more or less handed Sandra over to my mother-in-law, but I had fun with her. She wasn't a fussy baby. She slept all the time, she slept a lot. She'd sleep twelve hours sometimes, right through the night, not get up. I had to keep waking her up to breast-feed her. Sometimes it would be hard to wake her, I'd poke her and try to wake her up. She didn't get very fat. That was a nice spring, that year, '73. It was a beautiful spring. It was very warm, but I don't think the ice went away as quickly as it did this year. It was a beautiful spring.

WHEN I WAS HAVING MY BABIES

It didn't matter to me much when I was having my babies whether I had my babies in a hospital or at home. I don't think I cared much either way. I am kind of private about childbirth. I don't want a whole bunch of people watching me, so for me, I don't think I've ever really wanted a midwife next to my bed. When I had Mona, I decided I was staying at home, I was going to have the baby here. When I told my mother-in-law that I was having labour pains with Mona, she lost her

marbles. She called the next-door neighbour. She was an old lady, the
next-door neighbour. She called the next-door neighbour to see what
she should do. The lady told me to go to the nursing station right away.
My mother-in-law, she wasn't going to sit around and hold my hand.

I had Mona, then I didn't have any children for six years until I had
Sheila. By the time I had Sheila, the nurses were thinking that since I
hadn't been pregnant for so long, there might be complications. They
said that just to make sure that everything went all right, I had better
go to the hospital. Mona, she was getting her tonsils removed at that
time, so I went down with her to go the hospital. I had Sheila, and then
not too long after I had Dawn. Dawn was premature, so I went down
to the hospital again. This time I went as far as Montreal.

I had been sick with a very bad cold two weeks before the day that
I had to be rushed down to Montreal with Dawn. I had a very bad flu
with a very bad fever, and that's how the bleeding got started. So they
thought she had a chest infection, and that is why the baby was abort-
ing, because she was sick. I went down to Montreal because they were
trying to stop the birth from happening. I spent a week in Montreal in
this Jewish hospital, just lying down, taking this medication to stop me
from having contractions. Then they said, "Okay, you've quieted
down, go back to Iqaluit." When I got back to Iqaluit, the doctors
there still weren't sure if I was going to have the baby. They told me to
stick around until they knew for sure that I was not bleeding or going
into labour. I stuck around Iqaluit for another week. I was kind of
lethargic because I was taking all this medication to relax the muscles
around my uterus. The medication didn't help at all, because I ended
up going back to the hospital in Iqaluit to have Dawn. That was terrible. They kept trying to stop me from giving birth.

I didn't like the medication. It made me lethargic, and it gave me a
stomachache. When I went into labour for the second time, my labour
pains lasted all night and into the morning. By early morning I told the
doctor that I had enough. I told him, "Don't try to stop the contractions any more. I've had enough of this medication!" The pain wasn't
increasing, but it wasn't decreasing either. They took the IV out that
was giving me the medication, and not even fifteen minutes later I had
Dawn. She was bound and determined to come!

Dawn was born two months premature. She looked quite healthy
and fat when she was born, but she was very tiny. She was exactly three
pounds. She was small compared to the other babies, but she wasn't
skinny. I saw her when I had her, when I gave birth to her, I saw her
for about two minutes, and then they took her and rushed her away.
She went out that afternoon to Montreal. She was in Montreal for a
little bit over a month. The doctors asked me if I wanted to go down

and be with her, but I wanted to get home because Sheila was only a year old and Sandra and Mona were just kids. So I had to leave Dawn in Montreal and go back home.

They said that they wanted her at five pounds, I couldn't have her until she weighed five pounds at least. When I finally got her she was tiny, she hadn't grown much. She was five pounds, and we couldn't stretch any part of her skin. It was tight with fat. It seems like they just blew her up! And she was bald on the front half of her head because they shaved the head to put in the IVs and the monitors and all the neonatal things they use for premature babies. Also, that first month she spent in the hospital, they had been putting her head sideways. Like when she was born premature, her head wasn't fully developed, and down in Montreal they had been putting her head to the side all the time when they put her to sleep. She must have been left in a crib on her one side that whole month, because her eye got kind of droopy so she couldn't open it very well. We spent all that year exercising it, trying to help her keep it open, but she ended up being cross-eyed.

When she came home after that month, she was okay for about a year, and then she ended up developing rheumatoid arthritis. I think that's what it is called where your joints get affected and you get a fever? ... She was sick with that. This happened just when she should have been learning to walk. Her knee and shoulder were affected, so she couldn't walk. When she was just about a year old, she had to go down to the hospital again to have someone fix her arthritis. At that same time she also had eye surgery to repair the crossed eye. She ended up spending another month, month and a half in the Montreal hospital. When she was all finished with the sicknesses, she had been through surgery seven times. We were always waiting for her to heal. It was hard for me to go down with her. I was in Iqaluit when she got sick with arthritis. I was down having Lucas, so I was in Iqaluit when she was in Montreal.

I had Lucas, and then I came back to Pond Inlet. Dawn came back about a week later. So I had this brand new baby and another baby who was a year old but couldn't walk. She couldn't walk because of her arthritis. She was kind of standing up, but that was about all. Plus, she had developed an allergy to milk that I didn't know about. She had been on a bottle with formula ever since she was born, so she had developed an allergy to milk. When she got home I started giving her the milk she had before, and she had diarrhoea all week.

Around this same time when I came back with Lucas, Josh left to go on a four-week course. I was all by myself, and I had this brand new baby, this baby that couldn't walk, with diarrhoea, another baby who was almost three, plus Mona and Sandra. Mona was nine and Sandra was ten, so they were no problem. They were a big help.

Finally when I could get out of the house I went to the nursing station to ask the nurses about Dawn. They told me that the hospital had informed them when they sent her home that she had developed an allergy to milk. They hadn't told me! I had to get all these special supplies like soya-bean milk and things like that through the Co-Op. She had that allergy for the whole year she was on the bottle. Then it went away.

WHEN MY KIDS WERE JUST BABIES

I didn't work for a little while after Sheila was born, I didn't work for one year. Then I went back to work as a secretary-treasurer for the Education Council. Then I found out I was pregnant with Dawn. By the time I had Dawn, there were so many complications with her birth and trips to the hospital I stopped working again. And then I became pregnant with Lucas. It was the same year that I was pregnant with Lucas that Josh and I started talking about getting a HAP house.[7] The criteria to get assistance to build a house under this program was that the whole income of the family couldn't be more than $35,000 or $40,000 a year, so I decided not to work for that first year when we were applying for assistance. We moved into a little yellow shack that year. It was an old house. It was hard for us at first. We had been used to our nice, clean prefab unit up on the hill. It had a spacious living room and two bedrooms. When we moved into this little shack it was kind of old and dirty. It was an old building, and all the edges were dirty, and the paint was peeling off.

I remember Dawn had a big accident there. The breaker for the electricity for the building was open, there was no cover to it, and she stuck her spoon in it and got herself electrocuted. She was screaming and screaming, but I couldn't touch her because it would have just gone through me. She was standing there on top of the counter with the spoon stuck in her hand because she couldn't take it away, it was like a magnet. Finally she dropped it, and the spoon fell. That was when we first moved into that shack and we had no phone. I didn't know what to do. Josh was down the street working on the HAP house. It was summertime and I was holding her under her arms. I could smell burned hair on her head. The electricity had burned the ends of her hair. She wasn't even three. I was surprised she was okay. She was fine. It was just the smell on her head, and that was it.

I had a tough time back then, when Sheila, Dawn, and Lucas were just babies, when my kids were just babies. I already told bits of stories from the other house, about having Lucas as a newborn when Dawn was not walking and Sheila just a toddler. In this shack they were just a few months older. Lucas was just a baby. Dawn had just begun to walk. I didn't have running water in that house for the first little while. Josh fixed it later on, but for the first while I had to keep using a pail to put water into the washing machine. I got sick of it one day, so I went down to the RCMP unit to get my washing done.

I remember there was this one afternoon when I was trying to pick up my dry clothes at the RCMP's dryer and transfer my wet clothes. I was on my way over to the RCMP's and I had this big pail of washing, I had Lucas on my back, and Sheila was in the doorway crying. Dawn was with her, I think. Yeah, Sheila was crying in the doorway with Dawn. I wanted to go to them, to make them stop crying, but I didn't want to go back and get them because I had all this stuff in my hands and was carrying Lucas on my back, so I couldn't have held them anyhow. Sandra and Mona were out somewhere, and I was stuck in the middle of the road, thinking, "This is ridiculous!" So Josh put a pump in our house that winter and I did my washing at home.

That was the winter my grandfather Uyarak died. I had gone to Igloolik a few months earlier, in the summer, to show them Lucas. I remember walking behind him on the road on the way to the Bay and thinking how much my grandfather had aged. He died just a few months later. We went to Igloolik in November for the funeral and then we came back.

Josh started building our new house at the end of August. He had put in the concrete blocks for the foundation in July, before the snow. He dug under the permafrost, laid insulation, and put in the concrete. We worked on it all through the winter, and we moved into it in mid-June 1987, ten months later. Josh had a full-time job the whole time we were building it. He was never home in the evenings. He would come in after work for long enough to have a little bit of supper, sometimes only for ten or fifteen minutes, then go back out again. When the time came to start filling in the drywall, we all helped out, filling in the cracks and stuff like that. There were jokes in town about my children being white all the time. They had drywall dust on their parkas and their kamiks.

When we moved in it was all complete. I ordered all this furniture from Ikea when we moved in, a couch, a table, some beds. It cost $1,000 in freight to bring it in – I think it was more like $1,500 in freight. We moved in June. It was a nice spring day, I think it was a Saturday. I have been down South a lot, so I am used to staying in apartments or high-rise buildings, hotels, two-storey, three-storey, eight-storey buildings – like, I am really used to it. But when we moved into the house we had an upstairs room for the first time. I lay down on the bed and I thought, just for two or three minutes, my only thought was, "I am going to fall through to the floor!" It was really nice moving into the house. We finally felt like we were home.

REFLECTIONS ON A CHILDHOOD:
THEY SPENT ALL THOSE YEARS TRYING TO CHANGE ME INTO A QALLUNAAQ

I NEVER REALLY THOUGHT ABOUT MONEY

I came in from the land to go to school when I was eight years old. I don't think I ever really thought about money back then ... I knew about it, I knew what it was, but it wasn't part of my life. I never felt poor. Even when we were really hungry in my childhood, I never felt poor. We might not have had food, but it wasn't that we couldn't get it, it was just that my father wasn't hunting.

Up to the age of eleven or twelve, I never really thought about money. I remember being a kid, when I first started going to school, my aunts and uncles, I remember they had pocket money in the settlement, because they had their parents with them, but we were staying at the hostel. I had food and I had clothing to wear every day, so I didn't think about money. I never really thought about having it or not having it.

When I was about eleven or twelve years old, my parents moved into the community. I remember around that time feeling kind of poor at times. I think it mostly had to do with my age, but I remember feeling poor because I didn't have the clothing that was the latest trend, the clothing that the other young girls were wearing at that time, the bell-bottom jeans and the jewellery and stuff. I didn't have this record or tape. My father couldn't afford those kinds of things. That was when I was made to feel poor. I wasn't poor, but I was made to feel poor. You know how kids are, they tease each other all the time, "You tramp from an outpost camp" type of attitude. But that didn't last all that long.

When my parents moved in off the land, I remember money becoming more of an issue for all of us. I remember my father playing games with us – he would give us a quarter or a dime for every grey hair we pulled out of his head, stuff like that. A quarter at that time could buy a pop, a chocolate bar, and some little pieces of gum! People thought about money a lot more then. Around that same time Panarctic Oil started hiring people. Two of my brothers went to work for them.

There was a lot more money around, I noticed. People were buying ski-doos. There were more ski-doos available, and people were buying different models all the time. A big part of what I remember around that time was the alcohol. There were so many more drunks in the settlement. People were spending all their money on alcohol.

I remember when I first started living with my husband and working, it took me a long time to start thinking about money. The first year that we had Sandra, we were still living with my mother-in-law, so there wasn't any pressure for us to provide our own food or our shelter. By my standards we were living quite comfortably. We had our own room in my in-laws' house, my husband had a part-time job at the Co-Op, and he was doing very well. We had enough money to get some clothing now and then. I never felt poor at the time. Even today I don't feel poor.

I think for me I only felt money pressures when we had our second child and we moved into a little shack. When we moved out of my in-laws' house, we started having to get our own food. Before we moved out, Josh and I made a bed out of pieces of plywood. He drilled holes in it so we didn't have to buy a bed set. We brought a little table with us to our shack, that was about it. Mona was about two years old at the time. I was working at the time for a newspaper, a local newspaper here just to make extra money. After a while I switched jobs and started working for the hamlet office full time. I guess we felt like we needed the money. I think that is the first time I started really thinking about money a lot.

Things have really changed now that I have my own children. Things have changed so much from when I was a kid! My kids, they think about money every day. They are always saying things like, "Mom, do you have two dollars, three dollars, five dollars? Mom, how come you gave me only a dollar?" They are always in the Bay store or the Co-Op, seeing things they can buy. I am just thinking of my little child, Ruby, she is only three years old and she already knows what money is. She is already interested in coins.

Another thing I find with my kids and money is that if I don't have store-bought food on the table every day, my kids act like we have no food that day, no "real" food. It's called "real" food – chips and pops, pizza, hamburgers, tacos, spaghetti, that sort of thing. When we go to my mom's for lunch, my mother feeds us land food. She makes really nice cooked caribou soup. Maybe she'll have some seal fat to go with it. At certain times of the year she'll prepare a dish made with caribou fat and blueberries. If she doesn't have blueberries, she'll use raisins. For us that is dessert. So we have cooked caribou meat, a cup of tea, and dessert. That is fine by me. But if that's the only thing available, my kids will say there's nothing to eat because there's no rice, there's no fried chicken, there's no juice. They have different standards than I ever had. For them you're supposed to have toilet paper every day in your bathroom. You'll die if you don't have a toothbrush, you know, that sort of attitude. For them money is a way of life, they can't live without it. It has changed so much from when I was growing up.

THEY WANTED US TO BECOME QALLUNAAT

The stories we told – well, that I told, anyways – most of them are from a particular period. They are from the past I don't really talk about today, now that I am married with children, now that we are living in rural Canada, in small-town Canada.

These stories are about me and my life, but they aren't just my stories. I mean, they are mine, they have to do with my life, but they are the same stories a whole bunch of people my age have. It is the same with my mother's stories and the same with Sandra's. We are the same as a lot of people our ages. I don't think we are any special type of family. The details of our stories may be different, but a lot of the experiences are the same. My mother talks about how it was for people on the land. I talk more about the people who are the adults in the community right now, my generation, the Baby Boomers, the people who are making the community decisions, the politicians. The stories, most of the ones I have told anyways, they are from a transition period that we all lived through. It was very difficult for me, this period. I don't know about other people, but for me it was very difficult coming in off the land and going into school. It was difficult for me to learn when I was a child that there are other races, like the Qallunaat, who have the power, who have the authority. It was difficult for me.

When I went to school, when I came off the land, everything changed for me all at once. My parents didn't have a say anymore in the way I lived my life. When I came off the land, the people with any type of authority were Qallunaat. The teachers were Qallunaat, the principals were Qallunaat, the RCMP were Qallunaat, the administrators were Qallunaat, the nurses were Qallunaat, it was them who told us what to do. We were told to go to bed at ten o'clock at night and get up in the morning before school. Our parents used to get us to bed early when we were out on the land – they did it because they had hunting and sewing to do, not because the clock told them to. It was the teachers who taught us how to watch the clock. The nurses, they taught us that we weren't supposed to have lice in our hair. We had never thought that lice in our hair was necessarily a bad thing! When I got to town that very first day, they found lice in my hair, they took me to the nursing station and cut my long hair off. The nurses, they also taught us to take pills when we were sick, those sorts of things. The RCMP told us that we were not supposed to stay out late at night. We had a curfew at night, and if the RCMP saw us on the streets in the day, they could pick us up at any time to take us to school. They had that kind of authority. Same with the administrators, same with all of them.

Not only that but once we went to school, we had to comb our hair, brush our teeth, wash our hands, wash our faces, have breakfast, make our beds. We weren't allowed to leave the hostel in the morning until our beds were made. At the camps we used to be able to run outside when we woke in the morning, then come back a while later for some tea and bannock. It wasn't like that for us at school – we had to follow a certain routine and watch the clock. When we were in school, going to school, we had this group of people looking after us, and they weren't our parents. They acted like our parents, but they weren't our parents. It seemed to us at the time that the administrators, the nurses, the teachers, the principals, and whoever else was in authority were talking above our heads, talking about our welfare and not letting us have a say about it. They treated us like we belonged to them, not to our parents.

We didn't have a say, and our parents and grandparents didn't have a say. Well ... that is the impression I got anyways. As soon as I stepped into the school system, these rules were all forced upon me, and it was a very difficult period. They taught us a new culture, a different culture from our own. They taught us that we had to live like the white people, we had to become like the white people.

I moved in off the land and went to school when I was eight years old. That is when they started trying to teach me how to become a Qallunaaq. I don't quite know exactly how it was decided that I go to school. I think there must have been something forceful that went on for my father to let them take us away from the family at such a young age. I remember crying on his lap that first Christmas, crying for hours with my head in his lap, begging him to take me home. He said he couldn't. I don't know what happened, but it must have been forced on him to give me up and let me leave my family at that age.

That first day of school in Igloolik, when I was eight, I started doing everything in English. English was all around us. It wasn't so much that we were punished when we spoke Inuktitut – it might have been that way in earlier years, but there didn't seem to be that pressure for us. It was just that all there was at school was English, so we were more or less forced to learn it. The teachers were brand new in town, they were all from the South, and they didn't know any Inuktitut. We had to communicate with them. Also, all of the material was in English. *Fun with Dick and Jane, Dick, Jane, and Spot the Dog* – those books were what we were learning from, so we had to learn English pretty quick.

We had to learn to act according to Qallunaat standards and codes of ethics too, "thank you, excuse me, pardon me," that sort of thing. You say a sentence, and then you say "please." I could never remember "please." And like I said, there was a schedule to follow all the time. We had to be up by seven, get out of bed, comb our hair, and wash our face. We never did this in camp! Maybe we combed our hair once in a while but not every day. At school we would have breakfast, have recess mid-morning, go to lunch, have recess mid-afternoon, go to supper, have maybe a little bit of free time, and then be back in bed every night. All of that was kind of forced on us because they wanted us to become Qallunaat. We even had to wear skirts in school. They used to get pretty cold sometimes. We weren't allowed to go to school in our caribou clothing, even if it was freezing outside. We even had Brownies and Girl Scouts when we were young. We even had the uniforms.

When I was young I used to have dreams about my future, about what I wanted to be when I grew up. I always thought of people from the South, movie stars and musicians like the Supremes. They were my idols! I would have given anything to be able to sing like them, or look like them, or be as popular as them at that time. People loved Elvis Presley. I wasn't too crazy about him, but other people were. Then there were movie stars like Clark Gable and Tony Curtis. We fell in love with those guys.

There were a lot of different things going on back then, things going on to make us look up to the Qallunaat. We were taught in school that it was Columbus who discovered America. We were told that Franklin and Frobisher discovered Frobisher Bay. There was this mentality that Columbus discovered America, therefore he discovered you, you came from him, that type of thing. Frobisher discovered Frobisher Bay and all this area, so we kind of owe something to him, we are like his children. It wasn't said literally, but that was the mentality. We were supposed to look up to him. We grew up thinking that we should try to be Qallunaat, and that is why we had Qallunaat idols, idols like the Supremes, like Elvis, like Frobisher. We didn't have Inuit idols, we weren't told at school about people like Attagutaaluk who almost starved to death in this area – our heroes were all Qallunaat. It is difficult even today to change that mentality, to change it even to a point where you think, "I am an Inuk, I am a good enough person as I am." When we were growing up, the Qallunaat were the better people. We

were supposed to look up to them. You didn't visit their houses unan-
nounced, you had to knock when you went in, you had to say "please"
and "thank you" if you were talking to a Qallunaaq. It was like we
were bowing to royalty. We even had to sing "God Save the Queen"
every day in school, "God Save the Queen" and "Oh, Canada." That
is why I got mad at Trudeau when I was young. I was mad at the
authority he represented. I don't mind him now, but back then I was
pretty angry.

That whole time from when I was eight to when I was about thirteen or fourteen, all my learning was geared towards the Qallunaat
way of life, learning how to speak the language the Qallunaat wanted
us to speak, learning the mannerisms and ethics and morals that fit
Qallunaat standards. I am not saying that this was totally bad. It might
have been good for some people, but not for me, maybe for someone
else. Education and learning a new culture is good in itself, but at that
time it was forced on us, we didn't have a choice. For example, today
if I decided that I wanted to learn about the French culture, I might
decide to go live in Paris, learn about the French language and their
customs, I would be quite interested in that! But it was different back
then because it was forced on me, I didn't have a choice. The standards
of living today have been set by the Qallunaat. All that changes your
life after a while.

❀ ❀ ❀

It is only within the last few years that I have matured to a point where
I feel that I have a choice about how I want to live. Like, when I say
that I think that I have a choice now, I am thinking about both the new
and the old culture. Now I have a choice which culture I want to learn
about. Lately I have been learning all that I can about the old culture.
They didn't teach us much of that in school.

In just the past few years I have really taken an interest in sewing. I
picked it up when I went out with Josh in the middle of winter in a
down parka and I thought that I was going to freeze to death. I almost
burned my face off, it was so cold. All of my early years, before I
moved in, I had caribou clothing. When I moved into town, I think I
forgot how cold it can get out there. Even down jackets are kind of
useless in severe winters up here. Well, in town they are okay, but if
you are going to go out on the land for six or eight hours, or if you are
going to spend a whole day outside, Qallunaat clothing is very cold,
especially for your feet because they are touching the snow. All this surprised me. I didn't know how cold it gets because I had been in school
in a warm hostel all the winters since I was eight. I decided not long

after I went out that time that I had better start learning how to sew caribou skins. We need caribou skins to keep warm. Josh, he needs them because he hunts every weekend. He is not about to start staying here in town and buying steaks at the Bay. It is up to me to sew for Josh and for my kids.

My mother, for the past few years she has been teaching me how to prepare and sew with skins, caribou skins. She loves doing caribou skins. Other skins, she is not too keen on them, but she loves working with caribou fur, doing different designs with them, making different types of clothing with them. She teaches me all that. I have also learned a lot about sealskins from my mother-in-law and from Josh's aunt too. I still don't know how to do caribou kamiks, but I know about the mitts and the parkas and the wind pants. I know how to prepare the skins and sew them up. Also, just recently I learned how to do caribou-fat dessert. Sometimes it is called Eskimo ice cream. We make it with blueberries. Just recently I learned this. How old am I ... thirty-six? If I had known how to make this when I was fourteen or fifteen, just when I started having children, my children would have been used to eating it. They would have been comfortable eating it. It is the same with other traditional foods, and it is the same with learning how to sew. I do it and I realize that our traditional culture is still very much a part of our lives.

Us parents today, we were brought up to be assimilated. Our children are being brought up the same way that we were brought up ... kind of ... almost ... We aren't teaching them that Qallunaat are better people ... we are not teaching them that any more, but the standards of living and Qallunaat ethics are still there as a pressure for them. It seems as if, just like we were taught to throw ourselves in the Qallunaat culture, we are forcing that same culture on our children. Our children all go to school. I insist that my children be home at night. I am always telling my kids to clean their hands, to clean their rooms. I wash their clothes. Even when I was first married, almost all of my life I was told that I had to try to be a Qallunaat, so when I had my babies, I read Qallunaat books which showed me how to raise them, books like *Canadian Family*. There are others. I think I still have the books somewhere. I didn't learn about childbirth and child-rearing from my parents. I didn't have time. I was in school all the time, and I didn't see my parents. We learned in school that we had to try and unlearn what we were first taught by our parents, things like no bed-times, eating when we wanted to, the way we cleaned ...

So when it came time to have our kids, we went to Qallunaat books to try and find out what we needed to do to be good parents. We learned about things like bottle feeding, Pablum, straining food, bottled milk, apple juice, Pampers, diapers, ways to clean the baby, whatever. I am not against doing those things. I am not going to literally have my child dirty or underfed or whatever. But I wonder sometimes, if Sandra had been fed real meat – "real" meat, the word makes me laugh – country-food meat when she was four or five months old, country food when she started teething, I wonder if I had raised her in a bit more of a traditional manner with values from the Inuit culture, I wonder whether she would have had more of a desire to keep the Inuit culture herself, learn about the Inuit culture. I am thinking about things like eating country food, using caribou fur, things like that. I don't know ... I don't know whether all the learning I did when I was a child was a good thing or a bad thing.

Like I said before, I feel as if I have a choice now. I am learning how to sew skins, speaking Inuktitut as much as I can. I am making traditional foods like caribou-fat ice cream, things like that. After all of that learning I did in school, after all those years learning how to be a proper Qallunaaq, I have decided now that this is the kind of lifestyle I want to have. I seem to have a choice now, and I am becoming more traditional. There are people who are a little bit younger than me who are very confused. They don't know what culture they value most, they are stuck. They can't hunt, not because they can't, it is just that they don't understand the importance. They don't sew traditional clothing. They don't understand the importance.

It is not that I hate the Qallunaat. I was always a bit of a rebel growing up, so I never thought that Qallunaat were the perfect human beings, I have never thought that in my whole life, but I have never hated them. I have had some very good friends in my life who have been Qallunaat. There was a nurse from Montreal who was here for a while. She was black, but she was Qallunaat because she spoke the English language. Also, I had a good friend, Cheryl, when I was fourteen. I don't even have any hatred towards Qallunaat who were a part of my life when I was growing up, the teachers and the administrators who were here. I have nothing against them. I don't even remember who they are. I don't hate the Qallunaat, but sometimes, though, I get angry. I get angry not at the specific individuals but at the people who decided to do that to us back then. Those people, I have no idea who they were, the people who decided to move us all off the land, but it is them who I get angry at.

I am trying to say this very clearly ... I think about all those incidents in my life, I think about my life now and how I am trying so hard to learn things from the old culture, things like sewing skins, making traditional foods, learning about my relatives, all these things. I think of all this information that I am trying so hard to learn now, that I really should have learned as a child. Then I think of the life my children have now, school, the schedules, TV, video games, junk food, all the Qallunaat values and expectations. When I look at all that, when I put it all together, I start to question whether or not it was such a good thing to be totally immersed in Qallunaat culture. I mean, looking back and hearing my parents' and grandparents' stories, what is so bad about my own culture, what is so wrong with Inuit culture, that it has to be removed? Why did I spend almost all of my life trying to get away from it? It's like ... they spent all those years trying to change me into a Qallunaaq, and they couldn't. Was my life wasted?

That is about it ... I guess we are done.

Apphia Agalakti Awa in the living room of her house in Pond Inlet,
summer 1991. (Photograph, Nancy Wachowich)

An air shot of Pond Inlet, summer 1991. Apphia Awa's house was at the top of the hill, before the road that heads in the direction of the oil reservoirs and Mount Herodier. Rhoda and Josh Katsak live along the beach, a few houses down from the old Hudson's Bay Company store (the white building on the waterfront) and the RCMP detachment (the building beside it). The two schools sit at the top of the hill, alongside the hamlet office, nursing station, and Anglican Church on the northeastern edge of the settlement, past the long road running parallel to the beach. (Photograph, Nancy Wachowich)

Pond Inlet, summer 1991. A shot taken from the water of the original Hudson's Bay Company Post. The 1991 HBC staff house sits to its left. The small white building on the far right is the old Roman Catholic mission, which burned in 1994. (Photograph, Nancy Wachowich)

Apphia Awa beside her house in Pond Inlet, spring 1993. A polar bear skin is being stretched and dried against her neighbour's house in the background. (Photograph, Nancy Wachowich)

Apphia Awa and her husband, Mathias Awa, Spring 1993. Awa is wearing his hamlet employee coveralls, hard-hat, and safety glasses. (Photograph, Nancy Wachowich)

Apphia Awa and Rhoda Katsak, spring 1993. They are standing beside
Apphia's canvas tent which is pitched next to her house in Pond Inlet. She
used this tent as a cool and quiet place to prepare and sew traditional skin
clothing and pass on these skills to young people. (Photograph, Nancy
Wachowich)

Apphia and Sandra's kamiks (skin boots), 1993. (Photograph, Nancy Wachowich)

Apphia's grandchildren, John Awa and Ruby Katsak, spring 1993, outside her house in Pond Inlet. (Photograph, Nancy Wachowich)

Rhoda Katsak and her children, spring 1993, on a weekend day trip by snow-mobile and qamutik to the old coal mine near Pond Inlet. *From left to right*: Sandra Katsak, Mona Katsak with Terry in her amautik, Silas Katsak (a cousin), Rhoda, Dawn, Ruby, and Lucas. (Photograph, Nancy Wachowich)

Mona Katsak and her son Terry Milton, spring 1993, the same day. Mona's caribou-skin amautik was designed and sewn by Apphia. (Photograph, Nancy Wachowich)

Pond Inlet, the beach road, spring 1997. The Katsak house is among a group of two-storey beach houses to the left. Apphia's brother Maktaaq's house is on the right side of the road. (Photograph, Nancy Wachowich)

Nancy Wachowich, spring 1997. (Photograph, Kerri Wylie)

PART THREE

✣ ✣ ✣

Sandra Pikujak Katsak, 1993.
(Photograph, Nancy Wachowich)

Sandra Pikujak Katsak

�֎ ֎ ֎

A lot of times I really don't know what to do. I think about a career,
about having a family, about acting Inuit or acting Qallunaat.
I really don't know what I'll do.

INTRODUCTION

Sandra is the oldest of Rhoda's six children. She was born on 20 July 1973 at Iqaluit's Baffin Regional Hospital, when her mother was sixteen. She has lived her entire life in the settlement. As one of the oldest grandchildren in the settlement on both sides of the family, she was partially raised by her father's mother, Angutainuk Katsak, and feels close to both sets of grandparents. Sandra attended school in Pond Inlet beginning in kindergarten and skipped several grades during her elementary years. She remained in Grade Nine for three years between 1986 and 1989 and then continued with the rest of her age group into high school. Halfway through her last year of high school she stopped to take a part-time job. At the time that we began recording her life history, she had recently returned to school to complete the last two courses of her high-school diploma.

Sandra was nineteen years old when we began working together. A kind, sensitive, and introspective person, she described in her narratives problems faced by women her age who try to juggle the values and demands of Inuit and Qallunaat cultures. Like those of her mother and her grandmother, Sandra's life stories are honest and personal. She talks about her childhood, the pressures of school, and the anxiety she feels poised between "acting traditional" and "making it in the modern world." Her stories reflect upon hunting, smoking, drugs, health, religion, her relationships with her grandparents, her trips on the land, and her trips south. Sandra's stories provide insight into the perspectives and challenges faced by teenage women in contemporary Inuit settlements. When I initially spoke to her about participating in this project, she said, "It will be good for people to know what is happening up here with the younger people."

During most of our interviews Sandra was working part time as a receptionist and attending high school. She spent much of her free time helping care for her little sisters and brother, going to teen dances at the community hall, reading, watching NHL hockey games on CBC Television, and learning to sew caribou and sealskin mittens and kamiks. She arrived at my house for our first recording session wearing a hockey jacket, jeans, and kamiks, with her three-year old sister Ruby in tow. We sat around for a few hours, ate potato chips, listened to music, played with Ruby, and talked about our project, about life histories, and about other things while she drafted out her opening story in a notebook she had brought with her in a bag.

GROWING UP IN THE SETTLEMENT: I AM THE OLDEST

MOST PEOPLE JUST CALL ME SANDRA

My name is Alexandra Pikujak Qiliqti Katsak. I was born on the 20th of July, 1973, at Iqaluit's Baffin Regional Hospital. I am named after my maternal grandfather's late sister, Pikujak, and after my paternal grandfather's late father, Qiliqti. Most people just call me Sandra. There are six children in my family, five girls and one boy. I am the oldest.

My mother, Rhoda Kaukjak Awa, was sixteen and my father, Joshua Inuksuk Katsak, was twenty-three when I was born. They met at the federal day school in Pond Inlet, I think. My father said he started Grade One at the age of fourteen. He went on until Grade Eight or Nine. My mother quit school at Grade Eight when she became pregnant with me. When I ask her, though, she always tells me she didn't quit. The federal day school in Pond Inlet only went up to Grade Eight or Nine, and she would have had to go to a different community to finish her schooling. She just didn't want to leave. My father, I think he did go for a while. I hear a few stories of him going to Churchill, Manitoba, but that is all I know.

I have been living in Pond Inlet, Mittimatalik, all my life.[1] I am the eldest grandchild on my father's side and one of the eldest on my mother's side. Being the eldest gives you the advantage of knowing your great-grandparents before they die. I got to know Suula, my mother's maternal grandmother. I also got to know Uyarak, my mother's paternal grandfather, and Hannah, his second wife, who is still alive. They were married when my grandfather was very young, just an infant really, so she adopted Awa and treated him like he was her very own. My father's maternal grandmother, Tatiggaq, is the only great-grandparent on his side that I have known. She is still alive. My mother's parents, Apphia and Mathias Awa, have twelve children. My father's parents, Ishmailie and Jokepee Katsak, had six children. Two have died, so now they have four.

When I was a child, every year on birthdays my mother used to tell us stories about the day we were born. This story is kind of short. It is about when I was born, July 20th, 1973. My mother was sixteen. She lived in Pond Inlet and she had to go down to Iqaluit to have me. She went alone. She stayed at a stranger's place. I don't recall the names she mentioned. She didn't know them very well. When I was born she was all alone and she was scared. She was very young. She was just sixteen. I was her first baby and she didn't really know what to do. She was lying down on a hospital bed with me when this old man accidentally came in. He saw how young she was. He looked at her and then at me and he said, "I could keep the baby for you." He thought she was too young to have a child. My mother didn't say anything. I think she was too scared of him. I think she thought he was drunk. He was really old, and she was kind of scared because she didn't know him or what to do. She kept me in her arms, and the man just kept on staring at her, and then he finally closed the door and he left. That is all I know about that story.

I remember lots and lots of things from back then. When I start saying "back then" or "at the time," I am referring to the mid 1970s, that would be my early childhood. I remember the first house we moved into, just my parents, Mona, and I. I was four and Mona Lisa was two. Up until then we were living with my father's family. There were nine or ten of us living at my father's parents in a three-bedroom house. There are three main sections to Pond Inlet – Qaiqsuarjuk, the cliff area, Mittimatalik, the beach area, and Qaqqarmiut, the upper hill area. We were in Qaiqsuarjuk, the oldest part of town. I remember there was an old photo of my grandfather, Ishmailie Katsak, in a group picture. He is standing with a group of men that he worked with at a small coal mine a few miles from Pond Inlet. After that he became a sealskin trader for the Hudson's Bay Company. I would assume the mine closed down. Jokepee, my grandmother, would fondly tell me how he was a good hunter and made money trading the skins. The only recollection I have of him was as a stock clerk at the Bay. He would bring home sodas for us children after work. After some years he switched stores and started working at the Co-Op as a stock clerk again. He retired five years ago. My grandmother, Jokepee, has been a janitor at the health centre for the past fifteen years or so. She became a janitor after my family moved out of their house, and she is still working.

Both my grandparents do not have formal educations, but they have learned some things about reading and writing and English from the Bible. I am not very clear on this, but I think maybe at one point they did go to school. Jokepee told me once, just once, how she learned to read a little. We were in the bathroom, and we were scrubbing and cleaning. She picked up a Cow Brand baking soda box and read the English to me. I was very surprised! I asked her how she knew English writing. She told me they taught her to read a little when she was a child. I knew they had learned the Inuktitut alphabet as children. They learned syllabics from the Bibles given to them as kids.[2] Until she picked up that Cow Brand box, I didn't know she knew English.

My mother's family, the Awas, live just down the road from my father's parents. My mother's father, Mathias, has been a garbage-truck driver and pick-up for as long as I can remember. He is seventy-three and is still going at it. It does not look like he is slowing down at all. He also works around the hamlet garage working on heavy machinery. Apphia used to work as a janitor at the hamlet office and at the airport before her health got bad. Her health got bad when she got older, so now she stays at home.

I remember back when I was growing up, I was with my grand-mother all the time, my father's mother. I practically lived at her house until I was a teenager. I was really close to my mother's parents too, but Jokepee, she was like a mother to me. I remember my mom. I don't think I was all that dependent on her. I tried to be independent from her. I was proud of her, I was proud of her having a job, and I wanted her to think I was capable of taking care of myself and my sister. My mom was working a full-time job when I was growing up. She was working as the assistant manager at the hamlet office. My father was working too. He worked fixing up houses for the Housing Association. He is a carpenter. He was also a volunteer firefighter. He is now the deputy fire chief. When I was about ten, he switched jobs and left the Housing Association to work for the GNWT's Department of Public Works. He is still working there.

I don't think I cried much as a kid when my mom went away. Like I said, I was pretty attached to my grandparents. We also had a very good babysitter who lived very close, just next door. She took care of us when my parents went to work. I remember when my mom picked me up after work to take me home, I used to be really glad to see her. I remember sitting on her lap watching TV.

I remember the day that we moved out of my grandmother's house and into a house of our own. I was four and my mother was twenty. She was the age I am now ... The house had a slanted roof and a big slanted window on the front. Those same types of houses are still around now, but they are used as sheds for clothing and equipment and stuff. When we moved in I was so proud of our new home. I wanted to fix the porch floor, I remember hammering nails into it. It had one big room at the end of the house, the kitchen and the living room were at the other end, then it had one small bathroom. My father made a wooden bed, and they got nice new furniture, a couch, and a record player with a dome cover. Our house was above the creek.

My sister Mona, Mona Lisa Inuguk is her full name, she was born on the 1st of June, 1975. We are eighteen months apart. I was born and my mother got pregnant right after. I remember being with her all the time as a kid. I remember when Sheila was born, Sheila Suula. It was in 1983. She was different. She had big eyes compared to all of us. She was really pretty. When Dawn was born in 1984, Dawn Nuqallaq, my mom was away in Iqaluit for a while. It seemed like a long time, and I missed her. I was over at my grandparents when I heard Dawn was born. She was a girl. My grandparents heard the news and said, "Oh no, another girl!" I was so happy that Mom had another baby, it didn't matter to me that she was a girl. I couldn't express my joy, though, because everyone was saying, "Oh no, another girl!" Dawn was born cross-eyed and had to go down to Montreal for surgery. My mother came back, we went to the bedroom where she laid her on the bed. She was born premature so she was really tiny. We looked at her and they left the next day. Dawn didn't come home for a long, long time. She had an operation on her knee and her eye. Mom and Dawn went away for a long, long time. When my mother came back without Dawn, I thought Dawn had been adopted out, and I didn't think we'd ever see her again. She was down at the hospital in Montreal. I remember her coming home with her eyes still crossed, so she had to go back to Montreal again.

After Dawn came, Lucas Nattiq was born in 1985. Mom was away in Iqaluit again and phoned with the news. Everyone was really happy because my mom finally had a boy. I was happy for my mom because she had a boy, and nobody would bother her any more about having girls all the time. It was kind of tough on my mom having girls, she was supposed to have boys. My mother's sixth and last child was another girl, Ruby Inuutiq. Ruby was born on the 18th of March, 1990. She will be four this year.

THE FIRST TIME I REMEMBER CAMPING

The first time I remember camping it was winter, but it wasn't that cold. I remember frost coming out of our mouths in the tent. I was about two years old. It was my first long trip so I thought we were camped really far away from the settlement. Apparently we were just five miles away.

We were fishing, me, my parents, and Mona. We set up a tent near a big hill, and my dad went hunting. My mother was telling stories about my father and how he was catching fish and geese. She was trying to teach us about hunting. My parents brought a tape-recorder with them on that trip and they taped us singing and talking baby-talk. We listened to that when we were older and laughed. I remember seeing my father coming down a hill carrying a ptarmigan or something like that. I thought that he walked the whole world, far, far away, to catch that ptarmigan, and I was so relieved he came back. Even though I was so young, I remember the feeling that I had then, my mother telling stories to me and my baby sister, and my father coming down that hill with the ptarmigan.

THE DAY MY FATHER'S YOUNGER BROTHER DIED

I remember the day my father's younger brother died. I was just a kid, but that is one incident I remember quite clearly. I was living with my grandparents on my dad's side, and I hadn't seen my parents for a long time. I was playing with my cousins on the living-room floor, and my grandparents were sitting on the couch. My parents came in and I ran up to greet them. My dad, he said something to my grandparents about the police. Everything got chaotic. I was trying to listen, but everyone started going crazy. My parents started crying, and my cousins all ran out of the house. I went outside with them. I was pestering them, asking them what had happened. Looking back, I must have sounded quite rude. I was asking them and asking them, and then my cousins told me that my uncle had died.

My uncle, they said he had committed suicide while taking pilot training in Iqaluit. He was twenty-seven years old. My grandmother had to fly to Iqaluit to identify the body. I remember the funeral took place a few days later, when the first snow came. We had a new minister at the time, and I remember during the graveyard service, I was thinking about how the minister was new and didn't know my uncle. I remember thinking that he shouldn't be there doing my uncle's funeral because he didn't know him.

There was an oriental tourist and photographer in town at that time.

During the long days after the funeral, he was at Grandma's. No one was minding him, he was just sitting around. He had his camera with him, and after a while he started taking pictures of people crying. He took one picture of Grandma sitting on the sofa. She was really worn down. Grandpa got really upset at this, he took the camera and started smashing it on the floor, cursing. The photographer tried to take the camera back from Grandpa before it got broken, but someone stopped him so he just watched.

Since then I have been quite apathetic whenever there is a funeral. There have been lots of deaths in town since then, but I haven't been to a funeral since then. I don't go to church that much anymore either. It always reminds me of that.

MY FIRST IMPRESSION OF THE SOUTH

My first impression of the South is from when my mother and I went to Toronto when I was seven. The thing I remember most about that trip south was the smell in the air and Coke sold everywhere. I was happy about that. The smell was very different than in the North. It was really hot down there, and there were lots of insects, there were lots of flies and crickets at night. I remember long drives and being so hot I had to wear pyjamas during the day. I remember golf balls in big baskets and swamps with frogs. I remember going shopping, and my mother bought me a Barbie doll in a swimsuit. I remember seeing so many trees. I tried to climb one but there were little insects on it. I remember seeing lots of vegetable gardens and learning how to peel corn. Mom and I tried to get around by ourselves but lots of times we got lost. I remember nice people helping us out.

My mother had a friend there at that time, Paul, I think he was an exchange student and a friend of my parents, and he invited her down there. My mother was supposed to go alone, but I was crying a lot so she took me with her. I don't remember that part, crying to go. You'd think I would remember that part – crying a lot. We went to Mississauga, and then after a while we drove a long ways and we went to his parents' place.

His mother, I thought she was very strict. I was patting her puppy and slapped his bum. Did she ever scold me! It was scary at first, but I wasn't too appalled. I was pretty used to Qallunaat ways and accepted them. It seemed like that was the way things were down South.

NARY AND I, WE GREW UP CLOSE

My grandma Apphia adopted a newborn a year prior to my birth. They named him Nary. He was the first adopted one in her family and the last of her children. He was number twelve. Nary and I, we grew up close. Some people thought he was spoiled, but he was always good to me, he always showed his goodness to me. We were really close. My grandmother, she adored him. He was the youngest, so he was treated very specially. He was even spoiled a little. He would lie down on the couch and say, "Mom, I want food, bring me water, bring me this, bring me that," and she would do it for him. Nary and I, we spent a lot of time together. It seemed as if everyone in my family, my aunts and uncles, were all into Mona. I felt left out a lot of the time. Nary, he always made sure I got some attention. When we were kids, all of my grandmother's children and grandchildren, we always helped ourselves to the food she prepared at lunch. There was always some shuffling. Nary, he was like the king of the house. Whenever I went to my grandmother's for lunch, Nary made sure I got food.

When we became teenagers, Nary became really protective of me with boys. He was a grade above me at school. Whenever I complained just a little about boys, he became really angry. When he became a preteen he started experimenting with drugs. He was into sniffing and drinking, smoking cigarettes. I was always curious about that kind of stuff, but whenever I asked him about drugs he wouldn't tell me anything. He told me that I shouldn't try myself. I was just curious but he didn't want to talk about it with me. He didn't want me to start. One time I visited him and saw him and a friend sniffing. His friend wanted me to sniff but Nary didn't want me near it. That friend kept persisting so I did, and Nary didn't like the idea very much. He got pretty angry.

When I was growing up, my grandmother, my father's mother, and my father, they always told me not to take drugs, not to smoke. They were really strict about that and I was afraid of them at that time so I tried not to get involved with that kind of stuff. My father is scary about that kind of stuff. For the past ten years or so Nary has been away a lot. After he was about thirteen or fourteen he was in juvenile detention centres and correctional centres. I never got to see him much after that.

WHEN WE WERE OUT ON THE LAND

I remember one story about when we were out on the land. It happened out on the ice, near an iceberg. I was with my grandparents and my uncle Nary, the youngest uncle. He is only one year older than me. We were on a trip headed across the ice, and we had four hours to go. We stopped for a while to take a rest, and we were having some tea and bannock, just the four of us. After some time my grandfather started packing the Coleman stove and the cups. I guess we were taking too much time for Grandpa's taste because he suddenly began to tell us to hurry up. We had to zip up our wind pants and scramble up on the qamutik. At this time my uncle decided to go to the bathroom. He took off his jacket and put it on the qamutik. He had to get through all his extra clothing. He had to un-zip his wind pants, then his jeans. My grandmother and I waited patiently on the qamutik thinking he would get on in time.

Without even looking back, my grandfather turned on the ski-doo. Us kids, we always loved this part. While the snowmobile and the qamutik slowly started moving, revving up, we would run behind the qamutik, even though we were supposed to be safely on already, and we'd compete to see who could run the longest before the snowmobile was going full throttle. It wasn't usually a very long run.

My uncle must have thought it would be like that for him because he didn't even move when the snowmobile sounded. Grandfather started driving and didn't look back at the qamutik behind him ... so we kept going and going. Still my uncle was peeing and peeing. It was not until my uncle was almost just a speck against the huge iceberg. He was trying to zip up his jeans, his wind pants. He started running for dear life! My grandmother and I were screaming at my grandfather to stop the snowmobile. It was not until he heard our screams that he stopped the machine.

This is the way my grandfather was raised. Out on the land and back in the past, everyone had to learn to get ready quickly. You were always supposed to be aware of what is going on, never let the others wait. There was always an urgency to get somewhere, whether you were going home, going to a new campsite. It is because we used to have to follow the land's changes. It might not be good travel conditions later on. Things like climate, ice, and water conditions can change so quickly.

MY ELEMENTARY YEARS

When I first went to school, I wasn't that scared. I wasn't surprised or amazed about the school. My uncles and aunts were in school ahead of me, and I sort of knew what to expect. Before I started, my mother took us, me and my sister, to the school, just to see what it was like. We went in and looked at the kindergarten class. There were two doors in that class. They were closed, but they had glass windows so I saw what was happening in there. My mother said that is what we were going to do. I don't know what happened but I got scared. I didn't want to leave my mom and Mona. I started crying. I got scared, just for a little bit.

When I went to kindergarten class that fall, I was shy and nervous. Our teacher came up to me and told me not to be scared. She told me her name was Sophie. I was looking at her hair, her hair was curly, and I had never seen curly hair before on an Inuk. She introduced me to her son who was also starting kindergarten. He was half Inuk and half Qallunaaq and I was really interested in what he looked like. We became friends and I wasn't so scared after that. We were neighbours so we visited each other quite a bit.

During my elementary years almost all of my teachers were Inuit. Our principal at that time in those early years, he was a Qallunaaq. He had a family. In Grade Two my first Qallunaat teacher was the principal's wife. She was pretty excitable, she was fun to be with. She would talk loudly and laugh a lot. After school or during recess I would watch her secretly. I wanted to see if she would kiss the principal at school. The only thing I ever saw her do was hug her husband. I was pretty disappointed.

I remember my Grade Two teacher very well. Today she teaches my younger brothers and sisters. She still looks very young. She is very pretty. I remember that year, in Grade Two, we had a Christmas concert. I was the Virgin Mary, and one of the boys in the class was Joseph. We just sat on the floor in front of the manger, but I was so shy. I wasn't trying to be shy. There were so many people looking at us that I just stared right ahead. All the other classmates sang behind us. All I could think about was my mom. I was wondering where she was in the crowd. I wanted her to see me.

I never went to Grade Three. I skipped Grade Three and went on to Grade Four when I was eight. I began going to the same classes as my uncle Nary. I made sure that I sat behind him or close to him. I was with older kids and I was pretty scared. I was eight years old. I was shy because there were so many older people in my class. After a while all the older kids, they started noticing me, paying attention to me, and I started hanging around them. I remember this one girl, she always wore eye-liner. One day she took me to the washroom and asked me if I would like to put some eye-liner on my eyes. I said, "No thank you." She kept insisting, so I finally said okay. She watched me do it and she nearly laughed her head off. That is about all I remember of those years.

GRADE FIVE

Grade Five is a grade I remember really well. I remember there were about twenty-five people in my class, and I became really close to all of them. We hung around a lot at school. I thought that nothing would change. That year, our teacher, he was a French-Canadian. He could speak French and he always included some French things when he was teaching. He had a gold ring, a big thick gold ring on his left hand. He had long hair and a long beard. We played with his beard a lot, because it was kind of a wonder to us. Sometimes after school he would put a pencil or a pen through his beard and it would just stay there. One summer he cut his hair and his beard, and we were disappointed. He looked like a totally different person.

I remember in the beginning of October he promised to read us a horror story for Halloween. On Halloween day at school we had a party and then he told us a story. I remember that party because we made a little tent you could go into. It was like a horror house. There was macaroni in containers and we pretended they were brains. The story that he read after the party went on and on until the middle of April. It was a very scary story and it went on for a very long time. He told it once a week. One of my favourite things about school that year was the horror story. It became a special event. Everyone got excited on the day he would tell the story. We would talk about the story all through the day, we couldn't wait to hear it. The story was about vampires and people with leprosy. The vampire in the story was a very fat vampire.

As this story went on I began to believe that vampires were real – not real now but a long time ago. I looked up vampires in books, I did research on vampires. The books said that vampires were regular people, they were people who had rare diseases. It was the people around them that made them into scary things. They made up things about them. This teacher told us that a long time ago in Europe people who had leprosy would be treated horribly. They were treated like garbage. Lepers were thrown into colonies, into prisons, so that they couldn't get out. They would be treated like prisoners. It is just amazing what people did back then. Vampires, the books said, were sort of like lepers. They had rare skin diseases and they couldn't go out into the sunlight because it would ruin their skin. Their blood wasn't that good, so they had to depend on other people's blood. The books said that vampires had normal teeth, they didn't have big fangs.

I started to think about vampires a lot during that year. I guess a lot I was so interested in them because of my eczema, my bad skin, because of my bad blood. During that year I was really into medical things, and it was around that same time that I started thinking about being a doctor. Since then I have read everything I can about medical things.

Anyways, I remember in that Grade Five class I had a lot of class-mates I became really close to. I had a big rivalry going with a boy in my class, Simon, he was the principal's son, we competed all the time. Sometimes things got so tense we would start hitting each other. He would talk pretty mean to me during class, when the teacher wasn't looking, and I would throw things at him. One time I hit him pretty hard with a stick and the teacher told me I was going to get the "golden hand." He said that I was going to get a spanking but all he did was scold me in front of all my classmates. I was so embarrassed! Having him yell at me like that, it was worse than getting the "golden hand." Simon and I stopped fighting a little while after that.

Simon and I competed all through Grade Six, then in Grade Seven the class split up. Some of the kids moved away, some went to different classrooms. My friend Simon moved back down South and finished high school there. I had no more competitors. It seems like a long time ago now ... I remember thinking back then that we would all be together forever, that we would all graduate together. Two of the kids from that year have committed suicide. Terry committed suicide two years ago in March. I don't know what happened, I hadn't seen him since Grade Six. Eva, she committed suicide just last spring. Those two, they always seemed like kids who would succeed. They were good students. Of that class, most of the kids dropped out of school in Grade Nine or Grade Ten. Only two have ever graduated, Simon and my friend Gabriel. Most of the other kids are still in town. None of them have graduated. Most of them don't have jobs.

TEENAGE YEARS: WHEN THE COFFEE SHOP CLOSED

A PLANE TICKET TO IGLOOLIK FOR MY THIRTEENTH BIRTHDAY

When I was twelve, I went to Igloolik for the Baffin Regional Games. They are held each year in different communities. Half of our class that year went to Brampton for an exchange trip, the rest of us went to Igloolik. We did a lot of fund-raising that year. We sold raffle tickets and had bake sales. We had a chart on the wall showing how we were doing. I remember getting on a plane, a tiny Twin Otter. There were about fifteen of us from different grades. Igloolik is about the same population as Pond Inlet. It is on a small island and is very flat. I was lucky because my great-grandparents lived in Igloolik, and I had family ties. I got to stay at their place. The games lasted a week. We did things like play volleyball, soccer, floor hockey, broomball. The best part, though, were the traditional Inuit games. I had such a good time there, I really wanted to go back. I wanted to move there. When I got back I began bugging my parents, pestering my parents to send me back there.

I got a plane ticket to Igloolik for my thirteenth birthday. I remember my parents were anxious about me going by myself. They were worried and warned me about things that could happen if I wasn't careful. I really wanted to go, and I thought they were wrong, but when I got to Igloolik it was worse than they had said. I wasn't in a group any more, and being by myself was hard. I got pretty hungry at times. I was there for a week, yeah, for a week, and I was staying with relatives. In Pond there are three main sections of town, but in Igloolik there are two, the hill and the lower shore. There are more Catholics there than here. When I got there they told me that the lower section was all Catholic people, and the upper one was all Anglican. They said that there was a big split between the Catholics and the Anglicans in Igloolik, they didn't hang around much together. I thought that was pretty strange. I didn't think it was true.

One day a friend of mine and I took a walk down to the lower section, and this guy came up and started yelling at us. He just started yelling, "Get out of this part! Get out, you're not Catholic, you don't belong here! What are you doing here? I'm going to beat you up pretty soon if you don't go away!" Nothing happened, but I was pretty amazed at this. I had never been exposed to that sort of thing in Pond Inlet. I had never heard about Anglicans and Catholics living in separate sections of town or fighting when I was growing up. I was so surprised. I guess things like that show you how many differences there are between communities.

I made a few new friends, but I had a terrible time that trip. I should have listened to my parents. I didn't question their judgment as much after that. I've been there lots of time since then. We go there quite a bit. I've had two birthdays there. My birthdays there ... here it would be like just another day, but in Igloolik it seemed as if the whole town made my birthday a very big, special event. It seems as if the people in Igloolik were more traditional, more Inuit. There are very nice people there. They are very kind. They always say "Hi." I've had wonderful times in Igloolik with my family when we go there, but being there alone was kind of hard.

ASKING MY PARENTS AND GRANDPARENTS, "WHAT WAS IT LIKE GOING HUNGRY?"

A few years ago when I was thirteen I got pretty hungry camping out on the land ... I have always heard stories about people in the old culture going hungry for long periods of time. I remember always asking my parents and grandparents, "What was it like going hungry?" Sometimes I really wish we could go back to how people used to live. There would be no TV, no cigarettes. I just want to know what the feeling would be like not to be dependent on Qallunaat things. I always tell elders that they are lucky that they grew up that way, in kamiks and skins and stuff like that. They always say negative things about back then. They talk about having lice in their hair, or they say it was too cold or that they didn't have enough wood. They are always saying negative things about the way things were. I've always wanted to tell them that I wish I were given the chance to live that way.

Some of the stories I used to hear from my grandparents' time were about people who were so hungry they had to eat a dead person. One of the people who did this was the wife of my grandma's uncle. I remember hearing that story. That lady, I heard she could never eat polar bear after that, because the taste reminded her of that dead person. That was a long time ago.

Every since I first started to hear these stories about near-starvation, I started bugging my parents to tell me more. When I was thirteen we went camping, the whole family and my mother's sister Salomie. That is when I had a taste of what it would be like to go hungry. It was only just a taste, really, but I started to understand why they never wanted to talk about it.

It was supposed to be a great trip. For one thing it was supposed to be a whole week long. Both my parents worked all week long so usually we used to only get out on weekends. We went to the floe edge and ran out of store-bought food. We were supposed to stay just one week and we ended up staying a week and a half. We had brought only enough food for one week. There were murre eggs and seal to eat, but I throw up raw eggs when I eat them and I didn't want to eat seal. For about two or three days I didn't eat. I got really weak and I couldn't walk. My father got angry at me for not eating seal even though I was really hungry. When we were packing to go back home I just sat there and didn't help pack. He refused to carry me to the qamutik, and he was angry all the way back to the settlement because I wouldn't eat seal. The other kids ate some seal so they were okay. I was happy that I finally got that feeling that they used to have all the time. I finally got to feel what it would be like to go hungry, to starve.

A LOT OF KIDS WERE HAVING BABIES

I guess I was around fifteen when I started to notice that a lot of kids were having babies – kids my own age, my friends, were having babies. Both my sister and I had boyfriends when I was around fifteen. I practically lived with my boyfriend, almost. I started using the pill when I was fourteen and I kept on using it. I remember talking to my mom at that time and saying to her, "Please, could I have a baby?" That's what I kept asking her. She said that I couldn't handle the responsibility. I used to answer that I had a lot of experience with Dawn and Sheila and Lucas. I thought that what she said was wrong. I thought that I could handle it. I kept asking my mom if I could please have a baby. That is exactly what I said. When she kept saying that I couldn't have a baby, I said to her, "Could you have a baby?" So they had Ruby. They said they were already thinking about having a baby when I brought that up, but they weren't sure. I kept pushing them into saying yes to what they had already thought of. Personally, sometimes I say, "Oh, wow, I got Ruby into this world." I'm sure they would say that I had nothing to do with it, but I know that I was pestering them a lot.

Ruby was born March 18th, 1990, and she was more than nine pounds. Now she is really small. She knows a lot more things than all of the other kids when they were that age, all my sisters and Lucas. She also has this great personality. She is very caring when you are alone with her, when you get up in the mornings. She is a very special friend. It is kind of amazing. She is more of a friend than a sister, and she is only four.

THE YEAR I STARTED SMOKING

When I was young, really young, when I was growing up, my aunts were always telling me not to smoke. I never thought I would smoke. I thought that it was idiotic of them to say that I might start smoking when I grew up. They told me not to smoke. They said it was bad for me. I was hanging out with our neighbour, she was a year older than me, and she smoked. She already had been smoking for a long, long time. She wasn't even shy smoking in front of her parents at all. She could ask them for cigarettes.

Grade Seven, that was the year I started smoking. I was ten years old at the time. I remember when I first started, it was during the summer, almost fall, and we were going out somewhere. We were going to walk somewhere. I wasn't even thinking about smoking cigarettes back then. I don't know why, but that day I felt like I had to impress that girl, so I said that I should try puffing. We went under the house – these houses are set way up on stilts so that you could stand straight up underneath the house – we went under the house, and she lit one. My first few puffs were pretty anti-climatic, so I asked for more. I said that I didn't taste it and that I wanted some more. She said that I had to puff it really good. I started puffing and puffing. I had this strange tingly feeling. Then she said that I had better stop and that we better go. I was in a very intoxicated state. I said no, to please give me some more. I was asking her while we were walking. She gave me a few more puffs. A few houses away from where she lived, I suddenly fell down and just couldn't get up. I felt very drunk even though I didn't know what being drunk was at the time. It was like that. I saw my friend walking away, she was just leaving me. I couldn't get up. I couldn't get my head up. I was watching her walk away, I was calling to her for help. I laid there for a few minutes and I kept saying to myself, "Sandra, get up. Get up!" She was laughing at me. After a while she came and picked me up. For a few minutes I took some fresh air and was okay and then I went with her.

After that incident I started smoking. I smoked a lot that year when I was ten. My sister Mona started smoking about the same time as I did. Actually she started experimenting with cigarettes when she was really young. I guess she always had a thing for them. I caught her one day, early in the morning hiding behind the sofa. She was trying to light a cigarette, but the lighter didn't work. She was doing that for a while. She didn't know that I was watching her. One time at night, I wasn't around to see it, but one time she was sleeping in my parents' bedroom and she lit up a cigarette. She was just a kid, so she didn't know about ashtrays or throwing cigarettes out the window. She threw it in the garbage and the garbage lit on fire. My parents woke up and threw the garbage out. She started experimenting when she was just a kid. I guess she was really curious.

Mona, she must have been eight or nine when she really started smoking. I didn't know that she had started smoking. She was as afraid of me finding out as much as I was afraid of her finding out. One day we were walking back to school after lunch. We were all going through the hill.³ There were lots of kids around. Some were smoking. I guess we got together on that hill. This boy said, "Here, Mona, here is the cigarette that you wanted." Mona said, "Not now," as quietly as she could. I heard it anyway. That is how I found out that she started smoking too. I think after school that day I told her that I smoked too.

I guess my mom didn't know what to do about me smoking. I knew that she knew that I smoked. One day when I was cleaning up my room, I put two cigarettes on my dresser. I should have hid them, I shouldn't have left them there. It was just before Grade Six graduation. That year I was doing okay at school, and I got several awards. On graduation day I had to dress up and get prepared for the ceremonies. I didn't like my teacher very much and I didn't want to go. My mom found out about the cigarettes. She saw them. I was sitting on the sofa. She was telling me to get dressed, but I was just sitting there, I didn't want to go. She came up to me, she sat on the coffee table and said that she knew about the cigarettes. She started crying. She wanted to know why I wasn't going to school, especially on graduation day where she said that she could be proud of me. She started hitting me with her fists, not hard. She was crying. I guess she didn't know what to do. I didn't go to the ceremonies that day. I kept on smoking and am still smoking.

Not that long ago, maybe a year or something, I read this article in a newspaper that said that 77 per cent of women in the NWT smoke. Or was it 77 per cent of all Inuit women smoke? ... Anyways, when you are living up here, that is not surprising. I still bum cigarettes off my parents. A few years ago when my dad quit smoking, I started telling my mom to quit smoking too. That was pretty hard and she just ignored me or made fun of me. I kept telling her that she was acting just like her mom when they lived at the outpost camp. She told me stories about Grandma wanting to smoke so much that she became crazy. My mom said that all her children used to say to her to please quit smoking. Grandmother used to say back then that she was young, that she could keep on smoking and still be okay. I kept telling her that she was acting just like that. Now Grandma has to go to the health centre a lot. My mother still ignores me.

There has to be something that will eventually stop this smoking. Sometimes I think all the smoking is probably one of the reasons why people are having so many tough times here, I mean with money and health problems. People just laugh, though. They kind of think, "I'm going to die anyway, so why quit smoking?" but that is really the wrong philosophy. That statement should be banned. If you are going to die, then you are going to die, but wouldn't you rather have a good life before? I don't like that statement at all.

Watching my little sister Sheila turn into a teenager, I knew that this was going to happen sooner or later, that she would be with a group that smokes cigarettes. Yesterday afternoon I smelled her and she smelled like cigarettes. For a long time I knew that this was going to happen. I wasn't that surprised. This afternoon I was coming home from work and I saw her with this new friend. Sheila was trying to put something in her pocket. The friend saw me and said very quietly, "Sheila, Sheila, look who is here!" Sheila put something really quickly into her pocket. I don't want her to start smoking. I don't know what to do because I have been through this myself. I say that I don't know what to do because the first thing that most people would do is scold a child for smoking, or try to reason with a child. I heard most of this when I started smoking. I have heard stories of parents who find out their kid is smoking and make the child smoke a whole pack in one sitting so the child knows how bad it is. That also doesn't work. It's pretty tough, because most things don't work.

WHEN I GOT TO GRADE NINE, EVERYTHING WENT DOWNHILL FOR A WHILE

In Grade Eight I moved from the elementary school to the school for the older kids. I was still the youngest in my class so I was still afraid of all those older kids. My uncles and my older cousins were in those classrooms. I was catching up to them. I remember my teacher back then ... He was like the professor type. He talked a lot, and he was a big philosopher. He took forever to explain things. Every day we would watch the CBC news. All the kids thought that watching the news was an un-cool thing, but he made it into a big event. Every morning at eleven we would watch the news. He taught us about stock exchanges and about the values of American and Canadian money. We did a graph on it. Even now, whenever I get the chance, I still watch the eleven o'clock news and see what the money value is.

Up until Grade Nine I was doing very good at school. I was having a great time all those years. School was a big thing. When I got to Grade Nine, everything went downhill for a while. All those years of doing well just withered away. I was in Grade Nine for three years. The first time I was in Grade Nine I guess it was hard for me because I was turning twelve and I was a pre-teen. I was smoking, staying out at night, never going home. I was always late for school. I was out with my friends all the time. I thought school was a burden. Everyone, my parents, my teachers, were asking me what was going on. Why was I missing out on school? Why was I doing poorly? I always made excuses, I never told them exactly what my problems were. I repeated Grade Nine three times. I was in Grade Nine for three years. I just couldn't get my mind on school. I wasn't that surprised the first time I failed, I knew that I was doing very poorly, and I expected bad grades when I got my report cards. I wasn't even all that surprised when I failed Grade Nine the second time. I dismissed it, I said, "To hell with it! It doesn't matter if I fail!" I told myself that I didn't care.

I had three different teachers my three different years in Grade Nine. The first two, well, they didn't do much for me. I had troubles getting along with them. The third teacher was a woman. That was better. She knew that I was doing poorly at school, and she tried to help me. She made us write journals and I wrote all the things that I felt. She encouraged me to write some more, and since then I have written lots of things in my journals. Finally I passed Grade Nine and went on to

Grade Ten. By failing three times I ended up back with my own age group, same peers, so it was really easy for me, Grade Ten. That year it was good. I worked hard and I learned a lot.

WHEN THE COFFEE SHOP CLOSED

Nineteen eighty-eight was kind of hard. That was when the coffee shop closed. That was ... I guess that was like the greyest day for me.

I remember when the coffee shop opened. A Qallunaaq in town started a video-game arcade, just at the back of the Co-Op, just a little corner at the back. People started coming in, and they expanded. They got more machines and tables and chairs and a juke-box, and they added a hamburger and ice-cream take-out. It had seven tables alto-gether, with chairs and eight machines. It was a really small place, but it was great to hang out in. There were two washrooms.

I remember this new guy came into town around that time. Every-one was crazy about him. At first I couldn't figure out why, and I started liking him too. I started going to the coffee shop, and I made some new friends there. The friends I made were older guys, but we were still just friends. They knew I was just a kid. This one guy and I started hanging out. He was almost six years older than me. We became almost like best friends. He was a special friend. We didn't talk much, we weren't like boyfriend and girlfriend, we just hung out. We went to the coffee shop every day, played games, played songs on the juke-box. We had this table together that we would never let anyone else sit there when we were there. It became like our own place, just this one table at the back. I was thirteen and he would have been nine-teen, so he was pretty old compared to me. It didn't matter to me that he was that old because he was just a friend. We went to the coffee shop after school, right after school until ten at night. On weekends it was open until midnight.

It was from this friend that I first found out about drugs. He was pretty into drugs. For the longest time I tried to keep him from doing drugs. I always said it was good not to take drugs and all that. I always encouraged him to be drug free. I was like that for a while, and then during the summer things got pretty boring around the settlement. I got my first job and I got some money. I paid a hundred bucks to buy myself some drugs. The year I was thirteen, it was a long, long year for me ...

When I went to go buy the drugs, that was my first time ever actu-ally seeing what they looked like. I bought five grams for a hundred bucks. Drugs were a lot cheaper back then. I got some pretty good pieces. When the guy gave them to me, I was kind of surprised and appalled. I guess I was a little wary, I mean, all year long I was telling this guy not to take drugs, telling him how bad they are for you, and then all of the sudden I had these big pieces in my hand. We went to my grandparents' house. He was good friends with my uncle, so we went there.

Before that I was always considered sort of like the straight kid in town. A lot of my friends had been doing drugs for a while, and I'd never tried them, I'd always said how bad they were for you. When everyone found out that I had spent a hundred bucks on drugs, a whole bunch of people showed up at my grandparents' house. I remember we were in my uncle's room and people started coming in. There were so many kids in there, like the coolest guys in town were there.

My first try I coughed a lot, but I was determined to get high like the rest of them. I took probably about two hits, I think. Everything was so different. I got pretty high and really scared, and I wanted to be alone. I wanted to be by myself and absorb it all, so I went to the living room and there was my grandma. She started yapping at me, she started talking to me, and I got scared and sweaty because I thought she'd notice what was happening to me. I thought it was really obvious. By this time I wanted to go home pretty bad. I tried calling someone to help me, someone to take me home ... I was looking at the telephone for the longest time trying to remember a phone number, and I was pretty lost, I guess. All of the sudden I realized I was on the phone, that I had the phone handle on my ear and that I was just sitting there. I got pretty scared because I thought that my grandmother would see me that way and wonder what was happening. I pretended to look for something to eat, and I realized I was staring at the fridge for the longest time. I was staring at it for a while, and then I closed it and went back into the room where everyone was.

I saw my friend there, and I saw his eyes were all puffy and red and he was slurring. I had never seen him like that before, and I didn't like what I was seeing. I mean, he was a totally different person. I left the room and asked my aunt Rosie to take me home. She was our age but she wasn't toking. She was in the other room. She was just staying home. We went to go leave, and once we were outside the house all the guys went to the window and asked why I was leaving so soon. I kind of grumbled something at them. I said I didn't like what I was doing. And then I realized that I had the pieces of hash in my hand. I had them with me so I gave them to the guys in the room. A hundred bucks down the drain!

I remember on the way home we passed this cool guy that I had always had a crush on. I was walking by, and I didn't even notice that he was there – I was too stoned! He said "Hi," he had never said "Hi" to me before, but he did that night, and I didn't hear him. The next day he asked why didn't I answer back, and I said, "Were you there?" and he said, "Yeah, and I got pretty pissed off when you didn't say anything back." He said he passed pretty close to us but I didn't see him. When I went home I went straight to my room and fell asleep. I didn't take drugs again until two summers later. I hated that night.

Oh yeah ... yeah ... the coffee shop ... That is what I was talking about. When I found out the coffee shop was closing I was pretty sad. I was working at the Co-Op. It was attached to the coffee shop. I worked there as a store clerk. This is back when I was thirteen. I'd finish work every night and go spend my money at the coffee shop. I'd spend twenty dollars a night there playing the video games. In February my family went to Mexico for a couple of weeks. When we came back, I started hanging out like I used to, and some guy came up to me and said that the coffee shop was closing. I got mad at him for saying that, I thought he was joking. A few days later my boss told me that it was true. I became really, really depressed about the coffee shop closing. I practically lived there – I was there from four o'clock in the afternoon until ten at night every day. I would eat there, stay there, do my homework there. When they decided to close it I began to think the members of the Co-Op were really, really mean. I remember thinking to myself about how they didn't think of the kids at all. They were like dictators, they just saw us as pests or something. I asked all the time why they were closing it, and I always got the same answers. Looking back now, I guess they were reasonable answers. Parents were complaining that kids were spending too much money there. It was mostly kids who went there. I always said it's only quarters, only quarters. I sort of realized a long time later that I was spending close to twenty bucks a night there on games.

For the whole month before it closed, I didn't work. I went to work but I just slacked off. I became obsessed with it closing. I was counting the days until it closed. I spent all of my time at the coffee shop. At this time they were cutting jobs at the Co-Op, laying people off. I was one of the lucky ones, I got to stay on part time. Even though I got to keep my job, I wasn't that happy about it. I said I couldn't keep going to work next to the coffee shop when it was about to close down. I said I wanted to quit, and the person they were laying off took over my job. My boss started asking me why I was depressed all the time – Was it because I was quitting my job, did I want to stay on? I said, "No, it's the coffee shop closing," and he thought I was joking. I mean, he didn't quite believe me, he didn't understand how I could be so serious about it.

I still remember the day that it closed. My friends don't, but I still do. It was March 31st, 1988, a Thursday night. They usually closed the coffee shop at ten on Thursdays but since it was closing for good, they closed it at twelve. It was really, really, really crowded in there that night, and you could barely walk. It was the very last night and it seems like everyone was there. Usually I was always the first one to play the games. I never used to let anyone play this one game until I had the most points, but there was so many people there that night and a lot of people had reserved the games, I mean they already paid in advance and were waiting their turn. So that whole night I waited and waited and I never played. I just sat there.

The coffee shop meant a lot to me. It was a place to go to, to see my friends, to hang out. It had music, you could talk to your friends there. That last night that it was open, I saw my friend there, my special friend. I was really sad, and I could see he was pretty depressed too. That night, that was the very last time we were close, I mean, real friends. When we were hanging out when the coffee shop was open, we used to always walk home together after it closed, but that night we didn't even say goodbye. I didn't talk to him much after that.

DANCES AT THE COMMUNITY HALL

After the coffee shop closed, the summer that I turned fifteen, I started noticing that there were a lot more drugs around the community. It was really sad to see so many around, because it seemed like everyone was doing them. Even people that you would never think would do them started doing them. I think the kids were getting bored, kind of restless, because they didn't have anywhere to go.

They had dances at the community hall at that time, like when I was thirteen, fourteen, but people weren't really into dancing the way they are today. We had the coffee shop, so it was mostly the older kids, older than teenagers, who went dancing. They danced to slow music back then. A lot of the people who were really into drugs used to hang out at the community hall. The back is really dark. The washroom area is really, really dark. There were so many dealers back there. The supervisor never did anything about it. He was an old man, he was fifty or sixty, and he thought that everyone was having fun. He didn't throw out the dealers. He didn't mind them. You could always see one or two dealers at the back, always waiting. It used to be scary in the dark areas of the community hall. There were always pushers there. I used to be uncomfortable going to the washrooms.

After the coffee shop closed, though, little by little everyone started going to the community hall, and there was this big boom on dancing. People started dancing a lot more. We started going there on weekends. They started letting younger kids in. Everyone started a really crazy kind of dancing, like really moving. We got a new DJ, and then we got a new supervisor. He was youngish, pretty young compared to that old man. That new supervisor really got tough on the dealers, and he threw them all out. He started kicking them out, and today you don't ever see any dealer out back. He stopped letting drunk people in, and there were no fights anymore. There hasn't been a fight there for a long, long time. There used to be a lot of heavy smoking there too. You don't see that any more either. Everyone just goes there to dance.

Back when the coffee shop was open, I spent all my time there. After a while I started doing the same with the C-hall, kind of like making it my home. The dance hall purchased a few of the video games, so I started going there to play games. My mom had seen how hung up I had been on the coffee shop, and she tried to stop me from being the same way again. She would mention it here and there to me, drop little hints about how I should stay home. After a while I started to listen to her, I started staying home for supper, spending time with my sisters and brother. Now I only really go about once a week or so. That's enough.

GRADES TEN, ELEVEN AND TWELVE

Those were really great years, Grades Ten and Eleven. I found out a lot of things about myself. In Grade Ten I started doing things for other people. I did so much I didn't have time for myself. I joined the student council when I was in Grade Nine. I was very active on it. I worked so hard on the student council that my school work suffered. I just didn't care about my studies when I was on the student council. At first I was just a secretary, and then the next year I became a treasurer, the next year vice-president, and in my last year, I became the president. When I became president, all my time was spent working on the student council. We held dances for kids and we started accumulating money. My sister Mona, she was the vice-president when I was the president, so we did a lot of things together.

Also those years, Grades Ten, Eleven, and Twelve, I became more aware of the problems around town. I knew certain kids were having very rough problems outside of school. I sort of became like a social worker for these kids. I started staying up late, talking to them. I listened to them. I was very sympathetic, and I tried my best to help them, or let them talk at least. Sometimes they would talk to me for hours at a time, days at a time. Most of these kids had suicidal thoughts, and bad things were happening to them. It became really important for me to be there for them. I wanted to be there for those kids twenty-four hours a day.

In Grade Eleven I would stay after school and clean up the class-room. I would try to make the classroom really nice for my other class-mates. I got a civic award that year. Sometimes other kids would stay after school, just to hang out, just to talk. Teachers didn't know that much about what was going on. We didn't want to be bored, we didn't want to go home, so we stayed around after school to hang out.

When I quit school, I had more time for my friends. I saw them a lot more. I could stay up late because I didn't have to worry about going to school in the morning. There were so many kids who had problems. When we got together, I always encouraged them to talk some more, but to older people, experienced people. There was a poster in the health centre that advertised a crisis line in the Baffin region. The poster said it was free and confidential, so we started going to the pay phone in the doorway of the health centre, the nursing station, to call.

I realize now how long it takes for people to get better. It is hard growing up, so it takes a while for things to get better. My closest friends are doing a lot better. They weren't my friends before, we didn't start out as friends, but after all the talking we did, that's what hap-pened. My closest friends, some of them were sexually abused. I can't believe some of the things that have happened to people! This particu-lar girl, I remember having to be with her all the time at one point to make sure that she was okay. At first I didn't believe her when she told me the things that were happening to her. She cried a lot the first few months, and I held her a lot. Now she is okay. She is happy. She has a child to take care of, but she is still in school. She won't give up going to school.

Usually every weekend I talk to some friends to see if they are okay. One weekend this spring I listened to three separate kids talking about suicide. That was one scary weekend. They were desperate, they were ready to act. They showed me marks from their attempts. I remember staying awake for a long, long time. I didn't go home for a long time. One girl, she was really crying, she couldn't talk any more, she was shaking. She is fourteen years old, she is just a kid. So many things have happened to her already in her life and she is just a kid.

WHEN MONA GOT PREGNANT

I never used to say much about my boyfriends to my parents. When my dad found out I was going out with a guy, he would always tell me that he thought the guy was on drugs. I used to go out secretly, not tell them much. They never said anything about Allan, Mona's boyfriend, though – even when Mona got pregnant. I thought that my parents would get pissed off when she told them. Mona said it in a vague sort of way, "Oh, Mom, I've been missing my periods lately," that kind of thing. And my mom said, "Well, you must be pregnant." That was about it. My dad, he was in the washroom at the time. Mom told him when he came out. His face was hidden for a while, he was quiet, then he turned around and had a big smile on his face. That really shocked me. She was fourteen, fifteen, something like that. I thought he would start screaming and yelling. He was smiling pretty hard.

When we were growing up, Mona and I, we didn't talk that much about sex and those kinds of things to my mom. It was embarrassing to talk about all that, so I always tried to be there for my sister with her boyfriend. I repeatedly told her to go to the nursing station and get some pills or do something. She was afraid to go – not really afraid, maybe shy or something, and she didn't think she'd get pregnant. She was with her boyfriend for a long time, probably about a year, when she had her baby. At first I was really disappointed in my sister for not listening to me, for not taking the pills. I was disappointed in my parents being casual about it. I guess I was disappointed also because Mona started changing – she started growing up – and it was hard to let go of her. It was hard to see her grow up. When we were twelve, thirteen, fourteen, my sister and I were inseparable, we were together all the time. At first I was a little upset with Allan for taking her away, but Terry, her son, he is like a gem or something, he's so sweet.

One time she did listen to us was when my mom was telling her to eat healthy and all that, when my mom was telling her to eat lots and lots of meat. She listened to all of my mom's advice about what she should eat. I remember telling her as well to eat lots of meat. When you are a teenager, eating traditional food is uncool, but when my sister got pregnant, she ate a lot of it and I was proud of her.

CHRONIC ECZEMA ALL OF MY LIFE

There is one thing that I want to talk about that I think is important. It's about my eczema. I've had chronic eczema all of my life. It runs in my family on my dad's side. My grandfather Ishmailie has it, so do his sister's children. His brother, my great-uncle has it, so do his sister's children, my dad's youngest brother and my aunt, so do my brother Lucas and my baby sister Ruby. My father's mother used to say my eczema was because I was "augluttuq" – she said I had bad blood. I think what she meant by "bad blood" was that I can't fight off the disease as well as the rest of the people in my family. I have it the worst.

When I was five or six years old, my mother took me to the nursing station. The nurses gave me a special cleansing soap and cream. She took me back over and over again throughout my childhood, because it never seemed to heal. My eczema is really bad. It is wherever there is skin. I have huge scars all over, mostly on my calves, and the climate here makes it worse. From the time the doctors first diagnosed it, I knew there was no cure. When I was about twelve, I started going to the nursing station by myself. The treatments they gave me were strong enough to heal the wounds for periods of time, but the eczema always flared up again. Most of the time it flares up in late fall.

I used to go see the nurses so much. I've seen so many different nurses over the years, and their opinions all range. I've seen three doctors ... I think a nurse here finally got tired of me bugging her so much. She wrote down my name and said that I could go see a real dermatologist who was going through Iqaluit the next month. This was seven years ago, when I was thirteen. When I was waiting that month before the trip, I thought that after it was all over, I'd finally have a normal life. I thought the appointment with a real dermatologist would end it all.

I remember going down to Iqaluit. I packed a few of my things in a suitcase and left on the morning plane. I went all by myself and stayed two days. I hadn't been to Iqaluit since I was seven and didn't remember much about it. It was my first trip to the hospital besides my birth. I had always wondered what it would be like to have an accident or routine surgery, like my sister with her tonsils, and go to Baffin Regional. You know, have a normal accident or something. I remember being there, sitting in the waiting room for out-patients. I waited for a few hours. I felt so grown up and hopeful. After a while I was sent to an examining room. The doctor, the dermatologist, had on this business-like suit, and she walked very fast. There was also someone else there, an intern. I have never had long fingernails in my life – I have always cut them short so I wouldn't hurt myself as much when I scratched – but I was excited about my trip to Iqaluit so I grew them just a little before I left. The doctor looked at me and said sarcastically to the intern, "No wonder she has skin problems, she has scabies." She had the gall to say they're scabies. Scabies all of my life? I thought to myself. I couldn't believe it! I knew what scabies were, and I knew she was wrong. I knew what my problem was. I had read about eczema and I knew I had it. I didn't say anything to her, though. They prescribed medication for me. They were in tubes. I never used them. I never even opened them.

When I went back home to Pond Inlet, I left the tubes on the dresser, and a friend asked me if they were vaginal creme for STDs. I didn't correct him. I was more embarrassed about having eczema than if I had had an STD! I didn't want to tell him that I had eczema. I'm still angry at him for asking if I had STDs. I was only thirteen.

When I was a kid my eczema was just a nuisance. When I turned ten or eleven, though, I started to become embarrassed about it. I became more shy. As I got older this shyness became worse. I remember one guy who I went out with even said I was too shy. I didn't tell him that I was the same with every boy, "too shy." I never let them get too close. Living in this small community, it is a big thing how many boyfriends you have or who they are.

Another doctor who I saw later on, after the dermatologist, said my eczema would get better as I grow older. It was that way with my aunt and uncle – theirs got better when they got older. It didn't happen with me, though. It seemed to get worse. It used to only be on my body, but as a teenager it spread to my hands and face. The eczema on my hands was different than the eczema on the other parts of my body. It "bled," meaning that the wounds were full of water. I kept trying to hide my hands with long sleeves and putting them out of sight. I was embarrassed, having to scratch all the time.

There was once a time when I was totally relieved of it. I went south for an exchange trip when I was thirteen. In that climate it was gone in less than a week. I was so surprised because that was when I didn't put much cream on. I was trying to keep all the drugs out of my blood. I felt so normal then – my skin was so smooth, I didn't itch. Ever since then I remember that time when I was down South. I tell my parents and the nurses that there has been a time when I didn't have eczema. I hint and hint, hoping that there will be a way for it to be like that again.

Grade Ten and Eleven were okay for me, but in Grade Twelve I became more and more shy. It became harder for me to associate with friends, harder to open up. I worked the whole summer before Grade Twelve. I saved up and went south for a while. I went to Ottawa. The first thing I wanted to do when I got down there was to see another dermatologist. As usual I was shy with the doctor and didn't want to spill out my feelings about how my eczema affected my whole life. I read in a magazine once about how doctors often act as psychiatrists. I didn't want to be a burden or thought of as another sad case. The doctor who I saw gave me a different kind of soap and a cream that actually worked. I was so happy when I was down there! I watched as my eczema healed. I thought of my life as carefree as my sister's, and I thought my senior year would be great.

Two weeks after all of this, after I got this cream, my eczema came back. It came back with a real vengeance. It was okay when I was down South, but when I was going home through Iqaluit, the airline lost my luggage with the cream inside and I had to do without it for two days. The first day I was in Iqaluit, I went to the hospital for another reason. While I was there I was still so happy about it going away. I wanted to look for the nurses who had said I had scabies. I wanted to find them and show them that I had never had scabies. I wanted to let them know what a caring doctor down South did for me. Well, I shouldn't have thought that way, thought about paying them back, because not long after that my illness came back. Not only that but my fingernails were eaten up by all the drugs in the new cream! I got back to Pond Inlet, and the new cream was sent to me in the mail. I put it on again. It worked a little bit but not as much as it did in the South. Now I was in the dryness and the cold and the wind. When I ran out of cream a few months later, the health centre didn't have it, so I went without.

After that trip, after my eczema came back with a real vengeance, I felt so exasperated, helpless. I didn't want to deal with the eczema another year. When I got into Grade Twelve, after that summer, my problems really started to get to me. I couldn't deal with waking up early enough to wash up, putting cream on my face, being late for school, washing at lunch, and then scratching my fingers all throughout the day. The itchiness kept me from concentrating, I couldn't write as quickly. I kept on thinking about going home and taking off my stuffy clothing and getting into my t-shirts and shorts. It was that bad. I remembered the nurse who said that everything would be okay when I got older. I became unhappy when I remembered that.

There was one day I felt overwhelmed. I couldn't deal with bathing and going through the same routine, so I stayed home from school in the morning. I thought I'd feel better at noon, when I had more time to bathe. I didn't go to school in the afternoon, or the next day. I thought that maybe I'd get better over the weekend. I thought I'd get better if I just stayed home. By Monday I had lost all hope. I stayed in bed. Two weeks later I still wasn't going to school. I got a notice from school, and they told me I had one more chance. I wanted so much to explain to them, I wanted to tell them that I hadn't planned this and that I never meant to miss school. I wanted to write back to them and say, "Hey, it is not what you think! I am not partying my life away! I am not sleeping my life away!" I wanted to tell them that I wasn't staying out of school because I felt bitterness towards my teachers. Everything was going crazy in my head. What was I supposed to do – go back to school and pretend nothing ever happened, pretend everything was great like I thought it would be?

In the middle of all this I remember thinking about failing and having to go to school the next year, going through Grade Twelve at twenty years old. I thought of not graduating at sixteen or even at nineteen. I said to myself, "You had better get your act in gear," so I bathed that day. I got ready to go to school, put on my stuffy clothing. At 9:30 a.m., I was crying. I saw my face in the mirror and knew I'd be miserable. Ever since then I have never looked forward to anything. I don't want to lift my hopes up.

Growing up with my sister who is carefree and confident, it has been hard on me to see her happy all the time. I've tried to encourage her to look good and dress good. That is how I always hid my eczema, by dressing fashionably. I used to tell her that she would look so great if she dressed up because she doesn't have eczema to worry about, but she doesn't seem to care as much. That is how I am with my sister and my mother. I think they probably think I am bossy – "Put make-up on, try this, buy that!" I try to make their lives more colourful even though they think everything is all right. My sister, she is a little absent-minded, and she is happy the way she is. I think that is how I became a perfectionist, though, from trying to hide my eczema.

For the most part when it comes to my eczema, people are sympathetic and understanding. They know it is not contagious. Still, I try hard to hide it. Some people who don't know about my eczema think I have it all, they think I have nothing to worry about. I remember thinking that when I was talking to this girl in town who has an obvious medical problem. I found out one day how it affects her life when we were walking from a dance. We started talking, and she explained that she would like to join in dancing too but she was too shy. Even though we have always known each other, this was the first time that she opened up to me. I wanted so badly to tell her that I have been going through the same thing with my eczema but I didn't want to talk and interrupt her. The next time I saw her, she acted embarrassed for having talked like that. I wanted her to be my friend, but she never talked to me like that again.

My grandmother, Apphia, she prayed for me once. That was when I was probably fifteen or sixteen. She asked God to spare me any more pain. Things didn't change much after that. I don't think of God much since then. To tell you the truth, I think of Inuit spirits probably more. Sometimes I think they are punishing me. I think they have been punishing me, trying to tell me something. I think about them even though I have no idea what they are, who they are. Even if it is wrong to think about them, I've made them into my imaginary friends. I'm a little comforted by that.

I have never told my mother or father why I became miserable. They asked and asked, "Qanuikkavit?"⁴ but I never answered back. I became sort of a hermit. I'd spend all my time in my room. Even before Grade Twelve I did this. In the summers and at Christmas I'd stay in my room with my books, my magazines, my imaginary friends, and my dance music. I'd see my friends once a week in the dance hall. They would exclaim, "Oh, how good to see you! Why did you quit school? Long time no see!" The only place I went was to the dance hall. When you dance you don't have to talk. It was dark there and nobody could see my puffy eyes. Dancing is a big part of life for young people here.

I've never exactly told my parents the main reason why one day I'd be smooching my baby sister or playing with my brother and sisters, and the next day I'd be a totally different person, why all of the sudden I'd start cursing at my mother and then stop talking altogether, why I'd stay in my room for days and days. This went on for months and months. I couldn't tell them it was because of my eczema. I didn't want them to think it was their fault – that is the last thing I wanted them to feel. I didn't want them to think that I blamed them for passing it down to me. They probably knew full well why I was like that, but I never said it outright. Mostly it was my mother doing the asking, but once in awhile my father asked, and I would be so surprised I'd almost burst. It cheered me up a little when he asked. Still, I never said much to them.

I went to the health centre less and less as I got older. I knew the medicines they gave me didn't work. Before I quit school, I'd always keep my room clean, not a thing out of place. That was my pride, always having everything in place around me, at school and at home. I'd keep all my stuffy clothing in place. When I say stuffy clothing, I mean everyday clothing. When I am at home, I always wear shorts and a T-shirt. I never wear jeans at home. My baby sister knows I am going out if I am wearing jeans. When I was having such a hard time last fall, I went into a dream world of my own. My room lost it too – I wouldn't clean it up for weeks at a time. I never finished my chores. I lost hope of having a normal life. The things I used to have for school – books, paper, pens – were now only constant reminders of my mistakes. I didn't think I'd ever have the need to find my watch or find my sweaters and my jeans. That is when I started thinking really bad thoughts, because my room was a mess.

Also, I began listening to the community radio, day in, day out. I was still reading and writing a lot in diaries. The things I'd hear or read about started to weigh me down more. My mother asked me once whether the books were the reason why I was so down, and I thought she was being idiotic. As an afterthought I guess she was right in a way. I remember reading things about the North, like "Eight hundred students a year quit school in the NWT," or "Teachers feel like Social Service workers in the NWT because so many kids in trouble have problems," or "Pond Inlet has its highest suicide rate ever." I read so many of these things ...

I felt like such a burden to so many people, nineteen and still living at home, no decent boyfriends, school drop-out. Around that same time I tried to get a job, but I couldn't work very well for the same reasons I couldn't go to school. Whenever my mother mentioned a job opportunity, she found out later that I hadn't even looked into it. On not-so-bad days I'd clean the house in a frenzy, bathe my brother and sisters, wash their clothing, trim their nails, take them out, play Super Nintendo with them. I'd give Mom tons of suggestions. I'd try to make it all up to her for being such a burden. Late in the night I'd go to see my grandparents.

I started taking my baby sister out to pre-school story hour at the library. I'd take her shopping. After a while she was the one I answered to. She'd ask me if I had been crying, and she would try to cheer me up. She and I read story-books all the time. She liked to help me clean up. She put make-up on herself although I told her not to. That girl is impossible to be depressed around – I don't know where I would be without her. I'd like to think I helped her into the world, she was one of my "suggestions," but I think my mother thought of her and I just coaxed her into the final decision. Whatever – I am happy beyond words she had Ruby.

I never really told my mother why this all came about because I never really thought she would understand. She was so pretty when she was my age. She is pretty even now. She told me once about all the "boyfriends" she had back then. I dread having to think about one, but also I don't want to feel left out. I know she knows what it is like to live with the pain of eczema, because three of her six kids have it. I used to whine to her when it got really bad, but I stopped doing that, it's like old news. If I told her, I think she'd think I was being petty or suddenly becoming hyped about it when I've been living with it my whole life. I think she'd wonder why suddenly I am depressed about it now.

I would read things, happy-ending stories, and sometimes I'd associate with them but I never believed that could happen to me. I'd think, "I have brought this upon myself, I'll get myself out of this hell-hole I've created." My mother suggested a psychiatrist. I made up a reason to not do that as well. They already have so many cases worse than mine! Of course I said this to myself. Also I thought a person who has gone through a lot could be an even stronger person who helps other people. So I willed myself to reason myself out of this state I was in.

I sometimes think I'm better. I try not to think about last autumn very much. That is when I have flare-ups, moods I can't get out of, when I remember those two weeks especially. I used to say to myself, "Dear goodness, I look twenty years older than Cher! Imagine when I am her age!" Now I think, "Who cares about Cher! Screw Cher!" Also I tell myself to take it one day at a time. There is always a chance a bomb like Hiroshima will come to Pond, so take your time, don't lose your peace of mind, don't get in such a fluff!

Some good things have come out of it. I never got myself into something I might regret. I was always careful and never got pregnant – although I don't think that is the right phrase, because babies are never a regret. That is what I think. So all I'll say is that I never got pregnant. To think that babies are ever regrets! ... Anyhow, also over the years I've been taking cortisone steroids in the creams and I don't know how much I have in my blood now. So when people ask me to toke up or drink, I say, "No, thanks," not only because it is the right thing to do but because I don't want any more stuff in my blood, no matter how little. If I didn't have any steroids in my blood, I'd probably be a tad bit tempted at times ...

It is going to be easier for my baby sister and my brother and their eczema, because I know beforehand the things that work and don't work. Hopefully their skin will heal nicer than mine as they grow older. If you are wondering, humidifiers, Ivory soap, and detergent didn't help much in my case. It is the climate that makes it so bad.

SETTLEMENT CULTURE:
AT FIRST NONE OF THE TEENAGERS WOULD SQUARE-DANCE

I USED TO GO TO CHURCH WITH MY GRANDMOTHER

I was baptized as a baby. My grandparents were devoted Christians. I always asked myself why I didn't consider myself a Christian when I was brought up with it. When I was a kid, my grandmother Jokeepee usually took me to the church service and Bible class for little kids. I used to have fun there. I was very young, and I was surprised at how many other little kids went. After Bible class the instructors usually gave us cake or cookies, and we always had tea. We were lined up and counted, and then we could go home. The class used to be a half-hour long. The elders ran them in their houses, and my dad's grandfather was an instructor. There were different phases for the different age groups.

When I got older, I started going to a real church with my grandmother. The Anglican church used to be down at the end of town. It was a grey brick building with a church bell and a steeple. It was beautiful. It had beautiful windows. I was pretty young, just a little kid when we went to that church, but I remember walking down the long road to get there. There was always a rush to get to church, everyone was in a hurry, and the road to church was usually crowded with people just before church. The church inside had big blue curtains at the front, a big altar and leather little things, whatever, that you could kneel down onto. The male choir was on one side, and the females were on the other side. They demolished this church a long time ago, probably around 1980, and put up a church made for the cold up here. It is just a square yellow thing with metal exterior walls. There is no steeple. The new church is more in the middle of the town, and there is a big hill beside it. Usually kids go outside and play instead of going to church. The old church was much closer to the graveyard, so you didn't have to go that far if there was a funeral. You could always hear the bells. There are no more bells now.

When I used to go to church with my grandmother, after church in the evenings we almost always went somewhere for tea and talked a bit. I mean, my grandmother talked with her friends. When I started growing up I began going less and less. My grandparents didn't like that – they wanted me to go to church. They kind of pressured me. They said that I was baptized Christian and that I should go. After awhile I stopped going altogether. I never went. I wanted to watch The Muppet Show that came on the TV at seven o'clock. I watched The Muppet Show every Sunday at seven. I didn't go to church much after that.

Besides church, I also learned about Christianity in school. It was around that time that we were doing that learning that I really began to doubt a lot. We learned about the missionaries and the settlers, and the more I learned, the more I felt that I had to resist Christianity. I wondered how my grandparents could believe so strongly when it is so different from what they used to believe, so different from the old Inuit spirits. I used to ask them about those old spirits, about shamans and stuff, but they wouldn't talk about those things. They are strong Christians. My friends didn't want me to think about them either.

I didn't want to be a Christian, because I wanted to get back at the Qallunaat for saying all those bad things about Inuit back then. I didn't like what I learned about the Qallunaat moving in and telling us what to believe in, telling us the old Inuit spirits were evil. It is like they tricked us into Christianity, into believing the same things they believed in. I guess now that I've thought about it a little, I don't feel as much one way or another. I am very careful about being banged over the head with anything, but I guess I do believe in God. I guess I do.

I ALWAYS WONDERED ABOUT THE ANGAKOKS, ABOUT THE SHAMANS

I was always curious about how it was back then, back when my grand-parents were growing up. I always wondered about the angakoks,[5] about the shamans. Nobody was willing to talk about them or answer my questions. I asked all the time. I asked my parents, I asked my grandparents, I asked a lot. I guess I was the kind of kid who asked a lot of questions. "Why? Why? Why?" I was genuinely curious, I really wanted to know. I guess that they got tired of all my questions. They thought that I was just a kid being curious. They never said much to me, my parents, my grand-parents, they never talked about shamans much when I was a kid.

My parents and my grandparents, they are really strong Christians. I think that is why they never talk about shamans. There was one time, though, I remember, it was the only time that anyone said anything about an angakok. It was springtime and we had been out camping, a whole group of us at our family's campsite. We stopped to have tea on our way home, and my grandfather, Apphia's husband, said that if you take off your clothes and walk far away and pray to the shaman's spirits, the shaman leader or something, and if you suffer the cold to do that, the shaman would answer you. It was really cold that time when we were out camping, it was windy, and he told his favourite grandson that he should go out and take off his clothes and walk into the wind. He should ask the angakok for mercy. Everyone just laughed. I was a kid when I heard that, and for a long time I honestly believed what he said, that you could talk to the angakoks. From that one inci-dent I based all my beliefs. I don't know much at all about that ... I must be wrong or something, I must be really wrong ...

That is what I remember hearing about shamans. Some people still believe that these sprits exist. Sometimes I wonder myself.

THE C-HALL

For as long as I can remember, there has been a community hall. People here call it the "C-hall." It is a recreation centre or pinguarvik.[6] Every community in the North has one. Most of the time people use it as a dance hall. We square-dance with Scottish jig music, accor-dions, and fiddles. You need a partner, and you dance in a large circle. Each community has its own type of square dancing. I cannot describe the steps very well, they are pretty complicated. There are usually lots of people participating. At first none of the teenagers would square-dance. It was only the adults who did the dancing. Teenagers thought it was uncool. They would only do modern-type dancing, disco dancing at the teen dances. Now young people are starting to get into square-dancing a little bit more. Now there is barely any room to move during community hall dances. Sometimes you can hear the adults complain about that. During the Christmas season it gets especially bad. It seems as if the whole town is dancing! For a few weeks during Christmas the C-hall is open all the time, and we dance almost twenty-four hours a day. During the spring festivals or other celebrations it is less intense.

UP TO THE AIRPORT TO GREET PEOPLE COMING IN

The C-hall and the activities here haven't changed much since I was a kid. Other things have changed, though. For example, there used to be a big hubbub about the airplane, the tingmisuuq, coming in on the ice. Back then, when I was an infant up until I was about two or three, there would be hordes of people going to the bulldozed snow strip, wanting to greet people who came in from out of town. When I was a couple of years older, the planes stopped landing on the ice. They bulldozed the gravel on the outskirts of town and made a runway and a permanent airport, a mivvik.[7] When I was a kid, it used to be like, "Where are you going?" "Where else? Mivvingmut!"[8] My grandmother and I used to go a lot. It seemed as if the whole town would go up to the airport to greet people coming in.

If it was one of my aunts or uncles from Panarctic or from the regional high school in Iqaluit, my grandmother and my aunts and I would clean the house all day and have it all nice and clean by eight at night when the plane came in. I learned how to operate laundry machines and do laundry very early on in my life. If none of our relatives were coming in, we would go anyway and greet the people. Sometimes we would go visit the people who had arrived once they left the airport. Everyone would be out visiting after a plane came in. It was a treat when we had new arrivals, because we would go see them at Grandma's super-clean, Spic-and-Span smelling house. Sometimes groups of people would come in, and it would be a big affair. Sometimes it was the Akukitturmiut,[9] the Greenlanders, who came in. Sometimes it was exchange students from the South, workers from Panarctic, sports competitors from other communities, or kids from the Iqaluit high school.

Now with four flights in, four flights out a week, and with people travelling in and out all the time, it is not as big a deal as it used to be to go to the airport. If we ask now, "Who's coming in?" people will say, "I don't know," or "I don't care." Sometimes we don't even know what time the plane comes in anymore.

A BASEBALL SEASON IN TOWN

There's a baseball season in town now. We play baseball in the summer.
The last couple of years there has been almost like a baseball revival.
People used to play baseball in the summer behind the high school
when I was growing up. It wasn't a big baseball diamond or anything
like that, but it was a nice open field. The Co-Op store and the pool
hall were adjacent to it. Lots of people went. It seemed like the only
thing to do during the summer if you weren't out on the land. With the
sunlight in the summer, we used to play at all hours of the day and
night. I don't know what happened, but people stopped after a while.
They built an elementary school where the baseball field was, and
people did not think of it for some years. The pool hall closed down
too. I don't know why ... maybe because of the vandalism. Also, my
beloved coffee shop closed down. I loved that place. A few years ago
someone thought about playing baseball again in the field right beside
the Northern Store. Now there are regular teams. I am old enough to
play now, except I am too shy.

BEGINNING TO LEARN HOW TO SEW

I'm still learning how to sew. In fact, I'm just beginning. I know how
to make duffle socks. I learned when I was in Grade Four. Last year my
family went on a big ski-doo trip to Igloolik. When we were on that
trip my grandmother taught me a little about how to prepare skins,
how to make them tender for sewing kamiks. I still don't know how to
sew them, though, and I don't know how to cut out the delicate patterns in the furs.

   This year I've really showed an interest in sewing. My grandmother
Apphia, she is happy to see that. She has taught me a little bit about
preparing skins, and she has taught me some things about how to
measure. Still she hasn't taught me anything about sewing. The reason
my grandmother has never taught me about sewing is that she thought
it would be too tough on my diseased hands, on my eczema.

   I have a beautiful pair of kamiks right now. My mother and my
grandmother made them for me in a week. They are my second pair. I
did all of the skins for them myself. I watched my grandmother
measure them and sew them, and I watched my mother sew the soles,
the alungit. While they were being made, I learned what kind of skins
you have to have for kamiks – summer caribou skins are the best for
women's kamiks – and I learned what kind of tools you need to make
them. Our neighbour and a good friend of my mother's also helped
us out.

I can't believe I am twenty and I am just beginning to learn how to sew. My grandmother and my mother learned to make kamiks in their teens. But then again, when I think about it, I am learning, and I guess that is what is important. My overworked mom and my busy grandmother are taking the time to teach me. I guess I've always felt a little alienated from those types of things before. I never thought when I was growing up that I would ever be learning how to sew kamiks and things. Now I realize that I should have learned how to sew as a child. That is when I should have started to learn.

SATURDAY-NIGHT FEASTS

Saturday nights, I can't believe how different things are now. Saturday nights back when I was a kid, Saturday nights were always a family time. Now, Saturday nights, you have to go, go, go, you have to get out, see people, see friends, go dance. Now it is a total bore just to stay home on Saturday nights.

My dad and my grandparents used to always go out hunting on weekends. The only time they could hunt was on the weekends because they worked at jobs during the week. On Saturday nights when I was growing up, while the men were out hunting, the women stayed home and cleaned up. There was always this rush before they left, a rush to make bread and tea and prepare for the food that the men were going to bring back. My grandmother made lots of bread back then. On Saturday nights it was always special. There was always this bread and clean-house smell in the air at home. If it was winter, spring, or fall, it would be dark at night, so it was really cosy. My grandfather and my dad would come in from hunting to all of this. To see my grandfather and my dad coming in the door announcing that they had gotten seals or caribou made it all the better, topped it all off, you know?

My dad's father used to be a really good hunter. He caught seals all the time. Every Saturday night he would come home with some. Now he can't go out because he has no job. He is too old to have a job to buy the things he needs to go out hunting, like a good snowmobile and gas. My grandmother doesn't make bread any more. She rarely cleans up like she used to on Saturday nights. My father, though, he still hunts every weekend. No matter how small a catch, my father always gives half of it, some of it, to his parents.

Sometimes if there is a lot, he will give some to my mother's parents too. He doesn't give as much to my mother's family because my mom's dad has a job, he can afford to go hunting. He gets his own meat. He just turned seventy-three, he still works as a garbage-truck driver, and he still goes out hunting. He has some pretty expensive things. It is pretty expensive to get equipment for hunting. He has a four-wheeler and a boat and rifles and a ski-doo. He has tents and lots of other camping equipment.

Saturday-night feasts were really, really special when I was growing up. I loved the feasts. People would come to my grandparents' house. There would be so many people you couldn't walk, or sometimes you would have to crawl through the legs, there would be so many people. People would be talking and laughing. There would be this fresh animal smell, it smelled good. I would listen to my grandparents talk about us, praise us in front of all these people, so it was a lot of fun.

For feasts to happen people would go on the radio and announce that they had fresh meat and invite people over. There would always be tea afterwards. It was fun listening to the radio and finding out who caught seals or caribou and where the feasts were. Elders usually had the feasts. Young people, like my parents' age, they never had feasts, older people would have them. My parents now, they might have a few friends over when my father catches something, but our house is too small to go on the radio and invite everyone. If we said on the radio that my dad caught some seal, our house wouldn't hold everyone who would come. We don't have room. Sometimes if my dad gets lots and lots of food, lots of fish or whatever, he might go on the radio and tell people that they can come over with bags and take some meat, but he wouldn't invite them over for a feast because there would be too many people here.

Community feasts at the community hall are really great too, but they only come once in a long, long while. The community hall smells a lot during those feasts because of all those foods. People just flock to them, they can't wait to get in. If the community hall people say that it will open at six and then announce again that they will postpone it until seven because they are not prepared yet, people get pretty angry or whatever. They can't wait. People are just crazy for seal. Baby seals are a pretty rare treat. One time there was this contest between my father's father and his good friend, his old hunting companion. Those two competed one night to see who could catch a seal first. My grandfather won the contest. He caught the seal first. They had a feast at the community hall. They both caught seals, but the next part of the contest was seeing whose wife could cut up the seal the fastest. My grandmother won. It was kind of hard, though, because the other competitor was my aunt. She was young. She was good at it even at that age when she was young. After they cut up the seal, everyone went running for it. The ladies were screaming, "Move away! Move away!" It was pretty amazing watching how fast people can run when they are headed for a seal.

PLEASANTRIES

There are many books that say Inuit don't use pleasantries much. They say we don't think it is necessary. This is true. Personally I think pleasantries are a waste of time.

Inuit don't say "hello," and we don't knock. Some say it is because there is a silent understanding, a silent communication going on. The person knows what the other is thinking. There is no need to say "hello," because the other person already knows that the person he is talking to is friendly. The same thing with saying "thank you." If, for instance, someone opens the door for another, the one who opens the door knows the other is already grateful, so he accepts his silence. He is not insulted if the other person doesn't say "thank you." If it is a small, little thing, there is no need. The other knows the other is grateful. They just sort of know.

Qallunaat who are up North, they shouldn't worry, though, if they are saying too much or too little. People, Inuit, understand these things. We know that Qallunaat are not always aware of these customs. Qallunaat shouldn't have to work at not saying pleasantries. Inuit will say "thank you" to a Qallunaaq because we know he or she doesn't know those things.

Sometimes I get a bit confused in myself, though. I hear a lot of pleasantries among us now, and sometimes I wonder if I should join in. When I stop in at my friends' houses, some of my friends might say, "Come on in, you are very welcome here!" When people come to my house I already assume that they feel welcome, that they feel at home at my house, so I don't say pleasantries. I don't have to worry much about that, though, because I don't have a home, I still live with my parents. It is not for me to say anyone's welcome. Anyhow, except when it comes to kids, I am uncomfortable with saying "hello." I am always in a dilemma, wondering if I should say "hi" or just smile to a friend, to someone who is passing by. There is this word I've been hearing, only in the past couple of years, I think it is a new word. It was adopted. It is "ilaali." It probably means "yes, yes." It is said after saying "thank you," sort of like, "you're welcome." People are saying that a lot these days. It isn't bad, it isn't good, just different.

This practice of non-pleasantries, it is hard to break when you are out of town down South. You expect people to know that you have this practice, but naturally they don't. In some written stories that I have read, Inuit are considered timid. I guess it is just that we are less talkative. We don't say all the things Qallunaat say ...

I've gotten into some trouble with those kind of things when I was in cities in the South. I remember one time when I was seven and visiting my aunt who lived in an apartment building, I tried opening some doors, but they were locked. I didn't think they were strangers that lived there, so I got a hairpin and tried unlocking them. I got into a couple of the rooms. I thought my aunt knew the people who lived there, but I found out later she didn't. When my aunt found me she apologized for me.

Another time I went to an apartment complex where another aunt lived. I got the number of her apartment confused and I went to the wrong apartment. It was unlocked so naturally I thought it was my aunt's place. I didn't knock and started taking my parka off without saying "hello." A lady started yelling at me. She was yelling, "Who are you, why didn't you knock?" She was cursing. Doorbells and knocking devices and locked doors, those are always confusing to me.

ONE STORY THAT I REMEMBER THE MOST

We used to live with my dad's parents when I was a kid, so I was pretty close to my dad's mom. There is one story that I remember the most, probably because it is one of the very few stories that I ever heard from my grandmother Jokeepee. One night after church service in the evening my grandmother and I went home alone. We usually went visiting somewhere after church, visiting her friends and having some tea, but that night we just went home, the two of us, and relaxed. She didn't turn the lights on so it was semi-dark and quiet. I remember the story she told me pretty clearly, because I thought it was real and was happening between us.

The story she told me goes like this. A grandchild kept pestering her grandmother to tell her a story but the grandmother didn't feel like it. I guess she was tired or pretty lazy. The grandchild kept asking her and asking her, and this went on for a while until the grandmother finally gave up. She started telling her grandchild a story. She was telling her a story very quietly – she was almost whispering. It was a story about the weasels. The grandmother kept telling the story until it reached a climax. She kept the grandchild's interest up. The grandmother was telling her about weasels in detail, saying that if someone did something bad or whatever, the weasel would go up someone's leg and into their anus when they went outside to pee. Just as she said that weasels would go into someone's anus, the grandmother went "Poof!" At that point the grandchild was so surprised that she turned into a little bird and just flew away. Her grandmother looked up and suddenly realized what she had done. She started calling out her granddaughter's name.

The grandmother, she started to become desperate and was very sorry for what she did. She was sorry that she scared her little grandchild. She didn't think that she would be so scared. She cried and cried and cried until her throat became hoarse and her eyelids became really, really red. She too became a bird, but a ptarmigan. She flew off and found her grandchild. My grandmother told me that is how ptarmigans came to be, that is how they got their cry and the red under their eyes, because an old granny cried so much when her grandchild turned into a bird.

✦ ✦ ✦

My father also told some stories when I was a kid. He would usually tell them at night, just before bed. When I got scared I used to go into my parents' bedroom and sleep with them. The stories he told me were make-believe stories. They weren't traditional stories – he usually made them up. There was one that was recurring. He told it over and over. It was with the same character but there were different stories on different nights. His stories were about a girl, Tikiq,[10] and her dog and her sled. Girls didn't have sleds back then so it was pretty nice of him to say that she had a sled. She was a very brave girl. When he was telling me these stories I always imagined that she lived outside and she didn't have any parents. She was doing okay.

✦ ✦ ✦

My mother's dad also told some stories while we were picking his grey-white hair with tweezers when we were in his bedroom. We used to sit like that, the grandchildren, in his room picking his grey hairs out with tweezers. The stories he told us those times were about animals, ravens and birds and all that. It is too bad that I don't remember the stories that well or in any detail, because they were marvellous and wonderful stories. I wish I could tell stories well, just as good as my grandparents. The stories they told us were very good stories, in-depth stories. They made you think a lot. They had interesting things in them like birds and animals.

In school they also told us some stories. We heard stories in Home-Ec class. We usually went to this little building, the Tech Centre. The girls would learn to cook and sew, and the boys would learn to build things. Once a week we would switch: we had a Bible class every week. Our sewing teachers were all elders, not real elders but older people, and they would tell us stories. Our cooking class had all Qallunaaq teachers. It is sad to see that the elders that taught us then are so old now. I can't believe how young they were even then. We loved those instructors.

REFLECTIONS ON THE FUTURE:
ACTING INUIT OR ACTING LIKE QALLUNAAT

WHEN I THINK ABOUT MY GRANDPARENTS

When I think about my grandparents, I can't imagine them not being around. I can't imagine my grandfather being dead. He is over seventy, and I guess it will happen one day, but I can't imagine it. I don't think that he will ever, ever die. My grandmother too ... she has been sick for a long time. She quit her job a long, long time ago, but I can't imagine her dead. It is hard to think about it. Even though you know that you have to prepare for death, I don't want to think about it.

I don't think that my grandparents ever scolded me. I don't remember, I am not aware of them scolding me. I remember every time a teacher ever scolded me. Even if the teacher was a kind teacher and only scolded me once, I still remember it today. I don't ever remember my grandparents scolding me. When they disciplined me, they said it in a very matter-of-fact way and in a nice voice. One time my grandmother, my mom's mom, told me not to take drugs. She made sure that I knew what the facts were about drugs and what they could do to you. She also told me to be careful about guys. She always said things like that very, very nicely but thoroughly. My mom's parents have so many grandchildren that I try not to be babyish with them. They are so busy at times, I try not to grab too much of their attention.

There was one time my grandma went out of her way to help me. She knew that I had bad eczema and she got sad seeing me like that, so she decided to pray for me. One time we were alone, she sat on the sofa and I sat on the coffee table in front of her and we talked for a while. She took my hands, and she said that I should give myself to Jesus. I should ask him to help me. We prayed for a while, but I wasn't really into it. I guess I wasn't ready to have faith. I was just too hesitant to believe. Just recently she asked me again if she could pray for me. Now I am a lot more willing to pray with her. Hopefully that will be some time soon. I think it might help. I believe now that it will help to pray.

These past few years I have been noticing that my grandmother, my mom's mom, has been noticing me more. I am not just one of her grandchildren now. I guess this is because most of her family is away now, and we are the only family living in the same town with her. You know how I like giving things to people, giving my time, buying things for family and friends? With my grandparents I have always felt like I never had to give them anything. They never asked for anything from me. They never patronized me or made me do things. It seems like that with my other grandparents – it is not nice to say, but it is true – they aren't patronizing or hard on us, but they are always telling us to visit them more. They say that it is nice to see us, but that is about it.

Maybe it is because I am one of the oldest grandchildren in town, but sometimes I feel as if my grandmother and I are the same age. At Christmas parties I help her with her make-up, fix her hair, and put perfume on her. Sometimes she acts like a teenager, and it is fun. She always asks for my advice about that sort of thing, make-up, southern clothes, that sort of thing. She doesn't ever treat me like a kid. She knows that I am pretty level-headed and sensible, just like my mom. She knows I can understand things. Sometimes we get together and go against my mom. We corner Mom. Mom says that we are both crazy at times.

SO MUCH OF THE OLD WAYS IN US

Today there's so much of the old ways in us. Even though today we live in a settlement, I was born, I realize, just a breath away from the old life. I always thought my grandparents lived in camps a long, long time ago. I always thought we had all been living in a modernized world for some time, my family, I mean. Now I realize that it hasn't been that long for them at all. They moved in 1968. When I ask my grandparents about why they don't want to go back to the old ways, they say they don't want to go back because it was too hard. I'd like to tell them, "It is just as hard for us now!" The modern world is just as hard today. There are high prices for food, clothing, gas, snowmobiles, hunting gear. Now we young people must work, work, work, work, if we are going to get anywhere.

WHEN I THINK ABOUT SETTLING DOWN

When I think about settling down and raising a family, I don't really know what I will do. I'm not afraid of having babies. I know that I know more about having babies, medically speaking, than my mother or my grandmother knew when they had their first few. They were so young. I grew up in a big family and watched my brothers and sisters being born. And I've had lots of experience taking care of newborns and toddlers because of my younger sisters and brother and cousins. I know that when I have kids, I won't be in the same position my mother and my grandmother were. Still, I am afraid of raising kids as wonderfully as my parents and my grandparents did. They are a tough act to follow.

When I think about raising a family, though, I am not really sure where I am at. My grandmother's generation grew up being told what to do, who to marry. Their lives were set by their parents – their parents did a lot of their decision-making for them. My mother's and father's generation, they were left alone. They got to choose who they wanted to marry because they were away from their parents most of the time. There was still a bit of traditional culture in them, though. They married so young.

A lot of elders now are so afraid of telling kids what to do, who to marry. They don't want to act backwards. It must have been so hard for people of that generation, not having a choice about who to marry. I think a lot of them have come to accept that their traditional upbringing and the way they think about marriage doesn't fit with the way things are today. I think they know that education and jobs are more important now than when they were growing up. They won't say much about people's marriages. They are afraid of getting nasty feedback.

I've had a few tiffs with my grandparents and my parents about boyfriends. Sometimes when I got a new boyfriend, my parents would drop little hints that they thought I had made the wrong choice. My grandmother has been much more direct. One time she chased a boyfriend of mine out of her house with a broom and told him not to come back. Other times she just told me which boy she thought I should be with.

Sometimes I don't know what to do ... I mean, I need advice and I care a lot what they think, I want their approval. Sometimes I almost want them to choose a husband for me. And then again ... I don't know if I would accept their choices. Sometimes the boys my grandmother points out to me, she doesn't know half of what I know about them. Some of them might act nice to my grandmother, but they would be terrible to live with. I've asked myself that before, if they chose someone for me, would I go along with it? I'm confused a lot lately so sometimes I think I would probably just go through with it just so I wouldn't have to go through all the hassles of worrying about who to marry ... On the other hand, sometimes I think I wouldn't go along with it because I'd be thinking about my future in today's career world. If I settled down and had a family right now, I don't know if I would I be able to finish my education. What if I had to go look for a job somewhere outside of Pond Inlet? If I gave up getting married for a career, though, I would have to leave my family. Maybe I'd even meet someone and raise a family far away. Having a family away from home would be so hard! Sometimes I think it would be easier to start one right now in Pond Inlet. I really don't know ...

A LOT OF THINGS TO LOOK FORWARD TO

A lot of times I really don't know what to do. I think about a career, about having a family, about acting Inuit or acting like Qallunaat. I really don't know what I'll do ... I guess I have always felt that I wasn't Inuit enough ... I never really learned how to sew. I never even owned an ulu. I especially felt this way during Inuktitut classes when all my other classmates were so good at Inuit things. They were more traditional, they had kamiks and ulus, and they knew so many Inuktitut words. They were "university level" Inuit in comparison to me. They were so gung-ho about it. I guess I was just shy. I felt very dumb.

I don't feel any real bitterness about the mistakes I've made so far. I look at my mom and her life – she is raising kids, housekeeping, sewing, working, and now she is taking an accounting course too. That is a tough act to follow! That is what I think. And my grandmother, she's got a lot of grandchildren around. She is always tending to them ... There are a lot of things to look forward to, a lot of things I'd like to do for Pond to make it a little better here. Hell, I even wanted it to be the capital of Nunavut, but then I looked more closely at the map and saw that is wasn't as central as I thought. Come to think of it, I don't think I'd want all those people moving here.

When I think about my career, I don't really know what to do. There are so many great people who have been inspirational to me. They are all so different in their lines of work. I admire different people all the time. I am interested in what they do. Sometimes I lean in one direction. I think to myself that I would like to be like a certain person I know. Then I meet someone else who does something different and I want to be like them. I can't seem to make up my mind. I'm sure there are people who have compromised with their split culture before. They did things so that they could have a little from both. Iqaluit is a very good example of how these things from the two cultures have been combined. I know that what I'm doing right now is good, learning my roots, learning to sew, learning tough Inuktitut words. And when I think about moving, I realize I don't want to leave any of my family, not for a while. If I had graduated at sixteen, gone to pre-med and med-school and graduated eight, nine years later, I would have gotten home young enough to have a family and a career. Now, though, things are different. Now I don't know what I will do.

It was hard for me when my aunts and uncles started going away, when they started leaving the settlement to go to school, to look for jobs. I missed them very badly. I'm not saying that I never see them – I still do see them – it is just that I miss them so badly that I think to myself that I'd never want to leave the way they have. We were all together, a long time ago, we used to be all together. I'm not trying to sound overly sentimental. I'm not trying to dwell on the past to the point where I forget my life in the present. I'm not trying to make them feel guilty. My aunts and uncles, they are better off where they are, and they seem happy. Sometimes I think what I would like to do is to absorb as much traditional knowledge as I can and be like my name, be a Pikujak and take care of them.[11]

POSTSCRIPT

❊ ❊ ❊

The documentation of these life histories took place over six years.
The same period was marked by significant changes for the Awa and
Katsak families. Apphia died. Rhoda and her father, Awa, became
active in the local Anglican church. Sandra married, began working as
a legal assistant in Pond Inlet, and had a daughter, Carlene Apphia
Agalakti Omik. She is named after her great-grandmother.

Note about the Spelling

There are various and contesting ways to spell Inuktitut words in English Roman orthography. Depending on the region of the Arctic, the historical period, and the transcriber, Inuktitut names and words have historically been recorded using a number of phonetic conventions. Double o's have been used interchangeably with u's when writing Inuktitut names (i.e., Koobloo vs. Kublu, igloo vs. iglu), as have y/j, k/q, iq/erk, etc., and Inuktitut names and words have historically been written as they might be pronounced in English. For the purpose of this book (and to preserve as much as possible the integrity of Apphia's Inuktitut stories) we have decided to spell Inuktitut places and names of people as they would best be pronounced in Inuktitut. We make exceptions, however, when English speakers spell their names in a certain style; for example, we use Apphia's son James Arvaluk's contemporary legal name, spelling it differently than that of his unilingual grandfather, Arvaarluk, after whom he was named.

Of particular note is the exception we make for the title. "Saqiyuq" (sometimes spelled "saqijuq") Rhoda decided we should spell with a "y" rather than a "j" to flag the pronunciation of the title for a non-Inuit readership. In addition, we leave in Inuktitut certain words that have been adopted into English vocabulary in the North (iglivigaq, kamik, qamutik, and others), and at times, for clarity, we use their English rather than their Inuktitut plural forms (i.e., kamiks as opposed kamiit).

List of People Mentioned in the Stories

❊ ❊ ❊

Apphia Agalakti Siqpaapik and Mathias Awa's children:
Oopah, Arvaluk, Martha, Simon, Jake, Rhoda, Solomon, Joanna, Phillip, Salomie, Ida, and Nary.

Rhoda and Josh Katsak's children:
Sandra, Mona, Sheila, Dawn, Lucas, and Ruby. (Terry Milton, Rhoda's first grandchild, is Mona's son.)

Some of the people mentioned in the stories
Aaluluuq: Family friend who helped deliver Rhoda.
Aqaaq: Apphia's grandmother (Arvaarluk's mother).
Alurut: Apphia's adoptive younger brother who died young.
Amarualik: Apphia's husband's sister (Kalirraq's wife).
Angiliq: Apphia's uncle (Ingnirjuk's husband).
Angugaatiaq: Apphia's great-uncle (Qairniq's husband).
Angutainuk (Jokeepee Katsak): Rhoda's mother-in-law, Sandra's paternal grandmother.
Arnarjuaq: Apphia's great-grandmother (Nutarariaq and Ataguttaaluk's mother).
Arvaarluk: Apphia's adoptive father (James Arvaluk's atiq).
Ataguttaaluk: Apphia's great-aunt (Nutarariaq's sister).
Attaarjuat: Apphia's grandfather (Arvaarluk's father).
Attitaaq: Kunuk's father.
Bernadette Kublu: Apphia's younger sister.
Ijituuq: Apphia's brother-in-law (her stepsister Nattiq's husband).
Ilupaalik: Apphia's adoptive mother (Oopah's atiq).

Ingnirjuk: Apphia's aunt (Angiliq's wife).

Ipiksaut: Apphia's sister-in-law (Qayaarjuaq's wife).

Iqallijuk: Apphia's older stepsister (Arvaarluk's daughter from his first marriage).

Ippiaq: Apphia's paternal grandfather (Kublu's father).

Ituksaarjuat: Ataguttaaluk's husband.

Kalirraq: Apphia's brother-in-law (Amarualik's husband).

Katsak, Ishmailie: Rhoda's father-in-law, Sandra's paternal grandfather.

Kaukjak: Apphia's maternal grandmother (Suula's mother, Rhoda's atiq).

Kublu: Apphia's natural father.

Kunuk: Man who Apphia and Awa camped with when they were first married (Qaaqiuq's husband).

Kupaaq: Apphia's sister-in-law (Maktaaq's wife).

Kuutiq: Apphia's older stepbrother (Arvaaluk's son from a previous marriage).

Leeno Kublu: Apphia's youngest brother.

Lucy Kublu Quasa: Apphia's youngest sister (adopted by Suula from Maktaaq and Kupaaq).

Maktaaq: Apphia's natural brother (Suula and Nutarariaq's son).

Mala: Apphia's father-in-law's brother (Awa's uncle; Simon's atiq).

Mamatiaq: Kunuk's brother.

Nattiq (Ijituuq's wife): Apphia's older stepsister (Arvaarluk's daughter from his previous marriage).

Niqquttiaq: Apphia's sister-in-law, her stepbrother Kuutiq's wife.

Nutarariaq: Apphia's maternal grandfather (Suula's father).

Nutarariaq (Thomas): Apphia's natural brother.

Palluq: Awa's step-grandfather who took care of him when he was young (Rhoda's atiq).

Panikpakuttuk (Hanna Uyarak): Apphia's mother-in-law (Awa's stepmother).

Pikujak: Apphia's sister-in-law (Awa's stepsister, Sandra's atiq).

Piugaatuq: Ataguttaluk and Ituksaarjuat's son.

Qaaqiuq: Woman who Apphia and Awa went caribou hunting with when they were young (Kunuk's wife).

Qairniq: Apphia's great-aunt (her grandmother's younger sister).

Qajaaq: Apphia's older stepsister (Arvaarluk's daughter from his previous marriage).

Qayaarjuaq: Apphia's brother-in-law.

Quliik: Apphia's paternal grandmother (Kublu's mother).

Qulik: Apphia's natural brother

Quliik (Koolerk), Paul: Apphia's natural brother.

Suula Atagutsiak: Apphia's natural mother.

Ukumaaluk: Apphia's brother-in-law (Iqallijuk's husband).

Umik: Apphia's sister-in-law.

Uuyukuluk: Kunuk's stepbrother.

Uyarak: Awa's father, Apphia's father-in-law.

Significant Dates in Eastern High Arctic and Awa Family History

❄ ❄ ❄

1820   Scottish and American whalers start harvesting waters north of Pond Inlet.

1822   Two ships and crew from the British Naval Expedition, led by Captains Parry and Lyon, while searching for the Northwest Passage, become caught in drift ice and winter in the Igloolik region.

1900   George Washington Cleveland (Sakkuartirungniq) opens a whaling and trading station in the Amituq region.

1921   A Hudson's Bay Company trading post opens in Pond Inlet.

1921   Awa (Mathias Awa) is born.

1922   An RCMP post is set up in Pond Inlet.

1929   Anglican missionaries Turner and Duncan, along with Oblate priests Bazin and Girard, arrive in Pond Inlet.

1931   Agalakti Siqpaapik (Apphia Awa) is born.

1931   Oblate priest Bazin leaves Pond Inlet to set up a small mission at Avvajja, close to Igloolik.

1944   Agalakti Siqpaapik (Apphia) is married to Awa (Mathias).

1944   Family Allowance Act is passed by the House of Commons, and Inuit are given disk numbers.

1945   Canadian government launches an aggressive anti-TB, X-ray, and evacuation campaign in the Arctic.

1945   The rapid decline and eventual collapse in prices for Arctic fox furs begins.

1946   Oopah (Ilupaalik), Apphia's daughter and first child, is born.

1947   Arvaarluk, Apphia's father, dies.

1947   A permanent trading post is established in Igloolik.

1948   Arvaluk (James Arvaluk) is born.

1948   Ataguttaaluk dies.

1951   Martha (Umik) is born.

1953   Simon (Mala) is born.

1953   Ten Inuit families from Northern Quebec and Pond Inlet are relocated by Canadian government authorities to Grise Fiord and Resolute Bay.

1955   Six more Inuit families are relocated to Grise Fiord and Resolute Bay from Northern Quebec and Pond Inlet.

1955   Jacob (Siqujjuk) is born.

1955   Chesterfield Inlet Residential school is opened by Oblate missionaries.

1955   Hall Beach DEW-line site opens.

1955   Apphia and her children are flown to Igloolik for chest X-rays aboard the medical ship *The C.D. Howe.*

1957   Rhoda (Kaukjak Palluq) is born.

1957   Nursing station opens in Hall Beach.

1958   Solomon Awa is born.

1959   Federal day school opens in Igloolik.

1959   Anglican mission is established in Igloolik.

1960   Joanna Awa is born.

1961   Arvaluk and Simon are sent away to residential school in Churchill, Manitoba.

1961   Phillip Awa is born.

1962   Apphia and her family are afflicted with measles.

1963   Salomie Awa is born.

1965   Rhoda Katsak starts federal day school.

1965   Ida Awa is born.

1966   The Awa family moves off the land briefly for the first time.

1967   Apphia and Awa are legally married.

1968   Panarctic Oils starts hiring workers in Pond Inlet and Arctic Bay.

1968   The first scientists arrive in Igloolik to conduct tests for the four-year International Biological Programme Human Adaptability Project.

1969   Operation Surname is launched, and Inuit are legally registered with formal surnames. Aglakti becomes Apphia Awa; Kaukjak becomes Rhoda Awa.

1970   Pierre Trudeau visits Igloolik.

1971   The Inuit political organization Inuit Tapirisat of Canada (ITC) is established.

1972   The Awa family permanently moves off the land into Pond Inlet.

1972   Nary Awa is adopted.

1973   Sandra Pikujak Katsak is born.

1973   Rhoda Awa and Joshua Katsak marry.

1975   Mona Lisa Katsak is born.

1976   The first Nunavut land claim is presented to the Canadian government by ITC president James Arvaluk.

1982   Sheila Katsak is born.

1983   Dawn Katsak is born.

1985   Awa's father, Uyarak, dies.

1985   Lucas Katsak is born.

1985   The EEC extends indefinitely a 1983 ban on the importation of seal-skins to European markets.

1990   Ruby Katsak is born.

1992   Nunavut boundary is ratified by plebescite vote.

1993   The Nunavut Final Agreement is signed.

1996   Apphia Agalakti Siqpaapik Awa dies.

1999   The Nunavut Territorial Government is established.

An Overview of Iglulingmiut and Mittimatalingmiut Culture and History

✶ ✶ ✶

These stories, they are from a period of change that we all lived through.
They are not just our stories.

Rhoda Katsak

The stories that are told in this book are set against the backdrop of an old Arctic hunting culture in a vast land and seascape. The families in these narratives lived and travelled across the North Baffin region of the Eastern High Arctic, the Northern Foxe Basin, and the edge of Melville Peninsula (see map 1). Until her move into Pond Inlet in the fall of 1972, Apphia Agalakti spent more than two-thirds of her life travelling among camps scattered across this territory, from the flat tundra around Igloolik where both she and Rhoda were born to the mountains, glaciers, and high escarpments surrounding Pond Inlet where she lived the last twenty years of her life and where Sandra was raised. Apphia and her husband, Awa, travelled together to the shores of Baffin Bay east of Baffin Island, north to Eclipse Sound, Bylot Island, and Lancaster Sound, west to the Brodeur Peninsula, the Gulf of Boothia, and Melville Peninsula, and south to camps in the southern Foxe Basin.

Despite the extreme seasonal differences of temperature (ranging from -45°C in the winter to 20°C in the summer) and light, the Northern Foxe Basin is rich in natural resources, supporting many species of migratory and non-migratory animals. Access to game from both land and sea has supported one of the longest histories of human occupation in the Arctic.

PRE-EUROPEAN CONTACT

Radiocarbon dates of archaeological sites near Pond Inlet and Igloolik demonstrate almost 4,000 years of continuous human occupation of this region. The oldest sites are said to have been inhabited by the "Tuniit," a legendary people often identified with the archaeological Pre-Dorset and Dorset cultures of the

Paleo-Eskimos, who migrated into the Canadian Arctic from the west about 2000 B.C. By A.D. 1000, this culture was being replaced by the Thule people, who migrated along coastlines from Alaska, across the Canadian Arctic to Greenland. They carried with them specialized gear for hunting large sea mammals, especially the bowhead whale, from the umiak or open boat. They are the ancestors of the modern-day Inuit.

Before the changes brought on by the arrival of Qallunaat to the Arctic, the Iglulingmiut and Mittamatalingmiut lived and travelled along traditional routes determined by the seasonal cycles of the animals they hunted – large game like caribou, different species of seal, walrus, and whales, but also fish and migratory birds. People came together in larger camps and split apart into smaller family groups according to these cycles and the changing relationships among families. During summer and autumn, groups of younger hunters and their families would travel inland to small caribou-hunting camps on the land. Other families remained with elders on the coast, living in sod-houses and hunting walrus and other marine mammals. Before rifles became available, animals were taken with throwing and thrusting harpoons, bows and arrows, bird-darts, bolas, fishing spears, knives, and traps. These weapons and other equipment were commonly made from bone, antler, sinew, stone and metal (native copper and meteoric iron were mined at sources in the Arctic and traded, like wood, over long distances).[1]

Food was cached during the fall, and women sewed skin clothing such as parkas, pants, socks, mitts, and kamiks for their families to wear during the cold winter season. In the late fall the young and old gathered on the shore waiting for the ice to become thick enough for travel. The dark winter months were spent in large sealing villages made up of groups of igloos on the thick sea ice. With the lengthening days of sunlight in the spring, these larger camps would break up as meat caches became exhausted and weather and travel conditions improved. Small family groups set out to hunt seals on the land-fast ice, and there would be much visiting between camps. Before snowmobiles, travel was by dog team and qamutik during the winter and spring, and on foot or in small boats during the summer. Sod-houses, tents, and igluvigait were heated and lit by a seal or whale oil lamp called a qulliq, tended by the women and also used for cooking.

EXPLORERS AND WHALERS

Subsistence patterns of Thule Inuit were influenced by a changing climate and the arrival of Europeans in the Canadian Arctic. During the 1500s, explorers sailing along the coast of Baffin Island were looking for a passage through to the west. Inuit living in the High Arctic had most likely heard of these sporadic visits. The trade networks that carried the indigenous materials mentioned earlier would have provided indirect access to some European merchandise. However, the first "official" record of contact between Qallunaat and North Baffin and Northern Foxe Basin Inuit occurred almost three centuries later. In 1818 British Admiralty Captains John Ross and William Parry entered Lancaster Sound in search of the Northwest Passage. Parry returned to the region the following year, "discovering" Navy Board Inlet for the British and drawing up maps and expedition reports. He returned again in 1822 and spent the winter of 1822–23 among the Iglulingmiut, with his shipmate Captain George Lyon and the crew of the British Naval Expedition, after their ships became trapped in sea ice.[2]

In the following decades many British (and later, American) vessels set out to find and map the Northwest Passage and, after 1847, to search for John Franklin's missing expedition. This era of Arctic exploration coincided with the rapid growth of the whaling industry in the Eastern Arctic. Inuit families were employed as a seasonal workforce at shore whaling stations. Whalers supplemented their haul of whale products by trading southern goods such as rifles, ammunition, knives, sewing needles, flour, sugar, tea, tobacco, and metal pots for caribou meat, furs, skin clothing, artifacts, and ivory. Wood brought from the South aboard these ships began to permanently replace bone and antler, changing the style of qamutiks, tents, and sod-houses. Metal replaced the ivory, antler, bone, soapstone, slate, and other hard materials used for arrow and harpoon heads, knife blades, pots, and other items. Occasional stories of Inuit women acting as seasonal wives for whalers emerge in oral traditions and written records. Many of the whaling ships had Scottish crews who introduced accordion music, gramophones, and square-dancing to the Inuit.

The impact of this contact with whalers was significant. On the one hand, Inuit gained access to useful southern commodities. But foreign diseases, against which Inuit had no immunity, had devastating effects, severely reducing the Inuit population. Seasonal contact with whalers continued until the turn of the twentieth century when over-hunting drove bowhead whales almost to extinction and the whaling industry died.

TRADERS, RCMP, AND MISSIONARIES

Visits from whaling ships ceased in the early twentieth century, to be replaced by the arrival of independent traders to Arctic lands. Some traders were ex-whalers who stayed behind to exchange trade goods with Inuit in return for Arctic fox furs, in high demand in European and North American markets in the early 1900s. Hudson's Bay Company traders succeeded independent traders, establishing posts in Pond Inlet in 1921 and in Igloolik in the late 1930s. The Royal Canadian Mounted Police branched north at this time,

establishing a detachment in Pond Inlet in the summer of 1922. The RCMP did
not have a permanent post in Igloolik until the mid 1960s, when large numbers
of the population began moving off the land.

Anglican and Catholic missionaries arrived in the Eastern High Arctic
during this same period. In 1910 Anglican Bibles printed in the Inuit syllabic
writing system, developed by missionary Edward James Peck, began circulat-
ing in camps around the Pond Inlet region. The Roman Catholic gospel also
disseminated northwards at this time from the Hudson Bay region to camps
around Igloolik. In September 1929, two English Anglican (Church Missionary Society) and two French Roman Catholic (Oblate) missionaries arrived in
Pond Inlet, and a race began to proselytize Inuit families in the region. After
two years of intense competition in Pond Inlet (and allegations of pro-
Anglican favouritism by English Hudson's Bay Company traders), Oblate
priest Etienne Bazin left Pond Inlet and established a chapel at Avvajja, fifteen
kilometres northwest of the present-day settlement of Igloolik. There he baptized a highly respected and influential couple in the region, Ataguttaaluk and
her husband Ittuksaarjuat, and Roman Catholicism spread.

By the 1930s, when Apphia Aglakti was a small child, trading centres had
become permanent features of the Arctic landscape, and the Inuit economy
shifted from subsistence hunting and fishing (interrupted only sporadically and
seasonally by the whalers) to one based on both hunting-fishing and fox-trap-
ping. Families were still mobile, aggregating and dispersing as they had before
contact. Travel routes and seasonal rounds, however, now accommodated trap
lines and trading posts. Credit was arranged for hunters at specified posts.
Periods of hunger increased as game was gradually depleted where concentrations of people lived around these posts. Visits to the trade centres of Igloolik
and Pond Inlet increased as families came to rely on Euro-Canadian officials
for southern food staples, ammunition, and medical care. In the 1940s and
'50s the market for white fox furs in Europe declined and the cash value of furs
plummeted. Compounding these problems, epidemics of measles, tuberculosis,
and smallpox spread in camps across the Arctic, killing hundreds of people.

NORTHERN DEVELOPMENT AND THE ESTABLISHMENT OF SETTLEMENTS

In the period following the Second World War, the federal government implemented broad-scale policies for northern development. These had profound
effects for Inuit, who were made part of the modern welfare state. Hundreds
of people infected with tuberculosis were sent to southern Canadian hospitals
for treatment. Individual Inuit were assigned disks with identification
numbers. These numbers were later replaced with legal surnames, added to the
traditional name (atiq) given at birth. Church-run residential schools (both

Catholic and Anglican) were opened in the late 1950s in such faraway places as Chesterfield Inlet and later Churchill on the west coast of Hudson Bay. Many children from the Igloolik region, including the Awas' two oldest sons, were sent away for the school year. Classes in these residential schools were held exclusively in English, and Inuit children were taught with a curriculum oriented to students in southern Canadian schools. Day schools opened in Arctic Bay in 1959, and in Pond Inlet and Igloolik in 1960. Hostels were built to house children like Rhoda Katsak and her siblings whose parents continued to live on the land. Mandatory attendance was imposed: families like the Awas were denied family allowance payments if their children did not attend school full time. Officials and RCMP collected children by boat from camps where families failed to bring their children into the settlements for school at the end of the summer.

The establishment of permanent settlements such as Pond Inlet, Igloolik, and Arctic Bay (see map 1) facilitated the administration of programs of health care, education, and social assistance in the Arctic. To encourage year-round settlement, the government constructed small, low-rent houses with oil stoves, lights, and water tanks. These houses were poorly insulated, difficult to maintain, and often over-crowded. Living together in large groups year round was new to Inuit, and many found the confinement of western sedentary life stressful after living on the land. This was a period of great change for the Inuit, which is well documented in contemporary Inuit oral tradition. Many families like the Awas moved back and forth between the land and the settlement, but as government pressures intensified, more and more couples abandoned their camps to be with their school-aged children. By the early 1970s almost all Inuit were living year round in settlements. The last family from the Pond Inlet/Igloolik region to move off the land was that of Apphia Agalakti Siqpaapik Awa and her husband, Mathias Awa, in the fall of 1972.

In the 1970s the population of Pond Inlet and other settlements grew rapidly. Subsistence hunting and trapping were gradually supplemented by wage labour. Euro-Canadian values and world views became more common with exposure to television, formal education, and the attitudes and behaviour of non-Inuit in the settlement. The exploitation of oil fields in the High Arctic, as well as a lead and zinc mine in Nanisivik near Arctic Bay, employed Inuit men periodically, and sporadically brought large influxes of cash to communities. The economic viability of subsistence hunting weakened when in 1983, after years of anti-sealing campaigns, the European Economic Community instituted an embargo on importing sealskins. In Pond Inlet, prices dropped from $16 to less than $5 a skin. In 1985 this boycott was extended indefinitely. This affected many Inuit. Only those earning wages could afford to buy the equipment necessary to hunt.

The 1970s and '80s also brought expansion of government infrastructure in the North. A new nursing station, a school and gym, and a bigger airstrip were built in Pond Inlet. The Toonoonik-Sahoonik Co-Operative was opened, selling groceries, hardware, and clothing along with carvings and crafts. The Co-Op also took over a student hostel, turning it into a hotel for government employees and increasing numbers of tourists. In 1975 Pond Inlet was incorporated as a hamlet and began running many local services previously administered from Ottawa. Communications were transformed with the introduction of telephone service locally in 1970 and to communities beyond Pond Inlet in 1975. Television, introduced in the 1970s, began offering cable broadcasts from Yellowknife, Ottawa, Toronto, Edmonton, St Johns, Vancouver, and Detroit in the early 1990s.

In 1993 when Apphia Awa, Rhoda Katsak, Sandra Katsak, and I recorded these life histories, Pond Inlet was a community of a thousand people containing two hundred government-built houses, the hamlet office, two schools, two churches, a nursing station, the Northern Store (formerly the the Hudson's Bay Company), the Co-Operative store, a small hotel, the community hall, a skating rink, a curling arena, and an RCMP station. Since then, two new neighbourhoods have been built, along with a shopping mall, a new hamlet office and adjacent fire hall, and a new Catholic church.

During the 1990s the shifting winds of change have continued to blow. Inuit in Pond Inlet and across Canada's Eastern High Arctic have been preparing for the establishment of Nunavut Territory in April 1999. This new era of goverment and self-determination offers the prospect of continuing change for generations of Inuit into the twenty-first century, through their participation in a wider international network as well as a more meaningful political dialogue at home.

List of Stories

❊ ❊ ❊

APPHIA AGALAKTI SIQPAAPIK AWA

Suggested Readings

※ ※ ※

LITERATURE ON THE NORTH BAFFIN/NORTHERN FOXE BASIN INUIT CULTURE AND HISTORY

There is an extensive and longstanding written tradition describing Arctic lands and Arctic peoples. A list of ethnographic, historical, and oral history methodological texts has been included in the bibliography. A few works, however, stand out as particularly relevant to this life history collection.

LITERATURE ON EARLY-CONTACT CULTURE

Descriptions of Amitturmiut Inuit culture during the initial contact period were published in journals and reports by early visitors to their lands. British explorers William E. Parry and George F. Lyon both published accounts in 1824 describing their experiences among the Inuit in that region, as did ethnographers Therkel Mathiassen in 1928 and Knud Rasmussen in 1929. These writings chronicle early encounters with Inuit families and describe subsistence patterns, hunting strategies, technologies, folklore, rituals, and social organization as they were presented to outsiders. Awa family ancestors such as the shaman Awa, Palluq, Nutarariaq, other relatives, and historical figures are described in the pages of some of these early narratives. More recent anthropological scholarship including *The Handbook of North American Indians,* vol. 5, *Arctic* (Damas 1984), provides a useful overview of Arctic history and surveys Inuit cultures across North America and Greenland. Of particular interest is Guy Mary-Rousselière's chapter on the Iglulik Inuit in this volume, as well as his important book that documents a celebrated historical event in Eastern High Arctic history – the epic journey of a shaman, Qitdlarssuaq, who in the late 1800s led a group of Inuit to Greenland (1991). Traditional Inuit religion and shamanistic practices have been described in bits and pieces by Daniel Merkur (1991), Bernard Saladin d'Anglure (1977, 1978, 1994), Jarich Oosten (1988), and others. Adoption and naming practices have been written about by Lee Guemple (1965, 1979) and Valerie Alia (1994), among others. For a general overview of traditional Inuit material culture and social life, see Morrison and Germain (1995).

ETHNOGRAPHIC AND HISTORICAL WRITINGS ON EASTERN ARCTIC COLONIALISM

Numerous ethnographies and historical sources have chronicled changes brought to the Inuit by contact with outsiders. Some writings examine change across a broad spectrum of Inuit culture (Crowe 1970, Duffy 1988, Matthiasson 1992), while others look specifically at transforming Igluling-miut kinship structures (Damas 1963), the impact of whaling (Eber 1989, Stevenson 1997), disease and the Inuit incorporation into the Canadian health care system (Grygier 1994), and the justice system (Matthiasson 1967, Rasing 1994). Books have been written that illustrate modifications to the naming system (Alia 1994), the effects of environmental movements on Inuit economies (Wenzel 1991), and evolving socio-political and economic relations between Inuit and Qallunaat in the Eastern Arctic (Brody 1975, Paine 1977, Mitchell 1996, and others). Coinciding with the 1992 Royal Commission on Aboriginal Peoples enquiry of the 1953–1955 High Arctic relocations, several books have explored Inuit relocations and Canadian Arctic policy-making (1940–1960s) (Tester and Kulchyski 1994, RCAP 1994).

INUIT ORAL HISTORIES AND LIFE HISTORIES LITERATURE

The stories and recollections of Apphia Awa, Rhoda Katsak, and Sandra Katsak contribute to a growing body of Inuit oral history writings and Inuit literature. Anthologies by Gedalof (1980) and Petrone (1988) speak to the interplay between spoken and written words and offer rich examples of how colonialism has affected Inuit oral and written traditions in the Eastern Arctic. Our work joins a body of collaborative life history texts including those between Washburne and Anauta (1940), Nuligak and Metayer (1966), Bodfish and Schneider (1991), Blackman and Neacock (1989), and Pitseolak and Eber (1993), as well as life histories published by the Inuit Cultural Institute (Ungalaaq 1985, Paungat 1988). Also of relevance is Minnie

Freeman's acclaimed autobiography (1978). Most Inuktitut legends, songs, memories, and family stories told on the land and in settlements, of course, never make it to print. This list and the published works cited in the bibliography is by no means inclusive.

Glossary of Inuktitut Terms

amautik	Woman's parka with an oversized hood, used for carrying babies and toddlers.
Amittuq	"The narrow place"; the Northern Foxe Basin region of the Eastern High Arctic. The term has recently been adopted as a designation for the Nunavut electoral district which includes Igloolik and Hall Beach.
Amitturmiut	"People of the narrow place"; people from the Igloolik/ Hall Beach region.
atiq	Name.
iglu (igloo)	House or snow-house.
Iglulingmiut	"People of the place where the houses are." The term is used in the Arctic to describe people living in and around the contemporary settlement of Igloolik. It has also been used by anthropologists and historians to refer to the Inuit "culture and dialect group" who inhabit the North Baffin, Northern Foxe Basin, and Melville Peninsula region (Pond Inlet, Igloolik, Arctic Bay).
igluvigaq, igluvigait (pl)	Snow-house(s)
Ikpiaqjuk	Arctic Bay.
Ikpiarjuk	Another name for Igloolik. Igloolik is in fact the island off Meville Peninsula where the settlement of Igloolik

was built. Ikpiarjuk is the bay on which the settlement is located.

Inuk, Inuit (pl.)	Person, people.
kamik	Traditional Inuit skin boot.
qaggiq, qaggiit (pl.)	Large ceremonial snow-house.
Qallunaaq, Qallunaat (pl.)	Non-Inuit person, persons.
qamutik	Sled.
qarmaq, qarmait (pl)	Sod-house(s), round structures traditionally made of sod, rocks, bone, wood, and other materials.
qulliq, qulliit (pl.)	Oil lamp(s) made of stone, used to heat and light dwellings and cook food
Sanirajak	Hall Beach
saqiyuq (saqijuq)	Wind that changes direction once while maintaining its velocity.
Tunnunirmiut	"People facing away from the sun"; people from the North Baffin/Pond Inlet Arctic Bay region.
Mittimatalik	"The place where Mittima is [buried]"; Pond Inlet.
Mittimatalingmiut	"People from the place where Mittima is [buried]"; people from Pond Inlet.
ulu	A woman's knife.

NOTES

❖ ❖ ❖

At various places in the three collections, readers will notice the symbol ❖ ❖ ❖ between two texts. This symbol represents a break in the narrative when the speaker shifted from one topic to another and then back again in the middle of a session. I also use this symbol when parallel stories recorded on different days were patched together under one story title.

PART ONE

1 This translates into "fox" in English.

2 In Inuit culture names are passed down through the generations. Individuals are given the atiqs (names) of recently deceased relatives or community members and are said to share characteristics, indeed, share souls, with the person whose name they have been given. Often namesakes are both addressed and treated according to kinship relations of the previous person with that name. Our interpreter, Lucy, for example, named her youngest son after her mother, Suula Atagutsiak. When she addresses him, she calls him "mother," and he calls her "daughter." The person's soul is thus inherited and kept alive in the name.

3 Christianity was first introduced to the Amitturmiut Inuit in the early 1900s, when Inuktitut syllabic Bibles from the Hudson Bay area were circulated to camps in the region and interpreted by Inuit lay preachers. On 2 September 1929 the Hudson's Bay ship *Nascopie* arrived in Pond Inlet

bringing the first missionaries to the North Baffin. Church Missionary Society Anglicans Reverends Turner and Duncan, and French Roman Catholic Oblates, Fathers Bazin and Girard. Competition between the two denominations to convert the Inuit was fierce. Reverend Duncan and Father Girard left the region shortly after arriving, and after two years of intense rivalry in and around Pond Inlet, Father Bazin moved to the Igloolik area.

4   These poetic Inuit songs were sung while travelling, or in snowhouses, tents, and sod-houses, or during winter gatherings, which took place in gaggiit, or ceremonial snowhouses. Sometimes accompanied by drum dancing, they were, for the most part, composed of short, often personalized lyrics celebrating some element of hunting or life on the land. Ajaa jaa songs roughly followed a common melody and rhythmic pattern with repeated "Ajaa jaa" refrains. A documented example of Ajaa jaa lyric, from the traditional period sung by Rhoda's grandfather Palluq's wife, Takornaq, to ethnographer Knud Rasmussen in 1922 [Takornaq in Rasmussen 1929:27] is

> Ajaja – aja – jaja
> The lands around my dwelling
> Are more beautiful
> From the day
> When it is given to me to see
> Faces I have never seen before.
> All is more beautiful
> All is more beautiful
> And life is thankfulness
> These guests of mine
> Make my house grand,
> Ajaja — aja — jaja.

5   This was likely to have been Oblate missionary Etienne Bazin who in 1931 established a mission chapel at Avvajja, 15 km northwest of the present day settlement of Igloolik.

6   Adoption is a common and open practice among Inuit. When people practised a hunting/trapping existence on the land, adoption served not only to form alliances between families but also to ensure the survival of the group by guaranteeing equal distribution of food, hunters, and seamstresses in Inuit families.

7   This was Oblate missionary Etienne Bazin.

8   The RCMP had been in the region for fourteen years, since 1922 when a magistrate and court party were sent to Pond Inlet to try two Inuit men for the shooting death of an erratic and volatile trader, Robert Janes.

9   Utagannaakulu is an endearing expression in North Baffin Inuktutit dialect translating roughly into "my little child."

10   The term atiq used here refers to "Arvaluk's name," the person who he
     was named after, the person with whom he shares a soul.

11   In North Baffin Inuktitut this translates roughly as "dear brother." Inuit
     often address each other according to how they are related – through
     marriage, family relations, namesakes, etc. One of the people Awa was
     named after was his stepmother's brother, so she referred to him as her
     aniannuk.

12   Compared to English, Inuktitut has highly specific kin terms. Older and
     younger brothers and sisters, paternal and maternal cousins, aunts,
     uncles, brothers-in-law and sisters-in-law, and so on all have different
     designations, and Inuit often use these terms to address each other.
     An English translation of this term is "my husband's elder brother's
     wife."

13   This is an Inuktitut word for father.

14   English names adopted by Inuit are sometimes altered to conform with
     linguistic structure and inflections of Inuktitut. For example, the English
     name Elizabeth is often changed to Elisapee, Jacob to Jakopie, and
     Simon to Simeonie.

15   In North Baffin dialect this translates roughly into "something scav-
     enged" or "something taken out of the garbage."

16   Ataguttaaluk's story of courage and survival is a celebrated tale in Amit-
     turmiut history. It has been decribed in a number of written accounts and
     is kept alive in Eastern Arctic oral tradition. Both elementary and senior
     level schools in Igloolik are named after Atagutaaluk.

17   A translation of uujuq is "cooked meat."

18   An English translation of niukittuq is "small legs" or "shorty."

19   Tuberculosis spread in epidemic proportions among Canadian Inuit
     throughout the 1940s and '50s. The government responded to this health
     crisis with a broad-scale X-ray program and evacuation of infected Inuit
     to southern hospitals. By the mid-1950s the Canadian government had
     transported close to one-seventh of the Inuit population to southern
     Canadian sanatoria for treatment of the disease.

20   The Family Allowance Act was passed by the Canadian House of
     Commons in 1944 and implemented in the Eastern Arctic in 1945. Des-
     ignated payments of trade goods were made for each child (up to sixteen
     years of age). Children were registered with a disk number, and back
     payments were made to their parents when a delay in registration was
     recorded.

21   Ajakuluk is a North Baffin Inuktitut term for "your mother's sister."

22   This translates into "doll."

23   Coppermine is a settlement directly north of Yellowknife, in the north-
     western (Qitiqmeot) region of Nunavut.

24   In the North Baffin Inuktitut dialect, an udjuuk is a great bearded seal.

25   This is an Inuktitut word for "mother."

26 A literal translation of this is "in the manner of the Qallunaat." It is an Inuktitut word for "English."

27 Ikpiarjuk is the bay where the settlement of Igloolik is located. Although the contemporary community is referred to as Igloolik, Igloolik (Iglulik) is actually the name of a point on the island off Melville Peninsula on which the settlement is located.

28 This was part of the Canadian government's concentrated response to the tuberculosis epidemic in Inuit camps in the late 1940s and '50s. Using small aircraft, government officials transported Inuit from their camps to board the medical coast-guard ship *The C.D. Howe*. There they performed X-rays and medical exams and singled out infected Inuit to be evacuated to sanatoria in the South. These individuals were often separated from their families for many years.

29 Located approximately sixty miles south of Igloolik, Hall Beach was an American military base constructed in 1955 during the height of the cold war as part of the DEW (Distant Early Warning) radar line that branched across the Arctic. Two colossal seventy-foot radar screen towers were built on that site. A nursing station and small hospital were opened in Hall Beach in 1957.

30 Churchill is a community of Inuit, Chipewyans, and Whites on the west coast of Hudson Bay at the mouth of the Churchill River in Northern Manitoba. A trading post since the seventeenth century, in the 1960s it had a residential school where Anglican Inuit from the East and other northern Aboriginal children were sent to school. Catholic Inuit from the Igloolik region were sent to residential school in Chesterfield Inlet.

31 Pangnialuk is an Inuktitut term for a "big male caribou."

32 Inuit Tapirisat of Canada (ITC) was established in 1971 as a national Inuit political organization founded by an emerging generation of young, southern-educated Inuit political leaders. ITC immediately began lobbying for increased involvement of Inuit in Arctic policy-making. In 1975 ITC commenced land-claims negotiations with the federal government, and in 1976, ITC (then headed by Apphia Awa's oldest son, James Arvaluk) submitted the first of a series of land claim proposals that eventually led to the establishment of a Nunavut territory.

33 Qiluqqisaaq was a man living in Pond Inlet. At that time he was Solomon's brother's father-in-law.

34 Between 1968 and 1972 Panarctic Oils Limited hired approximately two dozen workers from Pond Inlet and Arctic Bay for oil and gas drilling operations on islands in the Arctic archipelago. Panarctic operations continued throughout much of the 1970s, at times more than tripling the cash income brought into Inuit communities.

35 Since the first arrival of the RCMP, missionaries, and Hudson's Bay traders to the eastern High Arctic in the 1920s, sea-lift vessels have

annually supplied Inuit settlements with building materials, Hudson's Bay Company stock, etc. Unloading the ships provided Inuit from the region with access to cash and trade goods.

36 Trips between Pond Inlet and Igloolik by dog team and qamutik at that time usually took between seven to ten days. By snowmobile the trek can take anywhere from twenty-four hours (direct) to two to three days (with a family and supplies in tow).

37 In the winter of 1922 the renowned shaman Awa, his family, and other ancestors of the Awa and Katsak families spent three weeks with ethnographer Knud Rasmussen who stopped during his travels across the Arctic to record Iglulingmiut stories, songs, and shamanic words. Originally published in two lengthy (1929 and 1930) volumes of the *Report of the Fifth Thule Expedition (1921–1924)*, the shaman Awa's stories and poems have shaped Eastern Arctic oral and written traditions for the past six-and-a-half decades, appearing in countless ethnographies, academic articles, and anthologies of Inuit literature.

38 In the Netsilingmiut dialect George Washington Cleveland's Inuktitut name translates into "the harpoon thrower." Stories about Sakkuartirungniq appear in historical texts and in Inuit oral tradition. He was famous for his boisterous character and the number of children he left behind in the North.

39 This is a North Baffin Inuktitut word for "narwhal skin."

40 This is an Inuktitut word for "interpreter."

41 In the 1930s and '40s Canadian government administrators began using disk numbers intermittently as a way of registering individual Inuit whose Inuktitut names made them difficult for administrators to identify. With the passing of the Family Allowance Act in 1944 and the incorporation of Inuit into the Canadian child welfare system, payment of allowances became based on the registration of children. A federal proposal was passed at this time to register the entire Canadian Inuit population with numbers. The Canadian Arctic was divided between East (E) and West (W) and then into twelve regions with corresponding numbers. Disk numbers in the Igloolik/North Baffin region began with E-5. By 1950 almost all Eastern Arctic Inuit were registered with E-5 numbers.

42 This would have been Canon John Turner, who arrived in Pond Inlet in 1929 to establish the first Anglican mission in the region. He fatally shot himself by accident in 1947.

43 Canadian Inuit began taking two names in 1969 with the implementation of Project Surname. The design of this Canadian government program was to replace Inuktitut names and disk numbers with a western-style naming system using Christian names attached to surnames of male heads of households.

PART TWO

1 These DEW-line sites were part of a mechanical warning system built by the American government during the cold war to defend against the threat of an air attack from the North by Soviet long-range bombers. Between 1954 and 1957 more than twenty elaborate sites like Hall Beach were built from east to west across the Arctic, bringing with them an influx of American Army personnel, tradespeople, airstrips, domes, scanners, heavy equipment, bunkhouses, and recreational centres. The Hall Beach DEW-line site was built in 1955.

2 Special Constables were a distinct class of Inuit RCMP officers who were trained specifically to patrol Arctic settlements.

3 In 1970 the administration of Inuit schooling was transferred from the federal to the NWT government. In response to fervent lobbying on the part of a growing class of educated Inuit and Inuit political organizations such as Inuit Tapirisat of Canada (ITC), a new northern curriculum was developed with a goal to incorporate Inuit language and culture components into the school system. Among the curriculum changes implemented at this time was a program to teach elementary school classes in Inuktitut until Grade Three.

4 These tests were part of the *International Biological Programme Human Adaptability Project*, an extensive four-year study which took place in Igloolik and Hall Beach from 1968–1972. Academics and scientists from universities and research centres across North America arrived in Igloolik to perform a battery of tests on almost all the Inuit population living in the region (the combined Igloolik/Hall Beach population was listed as 753 in 1969). Individuals were subject to different combinations of tests. Most had standard medical examinations performed and medical histories recorded. They were photographed in different positions and had anthropometric measurements taken of their skulls, faces, and parts of their bodies. Blood pressures were tested, and blood, urine, and hair samples procurred. Over five hundred Inuit had chest and skull X-rays, and as many had hands, feet, and legs X-rays. Detailed sociological and psychological interviews took place on a number of topics, and tests were performed for everything from dental hygiene and cold tolerance to IQ and psychological and physical health. The skin-grafts to which Rhoda refers were performed on several sets of siblings by a team of doctors from the Department of Medicine at the University of Alberta. They were part of a study relating to white-blood cell (HL-A) antigens, their connection with organ transplants, and their ability to identify genetic markers in human populations. Four extensive volumes (and numerous theses and papers) were published from this four-year Human Adaptability Project, few of which have been read by Inuit from the region.

5 These dictates were part of a centuries-old religious rivalry between Anglican and Roman Catholic missionaries played out in the Eastern High Arctic since the 1930s. While most Mittimatalingmiut (Pond Inlet Inuit) were initially converted to Anglicanism, Iglulingmiut (Igloolik Inuit) were proselytized more intensely by Catholics, and the settlement has subsequently remained divided between the two churches. These divisions have persisted into the 1990s with Anglicans and Catholics in Igloolik occupying distinct sectors of the settlement and acknowledging denominational differences.

6 This was part of a Canadian government-initiated Inuit relocation program which took place in in the Eastern Arctic in 1953 and 1955. Motivated by, among other things, reports of poor hunting conditions in Northern Quebec, paternalist social policies of the period, and High Arctic sovereignty concerns, ninety-two Inuit – sixteen families from Inukjuak, Quebec (formerly Port Harrison), and five families from Pond Inlet – were relocated to settlements on two previously uninhabited lands: Resolute Bay on Cornwallis Island and Grise Fiord on Ellesmere Island. Inadequate housing, a more extreme climate than that to which they had been accustomed, feelings of isolation, and poor hunting conditions caused much suffering among the "Arctic Exiles." These relocations recently came to public light with the 1993 Royal Commission on Aboriginal Peoples hearings and in 1996 a $10 million compensation settlement was awarded by the Canadian government to the Arctic Exiles and their descendants.

7 These houses became available as part of the Home Ownership Assistance Program (HAP) launched by the federal government in the 1980s to provide Inuit with funding assistance for materials and labour to build their own homes.

PART THREE

1 Mittimatalik's literal translation is "there is a Mittima here," meaning "a place where a hunter called Mittima was buried."

2 The Peck syllabic orthography system is used across the Eastern Arctic and is taught in the schools. It was imported to the Eastern Arctic in the early 1900s, developed by Anglican missionary Edward James Peck (1850-1924), who in 1876 founded one of the first Anglican Arctic missions in Little Whale River on Hudson Bay. Peck adopted the syllabic writing system from colleagues working among the Cree and was the first to translate and transcribe portions of the Scriptures into Inuktitut.

3 Pond Inlet sits on an escarpment overlooking an inlet. A small valley runs through the centre of town, which people sometimes use as a short

cut to get from the schools, post office, and nursing station to the houses along the beach.

4 In North Baffin dialect, this translates into "What is with you?" or "What is the matter with you?"

5 Angakok is a North Baffin Inuktitut word for a shaman.

6 A literal translation of pinguarvik in North Baffin dialect is "place to play."

7 This translates as "a place to land."

8 This translates as "to the airport."

9 Akukittuq is an Inuktitut word for Greenland, and Akukitturmiut in North Baffin dialect means "the people from Greenland." In the late 1800s, Qitdlarssuaq, a shaman from the region, led a group of Inuit on an epic migration across Ellesmere Island to northern Greenland. A century later many Mittimatalingmiut still consider themselves related to people of Qaanaaq, Greenland, and regular exchange trips take place between the two settlements.

10 Tikiq, in North Baffin dialect, translates into "index finger."

11 Pikujak, the woman after whom Sandra was named, died of appendicitis in 1970. She was known as a kind-hearted, generous woman whose house was always open to visitors and who took care of many people.

OVERVIEW OF IGLULINGMIUT AND MITTIMATALINGMIUT CULTURE AND HISTORY

1 The early writings of Franz Boas (1888, 1901-07), Therkel Mathiassen (1928), and Knud Rasmussen (1929, 1930) offer detailed descriptions of early North Baffin/Iglulingmiut symbolic and material culture, as do the more recent writings of David Damas (1963), Guy Mary-Rousselière (1984), W.C.E. Rasing (1994) and others.

2 Guy Mary-Rousselière (1984b:443) describes the culture and history of Iglulingmiut contact with non-Inuit. Western accounts of early meetings have also been recorded in the travel narratives of Sir William E. Parry (1824), George F. Lyon (1824), Albert P. Low (1906), and others.

BIBLIOGRAPHY

❋ ❋ ❋

Alia, Valerie. 1994. *Names, Numbers, and Northern Policy: Inuit, Project Surname, and the Politics of Identity*. Halifax, NS: Fernwood Publishing.

Anders, G. 1965. *Northern Foxe Basin: An Area Economic Study*. Ottawa: Department of Northern Affairs and National Resources, Northern Administration Branch.

Bissett, D. 1967. *Northern Baffin Island: An Area Economic Survey*. 2 vols. Ottawa: Department of Indian Affairs and Northern Development.

Blackman, M. 1989. *Sadie Brower Neacock, An Inupiaq Woman*. Seattle: University of Washington Press.

– 1992. "Returning Home: Life Histories and the Native Community." *Journal of Narrative and Life History* 2:49–59.

Boas, F. 1888. *The Central Eskimo*. Sixth Annual Report of the Bureau of American Ethnology for the Years 1884–1885. Washington.

– 1901–1907. *The Eskimo of Baffin Land and Hudson Bay*. New York. Bulletin of the American Museum of Natural History. Vol. 5.

Bodfish, W. 1991. *Kusiq: An Eskimo Life History from the Arctic Coast of Alaska*. Fairbanks: University of Alaska Press.

Brody, H. 1975. *The People's Land*. New York: Penguin.

– 1976. "Inuit Land Use in North Baffin Island and Northern Foxe Basin." In *Inuit Land Use and Occupancy Project*, ed. M.M.R. Freeman. Vol. 1, 153–71. Ottawa: Department of Indian and Northern Affairs.

– 1987. *Living Arctic: Hunters of the Canadian North*. London: Faber and Faber.

Burch, E.S.J. 1994. "Rationality and Resource Use among Hunters." In *Circumpolar Religion and Ecology: An Anthropology of the North*, ed. T. Irimoto and T. Yamada, 163–85. Tokyo: University of Tokyo Press.

Condon, R.G. 1987. *Inuit Youth: Growth and Change in the Canadian Arctic*. New Brunswick: Rutgers University Press.

Cowan, S., ed. 1976. *We Don't Live in Snow Houses Now: Reflections of Arctic Bay*. Canadian Arctic Producers.

Crapanzano, V. 1984. "Life Histories." *American Anthropologist* 84:953–9.

Crowe, K. 1970. *A Cultural Geography of Northern Foxe Basin, N.W.T.* Ottawa: Department of Indian Affairs and Northern Development, Northern Science Research Group.

Cruikshank, J. 1990. *Life Lived Like a Story*. Vancouver: University of British Columbia Press.

Damas, D. 1963. *Iglulingmiut Kinship and Local Groupings: A Structural Approach*. Anthropological Series no. 64, National Museum of Canada Bulletin no. 196.

– ed. 1984. *Handbook of North American Indians*. Vol. 5, Arctic. Washington: Smithsonian Institution.

Dollard, J. 1934. *Criteria for the Life History*. New Haven: Yale University Press.

Dorais, Louis-J. 1978. *Iglulingmiut Uqausingit: The Inuit Language of Igloolik*. Quebec: Université Laval, Association Inuksiutit Katimajiit.

Duffy, Q. 1988. *The Road to Nunavut*. Montreal and Kingston: McGill-Queen's University Press.

Eber, D.H. 1989. *When the Whalers Were up North: Inuit Memories from the Eastern Arctic*. Montreal and Kingston: McGill-Queen's University Press.

Finnegan, R. 1992. *Oral Traditions and the Verbal Arts: A Guide to Research Practices*. London and New York: Routledge.

Francis, D. 1986. *Discovery of the North: The Exploitation of Canada's Arctic*. Edmonton: Hurtig.

Freeman, M. 1978. *Life among the Qallunaat*. Edmonton: Hurtig.

Gedalof, R., ed. 1980. *Paper Stays Put*. Edmonton: Hurtig.

Grygier, P.S. 1994. *A Long Way from Home: The Tuberculosis Epidemic among the Inuit*. Montreal and Kingston: McGill-Queen's University Press.

Guemple, L. 1965. "Saunik: Name Sharing As a Factor Governing Eskimo Kinship Terminology." *Ethnology* 4, no. 3:323-35.

– 1979. *Inuit Adoption*. Canadian Ethnology Service Paper no. 47. Ottawa: National Museum of Man.

Hall, C.F. 1864. *Life with the Esquimaux: The Narrative of Captain Charles Francis Hall, of the Whaling Barque "George Henry" from the 29th May, 1860, to the 13th September, 1862*. 2 vols. London: Sampson Low, Son, and Marston.

– 1865. *Arctic Researches and Life among the Esquimaux: Being the Narrative of an Expedition in Search of Sir John Franklin, in the Years 1860, 1861 and 1862*. New York: Harper and Brothers.

Hughes, D.R., ed. 1969–1972. *International Biological Programme Human Adaptability Project (Igloolik, NT)*. Annual Reports 1–4. Toronto: University of Toronto Press.

Iglauer, E. 1979. *Inuit Journey*. Vancouver: Douglas & McIntyre.

Jenness, D. 1959. *People of the Twilight*. Chicago: University of Chicago Press.

– 1964. *Eskimo Administration*. Vol. 2, *Canada*. Montreal: Arctic Institute of North America, Technical Paper no. 14.

– 1968. *Eskimo Administration*. Vol. 5, *Analysis and Reflections*. Montreal: Arctic Institute of North America, Technical Paper no. 21.

Low, A. 1906. *Report on the Dominion Government Expedition to Hudson Bay and the Arctic Islands on Board the D.G.S. Neptune, 1903–1904*. Ottawa: Government Printing Bureau.

Lyon, G. F. 1824. *A Brief Narrative of an Unsuccessful Attempt to Reach Repulse Bay, through Sir Thomas Rowe's "Welcome," in His Majesty's Ship Griper, in the Year MDCCCXXIV*. London: J. Murray.

Markoosie. 1970. *Harpoon of the Hunter*. Kingston and Montreal: McGill-Queen's University Press.

Mary-Rousseliére, G. 1966. "Toponomie Esquimaude de la Région de Pond Inlet." *Cahiers de Géographie de Québec* 8:301-11 (includes map).

– 1984a. "Exploration and Evangelization of the Great Canadian North: Vikings, Coureurs de Bois, and Missionaries." *Arctic* 37, no. 4:590–602.

– 1984b. "Iglulik." *Handbook of North American Indians*. Vol. 5, *Arctic*. Washington: Smithsonian Institute.

– 1991. *Qitdlarssuaq: The Story of a Polar Migration*. Winnipeg: Wuerz Publishing.

Mathiassen, T. 1928. *Material Culture of the Iglulik Eskimos. Report of the Fifth Thule Expedition, 1921–24*. Vol. 6, no.1. Copenhagen: Nordisk Forlag.

Matthiasson, J.S. 1967. "Eskimo Legal Acculturation: The Adjustment of Baffin Island Eskimos to Canadian Law." Doctoral Dissertation, Cornell University.

– 1992. *Living on the Land: Change among the Inuit of Baffin Island*. Peterborough: Broadview Press.

McGhee, R. 1996. *Ancient People of the Arctic*. Vancouver: University of British Columbia Press.

McGrath, R. 1984. *Canadian Inuit Literature: The Development of a Tradition*. Canadian Ethnology Service Paper no. 94. Ottawa: National Museums of Canada.

– 1987. "Oral Influences in Contemporary Inuit Literature." In *The Native in Literature*, ed. T. King, C. Calver, and H. Hoy, 159–73. Oakville, ON: ECW Press.

Merkur, D. 1991. *Powers Which We Do Not Know: The Gods and Spirits of the Inuit*. Moscow, ID: University of Idaho Press.

Mitchell, M. 1996. *From Talking Chiefs to a Native Corporate Elite: The Birth of Class and Nationalism among the Canadian Inuit*. Montreal and Kingston: McGill-Queen's University Press.

Morrison, D., and G. Germain. 1995. *Inuit: Glimpses of an Arctic Past*. Hull, PQ: Canadian Museum of Civilization.

Morrison, W. 1986. *Showing the Flag: The Mounted Police and Canadian Sovereignty in the North, 1894–1925*. Vancouver: University of British Columbia Press.

Nourse, J. E., ed. 1879. *Narrative of the Second Arctic Expedition Made by Charles F. Hall: His Voyage to Repulse Bay, Sledge Journeys to the Straits of Fury and Hecla and to King William's Land and Residence among the Eskimos during the Years 1864–69*. Washington: U.S. Government Printing Office.

Nuligak. 1966. *I, Nuligak*. Edited and translated by Maurice Metayer. Markham: Peter Martin Associates.

Oosten, J.G. 1988. "The Prime Mover and Fear in Inuit Religion: A Discussion of 'Native Views.'" In *Continuity and Identity in Native America*, ed. E.J. Brill, 69–81. Netherlands: Stichting Nederlands Museum.

Paine, R., ed. 1977. *The White Arctic: Anthropological Essays on Tutelage and Ethnicity*. St Johns, NF: Institute of Social and Economic Research, Memorial University of Newfoundland.

Parry, S.W. 1824. *Journal of a Second Voyage for the Discovery of a Northwest Passage from the Atlantic to the Pacific: Performed in the Years 1821–22–23, in His Majesty's Ships Fury and Hecla*. London: John Murray.

Paungat, H. 1988. *Recollections of Helen Paungat: A Life in the Keewatin*. Eskimo Point: Inuit Cultural Institute.

Petrone, P., ed. 1988. *Northern Voices: Inuit Writing in English*. Toronto: University of Toronto Press.

Pitseolak, P., and D.H. Eber. 1993. *People from Our Side*. 2nd ed. Montreal and Kingston: McGill-Queen's University Press.

Rasing, W.C.E. 1994. *"Too Many People": Order and Nonconformity in Iglulingmiut Social Process*. Nijmegen: Katholieke Universiteit, Faculteit Der Rechtsgeleerdheid.

Rasmussen, K. 1927. *Across Arctic America: Narrative of the Fifth Thule Expedition*. New York: G.P. Putnam and Sons.

– 1929. *Intellectual Culture of the Iglulik Eskimos. Report of the Fifth Thule Expedition 1921–1924*. Vol. 7, no. 1. Copenhagen: Gyldendalske, Boghandel, Nordisk, Forlag.

– 1930. *Iglulik and Caribou Eskimo Texts. Report of the Fifth Thule Expedition 1921–1924*. Vol. 7, no. 3. Copenhagen: Nordisk Forlag.

Royal Commission on Aboriginal Peoples. 1994. *The High Arctic Relocation: A Report on the 1953–1955 Relocation.* Ottawa: Canada Communication Group.

Saladin d'Anglure, B. 1977. "Iqallijuq ou les reminiscences d'une âme-nom
inuit." *Etudes Inuit Studies* 1, no. 1:33–63.

– 1978. "L'homme (*angut*), le fils (*irniq*), et la lumiere (*qau*), óut le cercle du
pouvoir masculin chez les Inuit de l'Arctique central canadien." *Anthropo-
logica* 20, nos. 1–2:85–94.

– 1994. "Brother Moon (*Taqqiq*), Sister Sun (*Siqiniq*), and the Direction of
the World (*Sila*): From Arctic Cosmography to Inuit Cosmology." In *Circumpolar Religion and Ecology: An Anthropology of the North*, ed. T.
Irimoto and T. Yamada, 187–211. Tokyo: University of Tokyo Press.

Stevenson, M. 1997. *Inuit, Whalers, and Cultural Persistence: Structure in
Cumberland Sound and Central Inuit Social Organization.* Toronto:
Oxford University Press.

Tester, F.J., and P. Kulchyski. 1994. *Tammarniit (Mistakes): Inuit Relocation
in the Eastern Arctic, 1939–1963.* Vancouver: University of British Columbia Press.

Ungalaaq, M.A. 1985. *Inuit Life Fifty Years Ago: Recollections of Martha
Angugatiaq Ungalaaq.* Autobiography Series no. 1. Eskimo Point, NT: Inuit
Cultural Institute.

Vansina, J. 1985. *Oral Tradition As History.* Madison, WI: The University of
Wisconsin Press.

Wachowich, N. 1992. "Unpacking from the Field: Reflections on Conversations with Inuit Women in Pond Inlet." Master's Thesis, University of
Western Ontario.

– 1994. "Pond Inlet Women Speak about Power." Report prepared for the
Royal Commission on Aboriginal Peoples Women's Traditional Gover-
nance Research Project.

Washburne, H.C., and Anauta. 1940. *Land of Good Shadows: The Life
Story of Anauta, an Eskimo Woman.* New York: John Day Company.

Watson, L.C., and M.B. Watson-Franke. 1985. *Interpreting Life Histories:
An Anthropological Inquiry.* New Brunswick: Rutgers University Press.

Weissling, L.E. 1991. "Inuit Life in the Eastern Canadian Arctic, 1922–1942:
Change As Recorded by the RCMP." *Canadian Geographer* 31,
no. 1:59–69.

Wenzel, G. 1991. *Animal Rights, Human Rights: Ecology, Economy, and
Ideology in the Canadian Arctic.* London: Belhaven Press.

INDEX

❖ ❖ ❖

MCGILL-QUEEN'S NATIVE AND NORTHERN SERIES
BRUCE G. TRIGGER, EDITOR